IN MEMORIAM
Konstantin Symmons-Symonolewicz

Brodzic

August 5, 1909 - October 29, 1986

The History of the
Russian Literary Language
from the
Seventeenth Century
to the Nineteenth

Vinogradov

The History of the
Russian Literary Language
from the
Seventeenth Century
to the Nineteenth

A CONDENSED ADAPTATION INTO ENGLISH

WITH AN INTRODUCTION BY

Lawrence L. Thomas

THE UNIVERSITY OF WISCONSIN PRESS

MADISON, MILWAUKEE, & LONDON 1969

PUBLISHED BY THE UNIVERSITY OF WISCONSIN PRESS

BOX 1379, MADISON, WISCONSIN 53701

THE UNIVERSITY OF WISCONSIN PRESS, LTD.

27–29 WHITFIELD STREET, LONDON, W.1

COPYRIGHT © 1969 BY THE REGENTS

OF THE UNIVERSITY OF WISCONSIN

PRINTED IN THE UNITED STATES OF AMERICA

STANDARD BOOK NUMBER 299–05260–5

LIBRARY OF CONGRESS CATALOG CARD NUMBER 69–16108

Preface

A condensed English version of V. V. Vinogradov's book (*Očerki po istorii russkogo literaturnogo jazyka XVII–XIX vv.*, 2nd ed. [Moscow, 1938]) was made by the members of a seminar at the University of California (Berkeley) some years ago and edited by Professor Francis J. Whitfield and myself. At that time, the work was issued in mimeographed form for local use. When colleagues expressed interest in my issuing the work in book form, I undertook the task of revision. It soon became evident that revision would be a rather dubious mode of procedure. The original (Berkeley) version had an uneven distribution of illustrative material, different writing styles (since each chapter was written by a different person), differing views as to what should be excluded and what should be retained, and somewhat uncoordinated transliteration systems. A revision would have been more difficult, and more liable to contain errors, than a completely new version. Consequently, the work has been done anew, with no utilization of the earlier version. I hope that the result is a more consistent, and more uniform, presentation.

This book is intended primarily for the use of the student of Slavic languages and literatures, although it may also be of interest to others who are engaged in either Russian studies or scholarship in other languages. Since the intent was to create a useful handbook, Vinogradov's work has been considerably abbreviated, without, it is hoped, the loss of any essential ideas. To keep the exposition proceeding as smoothly as possible, quotations from scholarly literature have been included, where appropriate, in the text itself, and bibliographical references have been dropped. Since the titles and numbers of the section headings have been retained, the interested scholar can easily find the bibliographical material by

referring to the Russian original. Quotations from writers and famous
literary critics, however, are always attributed to the writer or critic.
Quotations of *belles lettres* (poems, stories, etc.) are, where appropriate, identified by title, although I have not attempted to track
down sources for quotations which Vinogradov himself did not
identify. Critical judgments made by writers in letters to friends
and the like are not identified except for reference to the writer.
On rare occasions, the material of a footnote has been incorporated
into the text. All names, titles, and technical terms (e.g., *akan'e*,
virši) have been reproduced in a scientific transliteration.* All
examples (even when they involve only individual words) have been
left in Cyrillic. Since this book is a discussion of the history of the
Russian literary language, and since at least a rudimentary knowledge of Russian is necessary for a full understanding of it, purely
illustrative citations have not been translated into English, with
the exception of those citations in the Introduction which have to
do with Old Russian and, consequently, would present a difficulty
to people with a knowledge of only Modern Russian. It will be
noted, also, that Vinogradov's elaborate apparatus of technical
terms has been ignored, for the most part. There are several reasons
for this: Vinogradov rarely defines his terms; he uses them loosely,
so that there are instances of overlapping; on occasion, as when
he makes references to the various "languages" of the city, his
terminological coinages would lead one to assume strict distinctions
in areas where strict distinctions are scarcely possible.

In using this book, the reader should keep a number of things
in mind. First of all, the book constitutes something of a mixed
genre (a fact which Vinogradov has himself pointed out since its
publication). It is a combination of a history of the literary language
and studies of the styles of individual authors. This is true not only
of the chapters devoted to individual writers but also of many
sections of other chapters. Now, while it is true that the language
of a great author can *affect* the history of the literary language, it does
not follow that his language alone constitutes a *period* in the history
of the literary language—there are always other forces at work.
Secondly, and perhaps because of the fact that this is a book of

---

*The system of transliteration used in this book is that designated as System III in
J. Thomas Shaw, *The Transliteration of Modern Russian for English-Language Publications*
(Madison, 1967).

essays, Vinogradov fails to make clear that the development of a literary language is a *continuous* process. The Russian literary language has had its own peculiar problems to overcome, to be sure, but Vinogradov does not sufficiently stress the fact that new demands (because of changing sensibilities, etc.) are constantly being placed before *every* literary language. It is for this reason that, occasionally, the hero of one chapter or section of the book seems to become the whipping boy of the next; the solutions, or attempted solutions, put forward in one historical period are not necessarily satisfying for the next. Lastly, the reader should reserve judgment concerning Vinogradov's statements about the earliest occurrence of loan-words in Russian, their language of origin, and the direction of their penetration into Russian. Subsequent studies have, for example, established a much earlier occurrence of certain loan-words (cf. G. Hüttl-Worth, *Die Bereicherung des russischen Wortschatzes im XVIII Jahrhundert* [Vienna, 1956], and, by the same author, *Foreign Words in Russian: A Historical Sketch, 1550–1800*, University of California Publications in Linguistics, Vol. 28 [Berkeley, Los Angeles, 1963]).

The Introduction is meant to provide a short sketch of the Russian literary language up to the point where Vinogradov begins his study. I hope that it contains nothing which is not present in the standard handbooks. It relies heavily, even though not exclusively, on two of them: V. D. Levin, *Kratkij očerk istorii russkogo literaturnogo jazyka* (Moscow, 1964), and G. O. Vinokur, *Russkij jazyk: Istoričeskij očerk* (Moscow, 1945). (Vinokur's work was republished in a French translation, Paris, 1947, and in a German one, Leipzig, 1949. It was also republished in Russian, with some abbreviation, in his *Izbrannye raboty po russkomu jazyku* [Moscow, 1959].)

Non-Slavicists should note that I have followed Vinogradov in his use of the usual Russian convention of employing three dots, particularly at the end of the line, in the punctuation of short quotations from longer poems. These dots may signify *points de suspension* (i.e., the original author's indication of a thought incompletely expressed) or an ellipsis, short or long, or both at once. Since, in such instances, Vinogradov occasionally does not give the source of his quotation, or quotes from editions unavailable in this country, I have felt that it would be labor lost to attempt to establish a punctuation in keeping with standard American usage.

I would like to thank my colleagues in the Slavic Department at the University of Wisconsin—Harlan E. Marquess, J. Thomas Shaw, Robert W. Simmons, Jr., and Victor Terras. They were most helpful in their advice, encouragement, and their valuable comments on the typescript. Grateful acknowledgment is also due my wife, Doris, whose patient labors produced the typescript. Needless to say, responsibility for the final product is mine alone.

Lastly, I would like to dedicate this version to my friend and teacher, Francis J. Whitfield—who advised me to stay out of this whole business.

LAWRENCE L. THOMAS

Madison, Wisconsin
October 1968

Contents

INTRODUCTION: THE DEVELOPMENT OF THE RUSSIAN
LITERARY LANGUAGE UP TO THE SEVENTEENTH CENTURY   xi

1   THE SEVENTEENTH CENTURY: THE OLD AND THE NEW   3

The Old and the New in the Russian Literary Language
of the Seventeenth Century. The Disintegration of the
Church Slavonic Linguistic System. The Europeanization and Nationalization of the Literary Language

2   THE FIRST HALF OF THE EIGHTEENTH CENTURY: THE
MIXING OF STYLES   30

The Mixing of Styles in the Russian Literary Language
up to the Middle of the Eighteenth Century. The Role
of the Chancery and Technical Languages in this
Process. The Formation of New Literary Styles of
Narrative and Artistic Expression

3   THE MID-EIGHTEENTH CENTURY: NORMALIZATION AND DIS-
INTEGRATION OF THE THREE STYLES   55

The Normalization of the Three Styles on the Basis of a
Synthesis of the National and Church Slavonic Languages. The Disintegration of the Three Styles in Connection with the Expansion of National and West
European Elements in the Literary Language

4 THE SECOND HALF OF THE EIGHTEENTH CENTURY: THE
   SALON LITERARY STYLES   86

   The Process of Formation of Salon Literary Styles of
   Aristocratic Society on the Principle of Mixing the
   Russian Language with French

5 THE EARLY NINETEENTH CENTURY: STYLISTIC CONTRA-
   DICTIONS   110

   Stylistic Contradictions in the Literary Language of the
   First Quarter of the Nineteenth Century

6 THE LANGUAGE OF PUŠKIN   127

   The Language of Puškin and its Significance in the
   History of the Russian Literary Language

7 THE LANGUAGE OF LERMONTOV   158

8 MID-NINETEENTH-CENTURY LITERARY STYLES   178

   The Tension and Interaction Between Various Literary
   Styles in the Thirties and Forties of the Nineteenth
   Century. The Growth in Literary Importance of
   Raznočinec-Democratic Styles

9 THE LANGUAGE OF GOGOL'   209

   The Language of Gogol' and its Significance in the
   History of the Russian Literary Language of the Nineteenth Century

10 EXPANSION OF THE BASES OF THE LITERARY LANGUAGE   237

   The Broadening and Deepening of the National Demo-
   cratic Bases of the Russian Literary Language. The
   Process of Formation of a System of Styles in the Russian
   Scholarly and Publicistic Language

   INDEX   269

Introduction:
The Development of the
Russian Literary Language
up to the Seventeenth Century

THE WRITTEN LANGUAGE OF KIEV

At about the time that the East Slavs adopted Christianity, in 988 or 989, they also received their first written language. It was a Bulgarianized form of Old Church Slavonic, since Bulgaria, which had its so-called "Golden Age" under the rule of Tsar Simeon (893–927), became the chief purveyor to the East Slavs of translated Byzantine literature.

It is not to be assumed that the acquisition of a written language was a sudden event. The East Slavs had had, for a considerable time, trade, political, and martial relations with their neighbors, including Byzantium. It is quite likely that they became acquainted with writing systems long before Christianization, and it is also likely that some literary works had come to them, via Bulgaria, before official Christianization. It is also not to be assumed that a preliterary society is, *ipso facto*, a primitive one. Military organization, fortification, defense of trade routes, and the like, demand a rather well organized social and governmental structure. Furthermore, the East Slavs already had an oral folk literature and a legal code. All of these considerations argue for the existence, in East Slavdom, of at least the preconditions for the existence of a cultural elite. It is for this reason that an original literature developed in Kiev within an astonishingly short time after Christianization.

The importation of a written language did not mean the importation of an entirely *foreign* language. In the tenth century, the Slavic languages had not yet diverged from one another to any considerable extent. Consequently, Old Church Slavonic could serve as an *international* language. Its differences from East Slavic were few and systematic, even though they affected the entire grammar.

In the lexicon, several different layers of Church Slavonicism are to be distinguished (in what follows, examples will be in Modern Russian orthography wherever possible). There were Church Slavonicisms which were direct borrowings of Greek words (largely belonging to the realm of religious concepts): e.g., Библия, Евангелие, епископ, дьявол, икона, etc. There were also Slavonic calques on Greek terms, such as премудролюбление (philosophy) and звездозаконие (astronomy). There were a number of words which were simply Church Slavonic synonyms for native words (in the following pairs, the East Slavic word is given first): правда–истина, лоб–чело, щека–ланита, шея–выя, грудь–перси, etc.

Of more far-reaching significance than these, however, were the lexical doublets which came about as a result of the different phonological evolution of East Slavic and South Slavic. Most important in this connection were the differences in treatment of what are conventionally designated as Common Slavic $TorT$, $TerT$, $TolT$, and $TelT$ groups (i.e., a consonant followed by e or o, followed by r or l, followed by another consonant). East Slavic representations of them were, respectively, $ToroT$, $TereT$, $ToloT$, and $ToloT$ (after hushing sibilants, the last was $TeloT$); South Slavic representations of them were $TraT$, $TrěT$, $TlaT$, $TlěT$. This phenomenon in East Slavic is known by the term "full vocalization" (in Russian, полногласие). Examples are: East Slavic город, берег, молод, молоко, шелом, as compared to Old Church Slavonic град, брѣг, млад, млѣко, шлѣм. At first, such doublets were used indiscriminately; that is, both the Church Slavonic form and the native East Slavic form could appear in the same document without any distinction in meaning or stylistics. For example, East Slavic had the form волость, which had two meanings: "power" (in general) and "region under one's power." The Church Slavonic form, with the same two meanings, was власть, and, in the famous chronicle account of the blinding of Prince Vasil'ko, when Vasil'ko is made to say а мой Теребовль, моя власть и ныне и пождавше

("and my Terebovl' is my princedom, both now and in the future"),
we see that the doublets are still undifferentiated.

With the passage of time, however, such doublets were either
stylistically and semantically differentiated, or one or the other of
them was lost. The rate of such differentiation or loss depended
on social need. The end result, in Modern Russian, is that (1) the
native form has gone out of use (for example, Modern Russian
has only время, срам, среда, плен, храбрый, шлем; Old Russian
веремя, сором, середа, полон, хоробрый, шелом have totally disappeared); or (2) the Church Slavonic form has gone out of use
(for example, берег, дерево, мороз, середина, через; the Church
Slavonic equivalents брег, древо, мраз, средина, чрез may only be
used for special stylistic purposes); or (3) both forms are in use—in
which case they have undergone semantic specialization (compare
the following sets: власть–волость, страна–сторона, прах–порох,
краткий курс–короткий человек, хранить–хоронить, etc.).

The same sort of fate befell, *mutatis mutandis*, other types of
doublets. The most important of such doublets are the following:
(1) In South Slavic, all Common Slavic *or T-*, *ol T-* groups are
represented by *ra T-*, *la T-* groups; in East Slavic, under certain
conditions which need not concern us here, they are represented
by *ro T-*, *lo T-* groups. For example, in Old Russian one has forms
such as робота, розум, лодья; the Modern Russian forms работа,
разум, ладья are of Church Slavonic origin. Similarly, the prefix
роз- has retained its native vocalism when accented; otherwise, it
has the form **раз-**. (2) East Slavic differed from South Slavic in
not having an initial *j-* before *-u-*, a fact which led to such doublets
as уг–юг; уный, уноша–юный, юноша; утро–ютро. (3) On the other
hand, East Slavic regularly prefixed an initial *a-* with a *j-*: яз(я)–аз,
ягня–агня (lamb). (4) East Slavic replaced an original, Common
Slavic *je-* with *o-*, which led to the following kind of doublet in
Old Russian written monuments: один–един, олень–елень, озеро–
езеро, осень–есень. (5) The Common Slavic groups **tj* and **kt*
plus front vowel were represented in East Slavic by **ч**, but in Old
Church Slavonic by **шт** (which the East Slavs rendered as **щ**),
and this situation produced such competing forms as the following:
свеча–свеща (compare Modern Russian освещение), печи–пещи
(bake), and the like. The Modern Russian sign of the present
active participle, **-щ-**, is of Church Slavonic origin; the *native*

Russian forms of the present active participle have become pure adjectives (cf. летучий, горячий, могучий, etc.).

In the sphere of grammar, the following points deserve mention. (1) In East Slavic the long-form (definite) adjective was early influenced by the pronominal declension, so that, for example, the dative singular masculine was доброму, whereas the corresponding Church Slavonic (contracted) form was добруму. (2) The genitive singular and nominative-accusative plural of feminine soft-stem nouns, the accusative plural of masculine soft-stem nouns, the corresponding forms of the adjectives, as well as certain pronominal cases, all had the ending **-ѣ** in East Slavic; whereas the corresponding Church Slavonic ending was a nasalized front vowel. Thus, for example, East Slavic had землѣ (genitive singular, nominative-accusative plural), конѣ (accusative plural), новоѣ (genitive singular feminine), etc. The corresponding Church Slavonic forms (in their denasalized, East Slavic rendering) were земля, коня, новыя. (3) The East Slavic ending for the third person forms of the verb was **-ть**, as compared to Church Slavonic **-тъ**. (4) East Slavic had probably lost the declensional type слово, словесе; its existence in Old Russian written monuments was a result of Church Slavonic influence. (5) The reflexive pronoun and the pronoun of the second person singular had a different dative-locative stem vocalism in East Slavic; the forms were тобѣ, собѣ, as compared to Church Slavonic тебѣ, себѣ. (6) The short-form nominative singular masculine and neuter present active participle ended in **-a** in East Slavic, in contrast to Church Slavonic **-ы** (веда–веды). (7) Past active participles of the type хваль were Church Slavonicisms; East Slavic had only the type хвалив. (8) When the language began to be written, East Slavic completely lacked the **-омь** ending in the instrumental singular of masculine and neuter nouns and short-form adjectives. The endings were **-ъмь** (for hard-stem nouns and adjectives) and **-ьмь** (for soft-stem nouns and adjectives). There were also differences in word-forming elements: for example, many words with the suffixes **-ание, -ение, -ество, -енство, -енец, -тель**, etc., are of Church Slavonic origin or were constructed on Church Slavonic models.

Old East Slavic written monuments also give evidence for the interaction of spoken and bookish elements in syntax. The syntax of the spoken language tended toward parataxis; that is, individual

sentence elements were mechanically joined together on the same
plane, since there was no complex system of coordination and
subordination. For example, we read in the chronicle: Приде
Святославъ в Переяславець, и затворишася болгаре въ градѣ. И
излѣзоша болгаре на сѣчю противу Святославу, и бысть сѣча велика,
и одоляху болъгаре. ("Svjatoslav came to Perejaslavec, and the
Bulgarians barricaded themselves in the city. And the Bulgarians
came out to give battle against Svjatoslav, and there was a great
battle, and the Bulgarians began to win.") There was no device
for transmitting indirect speech; only direct speech was used, as
is evident in the following chronicle extract: В се же время придоша
людье ноугородьстии, просяще князя собѣ: "Аще не поидете к намъ,
то налѣземъ князя собѣ." И рече к нимъ Святославъ: "А бы
пошел кто к вамъ." И отпрѣся Ярополкъ и Олегъ. И рече Добрыня:
"Просите Володимера." ("At that time, the Novgorodians came
asking for a prince for themselves. 'If you don't come to us, we will
find a prince for ourselves.' And Svjatoslav said to them, 'And who
would go to you?' And Jaropolk and Oleg refused. And Dobrynja
said, 'Ask Volodimer.' ")

Also characteristic of the colloquial syntax was the repetition of
prepositions—да поиди за князь наш за Малъ ("marry our prince,
Mal"); and the use of the nominative case as object of an infinitive—
куна взяти ("a kuna [monetary unit] is to be exacted"). On the
other hand, such constructions as the dative absolute—Василкови
же сущю Володимери, на прежереченѣмь мѣстѣ ("Vasil'ko was then
in Volodimer, in the above-mentioned place"); the use of a substantivized neuter adjective in the plural—потрѣбьная имъ даяхъ
("I gave them what they needed"); and the use of the preposition
к with verbs of speaking—еже г[лаго]ла къ с[ы]нома своима ("what
he said to his two sons")—belonged solely to the written language.

The differences between the East Slavic and Old Church Slavonic
linguistic systems were, as we have seen, minimal; and the two
systems immediately began a varied and intricate interplay. We can
acquire some idea of this intricacy by merely considering the lexicon:
a particular term, for instance, might be purely East Slavic, with
no Old Church Slavonic parallel, while another might have no
East Slavic parallel; two terms might be both coexistent and
identical in their spheres of meaning, while two others, historically
doublets, might have developed totally different meanings in Old

Church Slavonic and East Slavic; finally, there could be historical doublets which had an added meaning component in either East Slavic or Old Church Slavonic. It is easy to see that great freedom of selection and stylistic manipulation was possible between the two linguistic structures.

The degree of interaction between the two systems, and the degree to which one system or the other predominated in a given written work, depended upon genre. It is customary, insofar as *language* is concerned, to differentiate three written genres during Kievan times: religious works (e.g., sermons, saints' lives), works having to do with everyday life (business documents, juridical works), and secular literary works. The linguistic system of religious works tended to be a highly sustained Old Church Slavonic; that of works having to do with everyday life tended toward pure East Slavic; and secular literary works were a varying, unstable combination of the two systems, in which we see the beginnings of their future fusion. In the examples which follow, the translations are meant to be as literal as possible.

The first example is from the oldest surviving copy of the *Russkaja pravda* (1282). The language is a very consistent East Slavic, with a very simple syntax. The extract cited here (with minor graphic changes) is from G. O. Vinokur, *Izbrannye raboty po russkomu jazyku* (Moscow, 1959), p. 47. *Prodaža* and *vira* were types of fines; the *grivna* and the *kuna* were monetary units.

Оже придеть кръвавъ муже на дворъ, или синь, то видока ему не искати, нъ платити ему продажю 3 гривны. Или не будеть на немь знамения, то привести ему видок, слово противу слова, а кто будеть началъ, тому платити 60 кунъ. Аче же и кръвавъ придеть, или будеть самъ почалъ, а выступять послуси, то то ему за платежь, оже и били. Аже ударить мечемь а не утнеть на смерть, то 3 гривны, а самому гривна за рану, оже лѣчебное. Потьнеть ли на смерть, то вира. Или пьхнеть мужь мужа любо къ собѣ, любо от себе, любо по лицю ударить, или жердью ударить а видока два выведуть, то 3 гривны продаже.

(If a man come to the [prince's] court bloody or [black and] blue, then he needs no witness, but is to be paid a prodaža of three grivnas. Or, if there be no marks on him, then he is to bring a witness [and there is to be] testimony against testimony, and whoever is the instigator is to pay sixty kunas. But even if he come bloodied and were himself the instigator, and witnesses come forward, then he is to pay the same fine, even if he were beaten. If [anyone] strike with a sword and do not cut to death, then [he is to pay] three grivnas, and the injured person [is to receive] a grivna for the healing of his wound. If he cut to death then [he is to pay] a vira. If a man push a man either toward or away from himself, or strike him in the face, or strike him with a staff, and two witnesses are brought forth [then he is to pay] a prodaža of three grivnas.)

The language of religious works, with their consistent Church Slavonic, was a stark contrast to the above. The example given here is from Kirill Turovskij, "Slovo v novuju nedělju po pascě." It is cited from N. K. Gudzij, *Xrestomatija po drevnej russkoj literature*, 5th ed. (Moscow, 1952), p. 53.

Ныня солнце красуяся къ высотѣ въсходить и радуяся землю огрѣваеть: възиде бо намъ отъ гроба праведное солнце Христосъ и вся вѣрующая ему съпасаеть. Ныня луна, съ вышьняго съступивъши степени, большему свѣтилу честь подаваеть: уже ветхый законъ, по писанию, съ суботами преста и пророкы Христову закону съ недѣлею честь подаеть. Ныня зима грѣховная покаяниемъ престала есть и ледъ невѣрия богоразумиемъ растаяся; зима убо язычьскаго кумирослужения апостольскымъ учениемъ и Христовою вѣрою престала есть, ледъ же Фомина невѣрия показаниемъ Христовъ ребръ растаяся. Днесь весна красуеться, оживляющи земное естьство: бурнии вѣтри, тихо повѣвающе, плоды гобьзують и земля, сѣмена питающи, зеленую траву ражаеть.

(Now the radiant sun rises on high and, rejoicing, warms the earth. For the true sun, Christ, has risen, for us, from the grave, and is saving all those who believe in him. Now the moon, having descended from its high place, gives honor to the greater luminary. Already the Old Testament, according to Writ, has stopped with its Sabbaths and its prophets and gives honor to Christ's Testament with its Sunday. Now the sinful winter has stopped in repentance and the ice of disbelief has melted in divine wisdom. For the winter of heathen idol-worshiping has stopped in the apostolic teaching and Christ's faith—and the ice of Thomas' disbelief has melted at the testimony of Christ's ribs. Today the spring is radiant and enlivens earthly existence. The turbulent winds, gently blowing, are multiplying the fruits; and the earth, nourishing the seeds, gives birth to green grass.)

Every degree of compromise between these two extremes was possible. Our next selection, from the biographical section of the "Poučenie" of Vladimir Monomax, contains relatively few Church Slavonicisms. The text is taken (as were the citations from the chronicle given above) from V. P. Adrianova-Peretc, ed., *Povest' vremennyx let*, Part I (Moscow, Leningrad, 1950), p. 162.

А се в Черниговѣ дѣялъ есмъ: конь диких своима рукама связалъ есмь въ пушах 10 и 20 живых конь, а кромѣ того же по ровни ѣздяималъ есмь своима рукама тѣ же кони дикиѣ. Тура мя 2 метала на розѣх и с конемъ, олень мя одинъ болъ, а 2 лоси, одинъ ногами топталъ, а другый рогома болъ, вепрь ми на бедрѣ мечь оттялъ, медвѣдь ми у колѣна подъклада укусилъ, лютый звѣрь скочилъ ко мнѣ на бедры и конь со мною поверже. И Богъ неврежена мя съблюде. И с коня много падах, голову си розбих дважды, и руцѣ и нозѣ свои вередих, въ уности своей вередих, не блюда живота своего, ни щадя головы своея.

(And this is what I did in Černigov: of wild horses, I tied up ten-twenty living horses in the thickets with my own hands and, moreover, riding through the steppe, I caught those same wild horses with my own hands. Two aurochses tossed me on their horns together with my horse; one stag gored me; and, as for two elks, one tread on me with his hooves and the other gored me with his horns; a boar cut my sword from my side; a bear bit the saddle-cloth at my knee; a wolf leaped at my side and knocked me down with my horse. And God preserved me unharmed. And I fell off my horse often; I twice split my head, and I injured my arms and legs—in youth I injured them, not taking care for my life, not sparing my head.)

The language of the thirteenth-century *Molenie Daniila Zatočnika* stands much closer to the high, Slavonic style. The selection given here is from N. K. Gudzij's *Xrestomatija*, p. 138.

Княже мои, господине! Богатъ муж вездѣ знаем есть и в чюжем граде: а убогъ мужь и во своемъ граде невѣдомъ ходит. Богат мужь возглаголет — вси молчатъ и слово его до облак вознесутъ; а убогъ мужь возглаголет, то вси на него воскликнут. Их же бо ризы свѣтлы, тѣхъ и рѣчи честны.
Княже мои, господине! Не возри на внѣшняя моя, но вонми внутренняя моя. Аз бо есмь одѣяниемъ скуденъ, но разумом обилен; юнъ возрастъ имыи, но стар смыслъ вложихъ вонь. И быхъ паря мыслию своею, аки орел по воздуху.

(Oh my prince, oh lord! A rich man is known everywhere, even in a foreign city; but a poor man walks unknown even in his own city. A rich man speaks forth—all are silent and praise his speech to the clouds; but if a poor man speaks forth, then everyone shouts at him. For those who have bright vestments also have honorable speeches.
Oh my prince, oh lord! Do not look at my external [qualities] but attend my internal [qualities]. For I am poor in clothing, but abundant in wit; having a youthful age, I have placed an old wisdom in it. And I would soar with my thought like an eagle through the air.)

Our last example is from translated literature—the *Izbornik* of 1076. This excerpt, with punctuation and minor graphic changes, is taken from the edition of V. S. Golyšenko, *et al.*, *Izbornik 1076 goda* (Moscow, 1965), pp. 475–477. (It is worth mentioning that, in the entire monument, the stem *vered-* occurs three times, while the stem *vrěd-* occurs twelve times; on the other hand, the stem *norov-* occurs ten times and the stem *nrav-* does not occur at all.)

Аз чадѣ реку вама: чловѣча жития отити хощю, вѣста бо како въ житии семь жихъ без лукы, како отъ вьсѣхъ чьстьнъ бѣхъ и лубимъ — не сана ради велика нъ норовъмь великъмь. Не укорихъ никого же ни вередихъ, и никого же не оклеветахъ, ни завидѣхъ никому же. Ни разгнѣвахъ ся ни на кого же, ни на мала ни на велика. Не оставихъ цьркъве божия вечеръ ни заутра ни полудьне. Не прѣзьрѣхъ нищих, ни оставихъ страньна, и печальна не прѣзьрѣхъ никъгда же; и иже въ тьмьницахъ заключении, потрѣбьная имъ даяхъ; и иже въ плѣнь-ницѣхъ избавихъ.

(I, children, say to you: I am about to leave human life. And you know how, in this life, I lived without deceit, how I was honored by all—not due to great rank, but because of great character. I did not reproach or harm anyone; I did not slander anyone or envy anyone. I never became angry at anyone, either great or small. I did not forsake God's church either in the evening, or in the morning, or in the afternoon. I did not despise the poor, I did not abandon the traveler, and I never despised the downcast. I gave those who were locked up in dungeons what they needed; and I rescued those who were in captivity.)

As can be seen from the above examples, a great range of variability in the mixture of East Slavic and Old Church Slavonic was possible. The relative preponderance of one or the other depended very much on *what was being talked about*. In this connection, the results of a special study of the language of Monomax's "Poučenie" made by a Soviet scholar (Jakubinskij) are interesting. The "Poučenie" consists of three sections of unequal length: the "instruction" proper, a biographical chronicle, and a section of religious meditations. Without going into details, and restricting ourselves to the relative frequency of East Slavic *ToroT*, etc., groups as compared to Old Church Slavonic *TraT*, etc., groups, the results of the study were as follows: in the "instruction," there are four instances of *ToroT* and four instances of *TraT*; in the biography, there are twenty-one instances of *ToroT* and only three instances of *TraT*; in the meditative section, there is one instance of *ToroT* and five instances of *TraT*. Since the sections are of unequal length, the absolute numbers are meaningless; it is the relative frequency that is important, allowing us to conclude that the coexistence of two linguistic systems permitted the East Slavic writer to use a high, Church Slavonic style when he was discussing elevated (religious) subjects, a low, East Slavic style for the description of everyday affairs, and an intermediate, mixed style for other written genres.

THE WRITTEN LANGUAGE OF MOSCOW FROM THE FOURTEENTH
CENTURY TO THE SEVENTEENTH

Moscow fell heir to the written language of Kiev. What is important to understand, however, is that the spoken language had continued to evolve while the written language had tended to remain stable. The differences, grammatical and otherwise, which had existed between the native linguistic system and Old Church Slavonic during the Kievan period were still present. To be sure, many Old Church Slavonic lexical items must have penetrated and been absorbed by the spoken language by this time, so that they were no longer identifiable by the native speaker as Slavonicisms. Moreover, many lexical doublets had ceased to be doublets because of specialization of meaning. In general, however, the grammatical differences remained and new differences were added, because of the fact that the spoken language had lost certain grammatical categories and developed new ones. In addition, certain developments in the phonological evolution had made possible the importation of new Church Slavonic doublets.

One such development was the loss and vocalization of the jers (ъ, ь), which allowed for new borrowings from Slavonic. In East Slavic, the Common Slavic group *dj had yielded ж; in Church Slavonic the result was жд. In Kievan times, it was not possible to borrow Slavonic words with this consonant cluster because East Slavic had no approximation of it (cf. the last word in the extract from Kirill Turovskij, above). The East Slavic form жьдати had to become ждати before the assimilation of such Church Slavonicisms as рождение, между, хождение, etc., was possible. Similarly, artificial church pronunciation of a vowel in the prefix въз-, въс-, in places where spoken Russian now had no vowel, led to new Church Slavonicisms. The form возраст was thus doubly a Church Slavonicism; were it not for the influence of Church Slavonic, the Modern Russian form of this word would have been взрост (cf. взрослый). By this time, also, a former e had become [o] under accent before a hard consonant (in modern orthography, it is inconsistently represented by the letter ё). Since church pronunciation tended to be a spelling pronunciation, however, it did not reflect this feature of the spoken language. Consequently, the pronunciation of the genitive plural жён as [žen] rather than [žon] was a Church Slavonicism. Semantic doublets were thus created; cf. Modern Russian небо (sky) as compared to нёбо (palate).

The grammar of the spoken language had also undergone many changes which led to new Church Slavonicisms in the written language. For example, a genitive plural form such as столъ was not a Church Slavonicism in Kievan times; the form was correct in *both* the written and the spoken language. By Muscovite times, however, this genitive plural had become столов in the spoken language, and the written use of the form столъ thus constituted a Church Slavonicism. The written forms of the adjective declension were full of Slavonicisms: for example, the nominative singular masculine ending **-ый, -ий** was Slavonic; the spoken form was **-ой, -ей**. The ending of the second person non-past of the verb (носиши) and the unaccented ending of the infinitive (носити) were Slavonicisms; the spoken language had, by now, lost the final unaccented vowel. Russian had eliminated the alternation of velars in the nominal and verbal paradigms by restoring a velar consonant to those forms where alternation had formerly taken place; forms such as the dative-locative руцѣ, нозѣ and imperatives such as помози are, therefore, purely written forms. Pronominals such as the genitive singular мене, тебе, себе, the short datives ми, ти, си, and the short accusatives мя, тя were also exclusively written forms. The colloquial language had lost the short pronominals, and the normal genitives had become меня, тебя, себя. Furthermore, the spoken language had lost the grammatical categories of the vocative (replaced by the nominative), dual number, the supine, the aorist, and the imperfect (both tenses had been supplanted by the simple past tense in **-л,** which had developed from the East Slavic perfect; one can see the beginnings of this evolution in the extract from Monomax in the preceding section). Use of such grammatical categories in the written language of Moscow was purely artificial.

There were many other phonological and morphological differences between the spoken and written languages of Moscow; but the examples given above should suffice to demonstrate that the written language was being cultivated largely according to Church Slavonic norms which were both artificial and foreign. Such norms, moreover, served to isolate the written from the spoken language— the language which should have been, to a far greater degree than it was, the structural base for the written language.

A factor which seriously complicated the development of the written language was a cultural and linguistic current which has come to be known as the "second South Slavic influence." It began, toward the end of the fourteenth century, with the resumption of intellectual relations with Serbia and Bulgaria (long interrupted by the Tatar yoke). It was intensified in the fifteenth century when Turkish conquests in the Balkan area forced many Serbian and Bulgarian scholars and churchmen to go into exile. It continued through most of the sixteenth century, and its effects were still very much present in the seventeenth. The Balkan scholars brought with them certain archaizing and decadent tendencies which Balkan literature had shared with Byzantine literature. They had a desire to cleanse the language of later "accretions," so as to bring it closer, in grammar and orthography, to the original form of Old Church Slavonic and to Greek; they wanted to remove all local characteristics from the language and separate the written language from its national substratum. They came armed with an almost mystical attitude toward the word and its semantics—and toward the letter of the word. Such an attitude found ready acceptance in a Moscow which at the time was seeking hegemony over other Russian principalities and cultivating the idea of itself as a "third Rome." For Moscow had need of a written language, and a literature, which would reflect its grandeur and assist it in realizing its political and cultural aspirations.

One result of the second South Slavic influence was that during the fifteenth century the character of Russian script changed drastically (the first Russian *printed* book to bear a date did not appear until 1564). Though some of these changes resulted from the influence of Greek miniscule writing, most were brought about by South Slavic writing styles. Some letters were dropped and others were added or reinstated (the intent often being to reestablish the "pristine" form of words borrowed from Greek). Some of the details of the spelling changes reflected an attempt to return to original Old Church Slavonic spellings, while others reflected South Slavic dialect characteristics. Writing of the jers was restored (but, since Serbian writers had no way of differentiating between them, they were often spelled unetymologically); the sign for the Old Church Slavonic back nasal vowel was restored (and sometimes confused with the sign for the front nasal vowel); a "non-jotized" spelling of [*ja*] was introduced (e.g., добраа); etc. The spelling system of a language is a purely surface phenomenon, however, and does not materially affect the language itself; other tendencies brought by the second South Slavic influence were to have a much more profound effect.

The great attention paid to semantics, etymology, and the phonological and grammatical forms of words resulted, for one thing, in a systematic replacement of colloquial (and dialectal) elements with learned terms. Slavonicisms which had become archaic were reintroduced into the written language. There were many new borrowings from South Slavic and from Greek, and many neologisms created on the model of Old Church Slavonic or Greek. New compounds were introduced (sometimes as calques on Greek terms), particularly for the expression of abstract ideas. Occasionally such compounds could have as many as three compounding elements: храбро-добро-побѣдный. Ordinary words were Slavonicized: works of this period tend, for instance, to have many more words, statistically, with the *TraT*, etc., form than works of the Kievan period had. It was probably at this time also that the Church Slavonic forms юный, юг gained ascendancy over the native Russian forms. The over-all effect of such changes was to make the written language more abstract and elevated, eradicating from it elements which had a mundane, everyday connotation.

In style, there was a tendency toward emotionalism, solemnity, splendor, and rhetorical and decorative expression. Much use was made of periphrasis, metaphor, simile, and analogy, and a great deal of attention was paid to accumulation of synonyms and repetition of epithets, often resulting in pleonasm and tautology. Because of such features, the style came to be known as "braiding" or "weaving" of words (извитие или плетение словес). Yet the motive behind it was not simply a striving for decorativeness. The word was supposed to reflect the essence of the object, to bring about a participation in the object's very being. The right word had to be discovered at all costs, and the object had to be described in all its facets.

It is natural that such a style would find its consummate expression in high-style genres—in panegyrics, religious instructions, and saints' lives. One master of the art, and a man with considerable literary talent, was Epifanij Premudryj (died c. 1420). The example

adduced here is from his *Žitie Stefana Permskogo* and is taken from
N. K. Gudzij, *Xrestomatija*, p. 193.

Коль много лѣтъ мнози философи еллинстии събирали и составливали грамоту
греческую и едва уставили мнозѣми труды и многыми времены едва сложили;
пермьскую же грамоту единъ чрьнець сложилъ, единъ составилъ, единъ счинилъ,
единъ калогеръ, единъ мнихъ, единъ инокъ, Стефанъ глаголю, приснопомнимыи
епископъ, единъ въ едино время, а не по многа времена и лѣта, якоже и они,
но единъ инокъ, единъ вьединеныи и уединяяся, единъ, уединеныи, единъ у
единого бога помощи прося, единъ единого бога на помощь призываа, единъ
единому богу моляся ...

(Once for many years many Greek philosophers were collecting and compiling
the Greek alphabet—and they barely established it with many labors, and they
barely composed it after much time. But the Permian alphabet—one monk
composed, one compiled, one contrived—one reverend, one father, one regular—
Stefan, I say, the ever-memorable bishop; one at one time and not after much
time and years, as [did] they, but one priest, alone, secluded and secluding
himself, alone, secluded, alone, asking for help from the one God, alone, appealing
to the one God for help, alone, praying to the one God ...)

When syntactic complexity was added to such a style, the exposition could become obscure and quite rococo in its over-all effect.
We find such a manner of writing in the *Vremennik* of Ivan Timofeev,
composed during the first quarter of the seventeenth century. The
passage chosen is an often-quoted one which occurs at the beginning
of his discussion of Ivan the Terrible's division of the land into
opričnina and *zemščina*, and is taken from V. P. Adrianova-Peretc,
ed., *Vremennik Ivana Timofeeva* (Moscow, Leningrad, 1951), pp. 11–12.

От умышления же зельныя ярости на своя рабы подвигся толик, яко вознена-
виде грады земля своея вся и во гневе своем разделением раздвоения едины
люди раздели и яко двоеверны сотвори, овы усвояя, овы же отметашася, яко
чюжи отрину, не смеющим отнюдь именем его мнозем градом нарицатися
запрещаемом им, и всю землю державы своея, яко секирою, наполы некако
разсече.

(Because of a conception [filled] with extraordinary rage against his subjects,
he became such that he hated all the cities of his land and, in his anger, he divided
a single people with a cleaving division and made it, so to speak, of two allegiances.
Some he befriended, others were rejected—he thrust them away as if [they were]
foreigners. Because of his interdiction, many cities did not in any way dare to
call themselves even by his name. And the whole land of his reign he, as if with
an axe, cut in half.)

The Soviet scholar Vinokur, who adduced these examples, has pointed out that they are extreme cases; for there were many gradations of complexity in the individual styles which were affected by the second South Slavic influence. Yet the examples clearly show the *direction* in which that influence carried the written language.

In addition to the heavily Church Slavonicized written language described above, Moscow had another, radically different, written language. This was the language developed in the government chanceries, from which fact it gets its name, "chancery language" (приказный язык). It was based, for the most part, on the spoken language of Moscow, and it became, as Moscow attained to power, the generally recognized norm for governmental transactions for the entire state.

Since the chancery language was based on the spoken language, its grammatical structure and lexicon reflected those of the spoken language. It had no vocative, no dual number, no aorist or imperfect. Its syntax tended to be paratactic, and it contained some of the features of the spoken language that we noted earlier: repetition of prepositions, use of the nominative for the object of the infinitive, etc. In addition, since it was not as effectively normalized as the Church Slavonicized written language, it contained numerous spelling errors which reflected actual pronunciation.

Despite its orientation toward spoken Russian, the chancery language still contained numerous Church Slavonicisms. Archaic legal formulas (which had Church Slavonicisms in their lexicon and grammar) were, of course, an integral part of the language of government and private documents—and they found their way into other written genres as well. There were Church Slavonic spellings in the inflection of the adjective, in the writing of the unaccented infinitive ending, in the ending of the second person singular of the non-past, and elsewhere. Moreover, the chancery language borrowed and retained a number of Church Slavonic prepositions—a feature which was later to be considered one of its hallmarks.

A good example of the chancery language is the *Domostroj* of the middle of the sixteenth century. In the sections devoted to man's moral and religious conduct, the *Domostroj* tends to have a rather large number of Slavonicisms; in the sections devoted to practical and domestic life, there are virtually none. The fragment chosen for illustration (taken from N. K. Gudzij, *Xrestomatija*, p. 278) is in the latter category. Of particular interest are the errors in the direction of a phonetic spelling.

А слуг своих заповедывай: о людех не переговаривати, и где в людех были и что видели недобро, тово дома не сказывали бы; а что дома деется, тово бы в людех не сказывали бы: о чем послано, то и паметуй, а о ином о чем учнут спрашивати, того не отвечевай и не ведай, и не знай того; борзее отделавшися, да домой ходи и дело кажи, а иных вестей не приноси, што не приказано; ино промежь государей никакой ссоры не будеть и неподобные речи и блудные то бы отнюдь не было; то доброму мужу похвала и жене, толко у них таковы служки вежливы. А пошлешь куды слушку или сына, и што накажешь говорити, или што зделати, или што купить, — и ты вороти да спроси ему, что ты ему наказал: что ему говорити, или что ему зделать, или что ему купити? И только по твоему наказу тебе все изговорит, ино добро.

(And instruct your servants that they not gossip about people and that they not relate at home where they were among people and what they saw [that was] reprehensible. And they should not tell abroad what is going on at home. "Remember what you were sent for, and if they start to ask you about anything else, do not answer, do not know, and do not acknowledge it; but, leaving quickly, return home and relate your business; and do not bring any information you were not asked to bring"—so that there be no quarrel between masters and so that there be absolutely no unseemly or iniquitous speeches. [Such a state of affairs] is an honor to a good man and his wife. Only they have such courteous servants. And if you send somewhere a servant or your son and order him to say something, or do something, or buy something—call him back and ask him what you ordered him to do: what he was to say, what he was to do, what he was to buy. Matters are in a good state only if he can relate everything to you at your behest.)

Another good example of the chancery language is the mid-seventeeth-century memoir of G. Kotošixin, *O Rossii v carstvovanie Alekseja Mixajloviča*. The excerpt presented here is from V. D. Levin, *Kratkij očerk istorii russkogo literaturnogo jazyka* (Moscow, 1964), p. 103.

А наутрѣе ѣздит жених с дружкою созывать к себѣ гостей к обѣду, своих и невѣстиных. А приѣхав к невѣстину отцу и матерѣ, бьет челом им за то, что они дочь свою вскормили и вспоили, и замуж выдали в добром здоровьѣ, и созывая гостей поѣдет к себѣ домовь. А как к нему всѣ гости съѣдутся, и новобрачная свадебным чиновным людем подносит дары. И перед обѣдом ѣздит он жених, со всем поѣздом, челом ударить царю.

(And in the morning the bridegroom and the best man go to invite the guests to dinner—their own guests and the bride's. And when he arrives at the [home of] the bride's mother and father, he pays his respects to them for bringing up their daughter and giving her in marriage in good health. He invites the guests and goes home. And when all the guests arrive, the bride offers gifts to the members of the wedding party. And before dinner, the bridegroom, along with the entire entourage, goes to pay his respects to the tsar.)

There was no generally recognized middle ground between the highly Church Slavonicized written language and the chancery language. Although elements of the two were mixed in such genres as chronicles, historical works, memoirs, travel narratives, and the like, there was no norm for the mixture. On the one hand, churchmen and scholars jealously guarded Church Slavonic against the incursion of colloquial elements, and, on the other hand, the chancery language could not win literary rights for itself except in some "low" genres. There was no recognized *Russian* literary norm, and the need for one was being felt more and more acutely. It is approximately at this point that Vinogradov begins his exposition.

The History of the
Russian Literary Language
from the
Seventeenth Century
to the Nineteenth

I

The Seventeenth Century: The Old and the New

1. THE CRISIS IN THE CHURCH SLAVONIC LINGUISTIC SYSTEM IN THE SEVENTEENTH CENTURY

The Russian literary language of the Middle Ages was Church Slavonic. In the second half of the seventeenth century an internal disintegration of its system, which had actually begun in the sixteenth century, became sharply evident. Changes in the structure of the church-book language were connected with the growth in literary significance of "lay" styles of the written language—that is, of business, publicistic, and narrative styles—and with a broadening of the literary rights of everyday speech. For example, the sixteenth-century revision of church books by Maksim Grek and others showed an interesting tendency to accommodate the Church Slavonic language to the Russian spoken language. In corrections of the Psalter, for instance, instead of цену мою совещаша отринути, one has честь мою совещаша отринути; instead of внегда разнствит Небесный цари на ней, one has егда разделит Небесный царей на ней. The aorist and imperfect are replaced by the compound past, especially in the second person singular: one has видел еси and текл еси instead of видяше, течаше. There are many such corrections and changes.

But these shifts did not erase the medieval dualism in literary expression. Church Slavonic (at basis a Byzantine-Bulgarian language, though it had already undergone a complicated evolution in Russia) continued to fulfill most literary functions. The business, publicistic, and narrative styles adapted themselves somewhat to

Church Slavonic and hence found themselves on the periphery of literariness; but more often they were restricted to the realm of commercial and everyday intercourse.

Heinrich Wilhelm Ludolph, the author of a Russian grammar published at Oxford in 1696, characterized the relationship of Russian and Slavonic thus: "For Russians, a knowledge of the Slavonic language is essential, for not only are their Holy Writ and liturgical books in Slavonic, but also it is impossible to discuss or write about questions of science or education without using it. Therefore, the more anyone wants to appear wise in the eyes of others, the more he fills his speech and writing with Slavonicisms— although there are some who deride those who make excessive use of the Slavonic language in ordinary conversation." Ludolph also observed that, "... on the other hand, in domestic and intimate talks no one could possibly make do with only the resources of the Slavonic language, because the terms for most things in common use cannot be found in the books from which one can derive one's knowledge of the Slavonic language." He laconically characterized the situation by saying, "It is necessary to converse in Russian, and write in Slavonic." He considered the only *Russian* book to be the *Uloženie* of Tsar Aleksej Mixajlovič, and the situation struck him as being abnormal. For this reason he expressed the wish that the Russians, like other European peoples, would elaborate their own language and publish books in it. Such a view is particularly compelling when one notes that Church Slavonic was incomprehensible to the majority of the people.

Meanwhile, the growth in political significance of new social classes—the increase in power of the landowners and the expansion of the merchant class—could not but be reflected in the relationship of the styles of the literary (Slavonic), social, and official (chancery) languages. On the one hand, it increased the demands that the national language play a more significant role in literary expression. But this process was accompanied on the other hand by an antithetical increase in the "Slavonicism" of the speech of the upper social strata of bookmen, clergy, and nobility, who tried artificially to return to a pure Slavonic, even though their everyday experience drew them away from it. The result was a new solidification in the literary position of Slavonic at a time when its inappropriateness was already evident.

At the same time another, parallel, process was taking place—the process of "Europeanization." The relationship of these processes among different social groups was different, complex, and contradictory, as various stylistic currents in the Russian literary language collided and mixed. Even Church Slavonic was penetrated by the European influences, experiencing, as a result, a variegated and discordant stratification that deepened the semantic, structural, and stylistic contradictions already present within it.

The important point here is that during the seventeenth century two basic centers of the Church Slavonic tradition, Moscow and Kiev, continued to exist, each with its own area of influence. Moreover, the two centers represented somewhat different traditions, and the Kievan tradition was preponderant. Kiev was not only the center of preservation of the Church Slavonic tradition, but also the place where the Church Slavonic language in its East Slavic version was first submitted to systematic normalization (the Ukrainian scholar Meletij Smotrickij first published his grammar in Vilnius in 1619). It was in Kiev, too, that the extension of the usage of Church Slavonic to secular literature was first and most clearly manifested: the first attempts to write rhymed verses (*virši*) in Church Slavonic were made by Ukrainian scholars; learned Ukrainian rhetoricians and preachers (who exerted a great influence on seventeenth-century rhetoric) used many Slavonicisms; and Ukrainian school dramas (to which Russian drama and comedy owe their existence) were written in Church Slavonic. It is important to note, however, that in adapting itself to new conditions of usage the Kievan Church Slavonic tradition did absorb certain features of the Muscovite tradition.

In the seventeenth century, and mainly through Kiev, the West European scholastic education which had triumphed over the Eastern, Byzantine education in the Ukraine came to Moscow. In the atmosphere of Muscovite literary and linguistic life, the tension between West and East was first to be manifested in a collision between the "Helleno-Slavonic" styles of the literary language of the church (that is, those styles that were founded on Byzantine Christian culture) and the church styles which emanated from the Ukraine and were oriented toward the Latin language—the scholarly and religious language of the West European Middle Ages. Other West European currents coming from Poland complicated the process of interaction between the ecclesiastical literary language and the secular and business language. The result was a crisis in the system of the Russian literary language.

These are the general features of the stylistic ferment in the Russian literary language of the seventeenth century. Its individual components must now be described and interpreted in greater detail.

2. THE BYZANTINE ("HELLENO-SLAVONIC") STYLES OF THE ECCLESIASTICAL LITERARY LANGUAGE

As a counterbalance to the on-coming wave of Europeanization, the archaic trend in the ecclesiastical literary language increased. Most of the higher clergy and nobility cultivated the elevated rhetorical styles of Church Slavonic, thus continuing the tradition of Byzantine oratory. Educated, conservative bookmen of the monkhood, clergy, and nobility had a vivid sense of an "internal, formal" connection between Muscovite Church Slavonic and Greek.

One interesting contemporary tract emphasizes the need for knowing Slavonic and Greek rather than Latin, and combines religious and historical considerations with confrontations of the grammatical structures of these languages. By analyzing the alphabet and the grammatical structures involved, the author concludes that Greek and Slavonic are related to each other as a "lamb to its mother," whereas Latin differs from both like a "strange goat." Both Slavonic and Latin, to be sure, lack a correspondent for the Greek article, but the author cleverly argues for the importance of the article for the Slavs as well, in that it aids them in distinguishing the general meaning of a term in a Greek text from its specifically religious meaning (*theos* as contrasted to *ho theos*). The fact that both Greek and Slavonic have a present participle from the verb "to be" (Slavonic сый), and Latin does not, is considered clear evidence of the religious inferiority of Latin, since Latin (and Polish), in using a periphrastic expression composed of pronoun and finite verb, cannot denote something eternal, but only something with a beginning and an end which therefore cannot be used to designate the Divine Being. The author bitterly notes the presence of Latin and Polish influence and warns against it: "The Latin teaching is as seductive as a knife smeared with honey; at first it seems sweet and safe to the one who licks it, but the more it is licked the closer it approaches to the gullet, where it will easily stab and kill the licker."

This author's further objections to Latin influence may be summarized as follows: Latin lacks equivalents for terms denoting Orthodox religious concepts and thus cannot distinguish ипостась from лицо. It is too poverty-stricken to be able to provide proper renditions of Greek words and has бискуп instead of епископ, кроника instead of хроника, поэтика instead of пиитика. It lacks an equivalent for Greek *eta* and therefore has метрополит instead of митрополит, академия instead of акадимия, and, worst of all, паче же самого Сына Божия спасительное имя Иисус глаголют Иезус. Finally, Latin has to have recourse to a circumlocution, *qui pluribus monachis praeest*, in order to render архимандрит.

The same tract stresses the lexical and semantic elements common to Greek and Slavonic, emphasizing, above all, the Greek words which had been borrowed and assimilated in the following spheres: liturgy (евангелие, апокалипсис, апостол), names of church dignitaries (патриарх, митрополит, игумен, диакон), names of saints (Алексий, Афанасий), liturgical accoutrements (стихарь, просфора, икона), and the extensive scholarly terminology (хронограф, грамматика, феология, арифметика, этимология, синтаксис, просодия). The ease with which Slavonic can make loan translations (calques) of Greek words is taken to be further evidence of the affinity of the two languages: богодар translates Theodor, отценачальник the Patriarch, and so on. It thus follows that Slavonic has an unusual capacity for translation from the Greek.

For the historian of the Russian literary language, these remarks are primarily interesting in that they show, albeit in a polemical, distorted fashion, the world outlook of a seventeenth-century Russian bookman of "Eastern" convictions. They are also of value as a key to the hidden religious symbolism of the grammatical categories which were being used to reinforce the conceptual system of the Muscovite church language. The tendency to represent the Greek element in the Church Slavonic language as an organic part of Russian culture and the Russian literary language is characteristic.

For Helleno-Slavonic styles, strict adherence to the Greek original was very important. A clear case in point is Epifanij Slavineckij's

defense of his use of укрестованный instead of распятый to mean
"crucified": "If пяло–распяло is identical with крест, then so are
распятый and укрестованный. If пяло is not identical with крест
then распятый is not identical with укрестованный. So, if пяло or
распяло differs from крест, then распятый also differs from укрестованный. Let them who judge judge correctly: it is either the
same or not the same to be распятый or укрестованный and, if it
is not the same, then let them lay aside распятый and accept
укрестованный—in concordance with the Greek original."

The Helleno-Slavonic styles were characterized by a complicated
syntax, an unusual number of Slavonicisms, "weaving of words,"
and pompous, often artificial compounds. Examples of the last are
Feodor Polikarpov's compounds разнопестровидный, верокрепи-
тельный; Epifanij Slavineckij's рукохудожествовать, адоплетенный;
and Karion Istomin's гордовысоковыйствовати, всевидомиротворо-
кружная. Grammatical forms were constructed and used with strict
adherence to the norms elaborated in Smotrickij's grammar—norms
which were arrived at by an artificial regularization of Church
Slavonic on the basis of later Russian and Ukrainian redactions of
religious works. Some of these norms were: a more or less consistent
differentiation, in the singular, of masculine inanimate and
masculine animate, and, in the plural, of masculine and feminine
animate and inanimate; formation, on the Greek model, of
"adverbs" (*pričastodetie*) like читательно; broad use of the adverbial
participle (*deepričastie*) as the indeclinable form of the short-form
participle (e.g., читая, читав, прочтущ, чтом, чтен, читаем); and the
differentiation of six verbal moods: *iz''javitel'nyj*, *povelitel'nyj* (бий,
чти, стой), *molitel'nyj* (услыши, воньми, призри), *soslagatel'nyj* (дал бы,
аще бы хотел), *podčinitel'nyj* (да бию), and *neopredelennyj* (бити,
стояти).

Smotrickij also differentiated, in imitation of Greek, six tenses,
of which four were past tenses. These four he called: *prexodjaščee*,
which he defined as an incompleted past action, and which corresponds, in general, to the unprefixed aorist (бих, бихся or биен есмь,
биен бых); *prešedšee*, which he defined as a completed past action,
and which resembles the imperfect, but clearly differs from it in
aspectual nuances (бияхся or биян есмь, биян бых); *mimošedšee*,
which he defined as a long-past action, and which resembles the
uncontracted forms of the imperfect (бѣях, бѣяхся or бѣяан бывах);

and *nepredel'noe*, which he defined as a recently completed past action, and which, for the most part, resembles the aorist from a prefixed perfective verb (побихся or побиен бых). The various forms of the Russian compound past, чел есмь, читал есмь, читаал есмь, прочел есмь, were grafted onto this scheme. Although the forms of these past tenses were adapted to the archaic paradigms of the aorist and the imperfect, it was verbal aspect that played the essential role in their differentiation.

All these verb forms were artificially cultivated in the high styles of the Church Slavonic language of the second half of the seventeenth century. For example, in a petition of unknown authorship we have the following: где же онех великих труды и всенощная пения *бяху*, тамо *благоволи* тебе Бог стати. In a tract entitled *O ispravlenii v prežde-pečatnyx knigax minejax*, not only are the tenses used in correspondence to Smotrickij's grammar, but they are also commented on in accordance with its rules. The protests of the Old Believers show a very different view of the tense forms, and are indicative of the linguistic disorder of the second half of the century. In the words of one such dissenter, "The correctors themselves don't know grammar, but they humiliate us; and they have the habit, with that petty grammar of theirs, of defining God with a long-past action ... In the troparion for Easter Sunday they used to print и на престоле *беаше* Христе со Отцом и Духом, but now in the new triodion they have printed the long-past tense: и на престоле *был еси* Христе со Отцом и Духом. As if He sometimes were and sometimes is. And they don't understand that it is fitting for God always to be."

In the Slavonic language of Smotrickij, it is necessary to differentiate the truly Slavonic from the pseudo-Slavonic. Among the latter are fictitious forms invented by Smotrickij on the analogy of Greek, Latin, or Slavonic itself, as well as Russian forms co-opted into Slavonic without justification. Examples are: preponderant use of the neuter plural rather than the singular of the substantivized adjective (cf. a seventeenth-century saying, крадый чужая не обогатеет); failure to use the negative with negative pronouns, adverbs, and particles (still present in Kantemir at the beginning of the eighteenth century: хотя внутрь никто видел живо тело); use of a preposition with article before the infinitive (in Polikarpov: слетайтеся ко еже созерцати красоту); and preponderant use of the nominative and accusative in the predication rather than the predicate instrumental, which had come into wide use under Polish influence.

Smotrickij's grammar had been the norm for Ukrainian bookmen as well, but in the Ukraine it had failed to become an overwhelming authority because of the great influence of noble and bourgeois tastes on the Ukrainian literary Slavonic language. In Moscow, however, the prescriptions of the grammar, republished with additions and revisions in 1648, became the unquestionable norm for conservative circles of "Easterners" (adherents of the Byzantine tradition), and, in some respects, for Muscovite "Westerners" from the higher levels of the clergy (defenders of Latin culture and Southwestern education). Thus, such a "Westerner" and adherent of Latin teaching as Sil'vestr Medvedev reveals a very close connection with the grammatical norms which were established under the influence of Smotrickij's grammar. For example, in explaining the "grammatical sense" of the form переложив, he repeats the argument of the grammar: "The word переложив is a past tense deepričastie; the deepričastie is formed from a participle and it differs from the participle just as short-form adjectives differ from the long-form ones: for example, праведный and праведен."

It is also interesting to note that Simeon Polockij, a product of the Kiev-Mogila Academy, tried to "purify" his language after coming to Moscow, by attempting to adapt it to the grammatical and lexical norms of Muscovite Church Slavonic. He spoke of this in the verse introduction to *Rifmologion*:

> Писах в начале по языку тому,
> Иже свойственный бе моему дому.
> Таже увидев многу пользу быти
> Славенскому ся чистому учити.
> Взях грамматику, прилежах читати;
> Бог же удобно даде ю ми знати ...
> Тако славенским речем приложихся;
> Елико дал Бог, знати научихся;
> Сочинение возмогох познати
> И образная в славенском держати.

The symbols and metaphors (образная) of which Polockij speaks in the last line, and, in general, semantics, phraseology, and syntax, put a sharp dividing line between the Helleno-Slavonic and Latin Slavonic styles. But in the morphological sphere, and partly also in the lexical, a strong tendency toward an archaic ordering of the high style was characteristic of both the "Easterners" and the ecclesiastical "Westerners" of the seventeenth century. And it was in this area that a rapprochement occurred between Muscovite and Southwestern (Kievan) Church Slavonic in the matter of revising the texts of liturgical books.

At the end of the seventeenth century, however, and particularly at the beginning of the eighteenth, the Helleno-Slavonic styles began to lose their regulative function. They continued to exist as a variant of the high styles, but they acquired a narrow, professional, religious character. As attempts were made to bring Church Slavonic closer to the native Russian language, the Greek features in it came to be considered foreign and superfluous—just as the knowledge of Greek itself was no longer considered indispensable for the educated man of the eighteenth century. This reaction against Hellenisms in Church Slavonic is clear evidence that the Eastern, Byzantine influence was giving way to a West European influence.

3. THE UNIFICATION OF CHURCH SLAVONIC DIALECTS. THE UNION
OF THE MUSCOVITE TRADITION WITH THE KIEVAN

Both the revision of Muscovite liturgical books according to Lvov and Kiev models and the ecclesiastical-administrative, theological, and philological activity of Kievan scholars in Moscow led to a rapprochement between the two varieties of Church Slavonic. Ukrainian influence supported certain phonetic features in the Moscow church pronunciation which were being eliminated in the spoken language. Examples are: the pronunciation of a velar fricative [γ] instead of the velar stop [g] that was characteristic of Moscow and northern Russian dialects; the pronunciation of [e] instead of colloquial Russian [o] in such words as пес, лен; and the differentiation of ѣ from е. Enthusiasm among the higher clergy and nobility for Kievan choruses and singers helped in establishing such Kievan traits in church pronunciation.

There were also significant morphological changes in the Muscovite church language. The use of the prefixes **во-, со-, воз-** broadened under the influence of church pronunciation of an [o] for a former **ъ**, which had disappeared in colloquial speech. The prefix **c-** was semantically differentiated from **co-**, with the latter acquiring the special meaning of participation (as in сообщество, соревнование, etc.).

Changes in lexicon and phraseology were particularly numerous: instead of от Него же всяк живот вдыхается, for example, one has всяко животно одушевляется. The protests of the Old Believers against such neologisms are indicative of what was taking place. They endowed the Church Slavonicisms with a concrete semantic content and compared them with corresponding expressions in everyday Russian. The normalization of the high Slavonic style, however, closely connected with the revision of church books, was expressed in the development of abstract, symbolic meanings in the sphere of religious dogmatics, in the differentiation of semantic nuances in synonyms, and in the creation of a solemn, metaphorical phraseology. In the tract *O ispravlenii v preždepečatnyx knigax*, for example, we find the following synonyms differentiated: тело–плоть, чрево–утроба, врач–лекарь, разум (*synēsis*)–знание (*gnōsis*).

This codification of the forms and norms of Church Slavonic had as its task not simply to "cleanse" the language of foreign admixtures and "inaccuracies," not simply to unify its terminology and phraseology, but also to safeguard it from influences of the secular, business language, the everyday colloquial language, and ideological systems foreign to Orthodoxy. But the Southwestern (Kievan) system, which was an important influence in bringing about a normalized, statewide Church Slavonic language, had, in addition to its archaizing tendencies (which, as we have seen, were not incompatible with a more "Eastern" view), other, "Europeanized" methods of expression and semantic forms, which had developed under Latin and Polish influence. And these, too, were to bring about changes in the literary language of Moscow.

4. THE LITERARY LANGUAGE OF THE SO-CALLED SOUTHWESTERN RUS' AND ITS INFLUENCE ON THE RUSSIAN LITERARY LANGUAGE

When, in the second half of the seventeenth century, Southwestern Rus' (Belorussia and the Ukraine) became an intermediary between Moscow and Western Europe, the Ukrainian literary language became a strong influence in the development of a Russian literary language. The social and historical causes of this mixing of languages were complex. In Southwestern Rus', the nobility and the bourgeoisie underwent Europeanization earlier than in Moscow. The influence of the Polish language, which was felt by the upper levels of the Russian nobility in the sixteenth and seventeenth centuries, had sent down its roots earlier and deeper here. In its struggle with Catholicism, the local clergy became proficient in the high philological culture of the Latin West. Latin gradually came to occupy a more important place in education. And it became indispensable in the civic life of Southwestern Rus', because of political dependence on the Polish government and the pressure of Catholic propaganda.

Church Slavonic, finding itself within the sphere of West European civilization, experienced a greater influence of the secular and literary styles of educated circles. However, Russian did not so much borrow the features characteristic of the Ukrainian national language (which were merely Russian provincialisms from the point of view of Muscovite chauvinism) as it borrowed forms of expression which had been worked out on the basis of church literature or adopted from Latin-Polish culture.

Before describing the changes made in the Russian literary language under the influence of Ukrainian, it is necessary to clarify the internal social and linguistic processes which took place in the Ukrainian literary language. The literary language of Southwestern Rus' of the seventeenth century had had a complex history, of which only certain elements are important for the history of Russian. Above all, the Church Slavonic of the region absorbed many of the constructive features of Latin—the language of medieval European religion, philosophy, and learning, and, for Poland, the language of the administration and the courts (before which the Southwestern nobility had to defend its interests). Grammar (particularly syntax) and rhetoric experienced a strong Latin and Polish influence. Both secular and religious oratory borrowed figures of speech foreign to Greek rhetorical practice, as well as Polish and Latin words and expressions. Then the influence of both Latin handbooks of rhetoric and collections of Catholic sermons led to imitation of all the devices of this extremely artificial and elegant oratory—an oratory which was at that time already frowned upon by the advocates of Greek rhetoric. In sermons, the Bible and the "deeds of the Holy Fathers" began to share their authority with philosophers and lay scholars. Alongside biblical legends one began to have historical and even mythological ones. Sacred figures were placed on a level with classical gods and heroes. Interest in content gave way to interest in form and secular scholarship. Didacticism gave way to entertainment. Thus, although one cannot deny the importance of the Greek language and Byzantine religious literature, their sphere of influence was restricted, in Southwestern Rus', to cult and liturgy, and even here they had to share their authority with Latin.

The following examples will give some idea of the Latin words which entered the Ukrainian secular language and, to some extent, the church literary language, either directly or through the intermediary of Polish. First of all, there were terms of the official language, business and juridical: апелляция, гонор, декрет, канцелярия, квестия, персона, фундамент, церемония, etc. Secondly, there were terms from rhetoric, and from scholarly and technical language: аффект (passion), доктор, литера, натура, оратор, суптельный, форма. Finally, there were school terms such as вакация, бурса.

There were, of course, loud voices in the Ukraine which decried the interest in Polish-Latin culture. But they had little effect against the strong political and social pressures favoring the Western influence.

Toward the middle of the sixteenth century, moreover, in Poland, the native language began to be the language of literature, law, and administration. This process also had its influence on Southwestern Rus', where the nobility imitated everything Polish. Thus, some written genres had Latinisms, Polonisms, *and* Church Slavonicisms, as the following lines from the poetry of P. Berynda will demonstrate:

> Христос Збавител ныне с Панны нароженый
> От Бога Отца ведлуг тела увелбеный
> Ныне в верных щасливе нехай завитает,
> И радос в сердцу каждово з нас проквитает.

Scholarly, publicistic, and belletristic works (verses and dramas) were written in this secular style.

The secularization of Church Slavonic had its antithesis in the broadening of the everyday functions of the church language. Thus, Ukrainian writers occasionally used Church Slavonic for topics which ordinarily called for a simpler and more natural language.

For example, P. Mogila used the same language when writing of everyday things that he used in composing church hymns and canons: В граде Белоцерковском Яну Пикгловскому родися дщи. По обычаю же баба, въсприемши отроча, пупок уреза, но недобре связа. Не внемши ж се баба, положи отроча в корытце, об нощь же кровь из отрочате течаше пупком, кровию же исплыв, умираше.

It was these secular and church literary styles of Southwestern Rus' that began to exercise a strong influence on the literary language of the Muscovite state in the second half of the seventeenth century.

5. UKRAINIAN STYLES OF THE CHURCH LITERARY LANGUAGE ON MUSCOVITE SOIL AND THEIR INFLUENCE ON THE RUSSIAN LITERARY LANGUAGE OF THE UPPER SOCIAL CLASSES

Muscovite styles connected with oratorical genres—sermons and theological, polemical, and publicistic works—were the first to experience Ukrainian influence. Before this could happen, however, the Ukrainian stylistic tradition had to be divested of those forms, words, and expressions which were most foreign to the Russian literary language. The complex task accomplished by Simeon Polockij in "Slavonicizing" his style, and in cleansing it of "the barbarisms of the literary language of Western Rus' and the provincialisms of his native land," is very interesting. One need only compare his writings before he came to Moscow with his later writings to be convinced of the depth of the transformation. The following extract (written in 1659) is very different from the extract from his *Rifmologion* quoted earlier in this chapter. Here, there is scarcely a line which does not contain a Ukrainianism, Polonism, or Latinism:

> Дай *абы* врази были побежденны,
> Пред *маестатом* его покоренны!
> Сокруши *пожных* людей выя, роги,
> Гордыя враги наклони под ноги ...
> Покрый покровом град сей православный,
> *Гды* обретает тебе *скарб* твой давный.

Also interesting are the changes which Sil'vestr Medvedev made in Polockij's verses, removing non-Russian lexical items (едно was

replaced by одно, як by как), and changing certain syntactic constructions (for instance, he replaced the participle with an adverbial participle: аз что принесу, ничтоже убо таково имуще, нищ инок суще, instead of имущий, сущий).

These same tendencies continued in the beginning of the eighteenth century. The language of Dimitrij Rostovskij underwent a similar "Russification": words like персона, казнодей, мовити, дяковати, господарь, скриня, власный were replaced by лицо, учитель, глаголати, благодарити, господин, кладовая, собственный. The change of national coloring is especially evident in the replacement of conjunctions: але, альбо, гды, еднак, ще gave way to но, или, когда (внегда), однако, еще.

Government instructions at the beginning of the eighteenth century also called for the removal of Ukrainianisms, both in the language of official business and in the literary language. But these were government decrees, and did little to change the state of affairs.

If the phonetic, morphological, and lexical peculiarities of colloquial Ukrainian found little support in the Russian literary language (although there were many Ukrainianisms in sermons and in poetry), phraseological and syntactic norms of the literary language of Southwestern Rus' had a great influence. Thus, for example, the Latinizing tendency to put the finite verb at the end of the phrase began to take root. The following type of construction is characteristic of the letters of Sil'vestr Medvedev: Яко сухая неплодная земля дождем на богатоплодие *прелагается* и гобзовательное доброплодие *произносит*, сице гласом твоего преподобия в человецех неплодствующаяся добродетель на всетучное благоплодие *претворилася*.

The accommodation of the syntactic structure of the Muscovite high style to the Ukrainian-Latin-Polish structure was accompanied by changes in the lexicon and semantics of the Russian literary language. One such change, which took place under the direct influence of the Southwestern tradition, was the morphological and semantic equation of Church Slavonic words with corresponding Latin terms and concepts. In Sil'vestr Medvedev's notes we have *contemplatio*–безмолствие (or, better, богомыслие), *speculatio*–зрение, *actus*–делание. It is important to note also that a certain amount of work had been done, in the Southwest, toward the adoption and translation of Latin philosophical terminology. The Church Slavonic

equivalents for philosophical terms in a seventeenth-century manuscript translation, from Latin, of Aristotle's *Physics* are interesting:
actu–действом, *affectio*–страсть, *compositio*–сложение, *continuum*–целое,
contradictio–противоречение, *essentia*–сущность, *modus*–наклонение,
subiectum–подлежащее.

But the influence of Southwestern rhetoric on the Russian literary
language was particularly great. Distinctive forms of abstract
symbolism, allegorical exposition, and refined parallels and comparisons became established in publicistic, religious-polemical, and
artistic styles. "Symbols and emblems" and punning devices contributed a unique nuance of intellectual play and rhetorical refinement to Church Slavonic and disturbed its semantics by giving it
a "secular" character. Father Superior Monastyrskij wrote to
Mazepa in 1688: Пречестного монаха Медведева веру, труды,
разум хвалю и почитаю ... Я того пречестного Медведя не от *медведя
зверя*, но от *ведомости меда* походити сужду ... And, in a 1689 letter
to Sil'vestr Medvedev himself, he derived his first name from Latin
sol vester. On the other hand, adherents of the Greek "party,"
mocking Sil'vestr, used the same etymological method to derive
his name from Latin *silva* and called him а дикий или леший
медведь. Echoes of the practice may even be found in Lomonosov's
Ritorika—for instance, in his derivation of кесарь from Latin *caedo:*

> Кесарь, ты сечешь врагов удобно.
> Имя в том делам твоим подобно.

At the same time, allegory, mythological accessories, and the
figures of speech of classicism intermingled with the Church
Slavonic lexicon and symbolic system. At first, of course, their
usage was quite limited, but gradually the neoclassical current
broadened and became a characteristic property of the high styles
of the Russian literary language. The adroitness of the rhetorician
was revealed by his clever bringing together of a religious theme
with historical facts, knowledge taken from the natural sciences,
and classical mythology. Ovid's *Metamorphoses* enjoyed a special
popularity as a model of this technique.

These various rhetorical devices worked together to develop new
genres, such as rhymed verses (*virši*), drama, and prose fiction.
And the new genres in turn complicated the process of mixture of
Church Slavonic with the styles of the official language and the

secular-literary language (which was oriented toward the official language).

6. THE PROCESS OF DISINTEGRATION AND TRANSFORMATION OF THE STYLISTIC SYSTEM OF CHURCH SLAVONIC—A CONSEQUENCE OF ITS MIXTURE WITH SECULAR AND OFFICIAL LANGUAGE, COLLOQUIAL LANGUAGE, AND FOREIGN ELEMENTS

The growth in significance of such genres as verse and drama, written, for the most part, in Church Slavonic, could not but entail changes in the stylistics of Slavonic, and could not but disturb the relationship which had existed between Slavonic and secular styles. Alongside and in interaction with Church Slavonic there existed an official language. It was the official state language of the Muscovite chanceries and, at the same time, was close to the spoken language of the bureaucracy and other classes of society. It therefore occupied what amounted to an intermediate position between the literary language and colloquial styles. The official language was used to write state acts, legal codices, and technical guide books (such as *Kniga ratnogo stroenija*). It was used also for certain works which made no pretense of "literariness," such as Kotošixin's pamphlet *O Rossii v carstvovanie Alekseja Mixajloviča*, or descriptions of journeys to foreign countries. But those works of religious, pedagogical, scholarly, or simply belletristic content which had literary pretensions were written mainly in Church Slavonic, with deviations in the direction of the official and colloquial languages. And the more or less consistent adherence to Church Slavonic gave even belletristic compositions a certain "height" of tone and a unique ideological and expressive nuance of solemnity or profundity, of religious moralization or abstract symbolism.

In the second half of the seventeenth century, influenced by the relationship which had been established between Church Slavonic and secular styles in the literature of the Southwest, there came about in Russian literature as well a dichotomy between the *use* of Church Slavonic and its *meaning*. It came to be used for such subjects and themes as would formerly have found their expression in the official language or in colloquial forms. K. S. Aksakov was the first to make this observation: "The Church Slavonic language becomes a tool for arbitrary fancy ... trivial foreign and folk words and expressions, which bear the stamp of contemporaneousness, sound startling in it since they are sharply opposed to its character and forms ... This disorder, this strange, apparently destructive state of affairs points to a new order, a new life ..." Thus the same social and linguistic contradictions that characterized the Ukrainian language of the sixteenth and seventeenth centuries were evident now in Moscow.

These new usages of Church Slavonic and new mixtures of it with other styles were most clearly apparent in dramatic works. In the seventeenth-century drama *Judif'*, for instance, there is a coarse mixture of archaic Slavonicisms with vulgarisms from everyday speech:

Ахиор: Имянуешь ныне **мя** милостивым господином; како же **мя** в то время имяновал, **егда мя** к дереву привязал еси?

Сусаким (сде тайно к себе говорит): О! когда **бых** его в то время удавил, то бы ныне не **возмогл** так **возвышатись.**

Ахиор: Что ворчишь ты, *собако?* Что **ропщешь?** Како **сице** молчиши, ты *скотина,* ты **осля?** Говори ты, *лютой ворище.*

On the other hand, in the same drama Slavonicisms collide with forms from the chancery language and with barbarisms:

Сомнас: **Аз бых** свиней не коснулся, но красную деву во изрядном одеянии **взял бых.**

Моссолом: Что же бы с нею хотел сотворити?

Сомнас: Одежду от нея взяв, про себя **бых держал**; но деву моему милостивому господину *капитану* **дарил бых.**

In the language of the late seventeenth-century dramas, one can see clear lexico-semantic adaptations of Slavonic to West European languages, mostly to German. It has been pointed out that many Slavonicisms in these dramas are semantic Germanisms—morphologically exact calques of German words. There are such examples in the drama *Judif'* (whose author was a German): живи благо (*lebe wohl*), отключити (*aufschliessen*), беспохвальный народ (*unlöbliches Volk*), etc.

7. THE INFLUENCE OF THE LATIN LANGUAGE

The influence of the Southwest brought with it a flood of borrowings. To be sure, the professional lexicon had been influenced even earlier by West European items brought in by Western artisans and craftsmen. And the rapid development, in the sixteenth century, of translation (largely from Latin, German, and Polish) led to further borrowing, particularly since the translators were often foreigners. Until the seventeenth century, however, these borrowings played no significant role in the literary language of Moscow. It was the literary and spoken tradition of the Southwest, coupled with increased translation activity, that produced the real flow of Latinisms. And it was the organization of Latin schools in Moscow, leading to an increased knowledge of Latin among the privileged classes, that finally served to "canonize" it alongside Greek and Slavonic. Latin thus paved the way for other West European languages.

Concerning seventeenth-century translation activity, A. I. Sobolevskij wrote: "It seems that the greatest portion of the translations of the century were made from Latin, that is, the language which at that time was the language of science in Poland and Western Europe. After Latin, we can place Polish, which the majority of our translators knew and which south and west Russian scholars often used. German, Belorussian, and Dutch must be put at the very end. We know of no translations from any other language of Western Europe, even though there were people among our chancery translators who had a command of French and English."

A whole series of scholarly and school terms entered the Russian language as a result of the Latin influence. They were largely terms pertaining to rhetoric (ексордиум, наррация, конклюзия, фабула), mathematics (вертикальный, цыркуль, нумерация), geography (глобус), astronomy (деклинация, минута, градус), military affairs (дистанция, фортеция), and administration (инструкция, церемония, фамилия). There were also calques and neologisms: междометие (*interjectio*), наклонность (*inclinatio*). It is interesting that words borrowed earlier from Greek now adopted a Latin form, even occasionally changing the position of the accent: центр instead of кентр, акадéмия instead of акадимúя. There were also syntactic influences: the placing of the verb at the end of the sentence, for instance, and constructions such as accusative plus infinitive and nominative plus infinitive.

8. POLISH INFLUENCE ON THE COURT ARISTOCRACY

Latin influence was aided by the spread of knowledge of the Polish language among the nobility. Interest in the Polish language, culture, and art increased during the Polish interventions of the seventeenth century. In the aristocracy and the court, a *"politesse in the Polish manner"* (политесс с манеру польского) developed. Many translations were made from Polish, and Polish words and phrases made decisive inroads into the literary language. A Polish-Slavonic dictionary was published in 1670, and by the end of the century a knowledge of Polish was characteristic of an educated nobleman.

Polonisms achieved a wide currency and became a component of the everyday lexicon of high society as well as of the literary language. They included purely Polish words, such as вензель, место (city), особа, опека, пекарь, писарь, весняк (villager); Polish borrowings from German, such as бляха, кухня, рисунок, рисовать; Polish calques of German words, such as духовенство (*Geistlichkeit*), правомочный (*rechtskräftig*), мещанин (*Bürger*), обыватель (*Bewohner*); words of general European currency in Polish dress, such as аптека, пачпорт, папа; and Latinisms in Polish form, such as суптельный, маестат, оказия, приватный, презентовать, мизерный. Polish also exercised some influence on Russian syntax.

9. TRACES OF MEDIEVAL FETISHISM CONCERNING "HOLY WRIT" IN THE SPHERE OF CHURCH LANGUAGE

The new, European influences disturbed the semantics of Church Slavonic by shaking the ideological and mythological bases of its conceptual structure. The Old Russian bookman of the clergy or feudal aristocracy was governed not only in his literary imagination but in his whole perception of life by the images and symbolic schemata of Church Slavonic. The change of a form or the replacement of a word seemed to distort the very essence of a religious concept. The judgments of the Old Believers are very indicative of the mythological process of a *real* perception of church phraseology. Nikita Dobrynin, one of the leaders and martyrs of the Schism,

could not bear the replacement of крест by древо or of церковь
by храм because, in his opinion, the change dishonored the objects
themselves. He objected also to the change of the words of a prayer
from Тебе молятся звезды to Тебе собеседуют звезды, because not
even angels, much less stars, could talk with God as with an equal.
Simeon Polockij, a Westerner and a rationalist, had to counter this
reasoning with a symbolic explanation. He explained that it was
simply a matter of a metaphorical depiction of nature's hymns to
God and not a quotation of actual conversation, "since stars have
neither mouth nor mind and are inanimate things."

Thus a social and stylistic contrast developed between a Russian
literary language undergoing reformation on Western models and
Old Muscovite Church Slavonic. The old Moscow tradition
gradually receded into the schismatic underground, where, however,
it was subjected to its own kind of simplification.

10. NATIONAL, DEMOCRATIC STYLES OF THE LITERARY LANGUAGE.
THE PROCESS OF ADAPTATION OF CHURCH SLAVONIC TO SPOKEN
RUSSIAN

Old Muscovite Church Slavonic was cultivated and preserved
among the Old Believers. Here, the high-flown bookish style and
"weaving of words" of the medieval liturgical language continued
to be developed. But since the archaic phraseological forms, free of
European refinements, were actually closer to native speech, there
took place, alongside a preservation of the tradition, a broad
introduction of living speech into literature; and a struggle for the
literary rights of the national language was carried forward.

The best examples of these democratic tendencies were the leaders
and ideologists of the Schismatics. Avvakum, for instance, emphasized his lack of concern for eloquence and called his language
popular and "natural" (i.e., native Russian), opposing it to
"philosophical verses," by which he meant the language of the
bookmen who followed Western models and West European
scholastic tradition. It is important to note that "popular speech"
was opposed to "eloquence," and not to Church Slavonic in general.
In this conception, popular speech included several varieties of
everyday language, as well as Church Slavonic without its ornate
component.

In his *Kniga tolkovanij i nravoučenij*, in an apostrophe to Tsar Aleksej Mixajlovič, Avvakum gave a more detailed exposition of his view of the Russian literary language:

Воздохни-тко по-старому ... добренько и рцы по русскому языку: *Господи, помилуи мя грешного* ... А ты ведь, Михайлович, русак, а не грек. Говори своим природным языком, не уничижай ево и в церкви, и в дому, и в пословицах. Как нас Христос научил, так и подобает говорить. Любит нас Бог не меньше греков; предал нам и грамоту нашим языком Кирилом Святым и братом его. Чево же нам еще хощется лутше тово? Разве языка ангельска?

Thus, popular speech was opposed both to high Helleno-Slavonic styles and to the contrivances of Southwestern rhetoric. Avvakum characterized his style as *vjakan'e*, by which he meant a familiar, everyday type of colloquial speech. The word evoked a scornful, ironic connotation, as is clear from this quotation: Ныне еще есть учитель, бедной старчик-черничек, учит по уставам диким и лешим, вякает же бедной, что кот заблудящей.

This seventeenth-century literary colloquial language did not follow the norms of Slavonic. It occasionally reflected living, and even dialect, pronunciations (e.g., *okan'e, akan'e, jakan'e*, etc.), as well as conversational declensional forms; and it made more frequent use of the simple past tense in **-л**, and rarely used aorists, imperfects, and participles. In syntax, it favored the simple sentence with a verb and its modifiers at the core and without complicating "digressions"; it avoided participial constructions; and it preferred coordination to subordination. The degree of display of the spoken element depended, on the one hand, on theme and situation, and, on the other, on the social position of the writer.

But what is of greatest importance is that, in those literary styles which were oriented toward the spoken language, there took place a "neutralization" of Church Slavonicisms. This was because, in the concrete, everyday application of such phrases, a selective process took place which tended to eliminate elements that were simply phraseological and syntactic niceties of the high styles of the upper classes. Moreover, in the "democratic" schismatic styles, the living national language was brought within the conceptual sphere of the church language and was, so to speak, "canonized" by it. The tension and interaction between the Muscovite and Kievan church language traditions were thus accompanied by a sharp social differentiation of the styles of the literary language.

A natural reaction against borrowed forms of expression was a turn to "indigenous" ones—to native Russian and to those Church Slavonicisms which were in more common use. The works of Avvakum show very clearly this type of mixture as well as the broad introduction into literature of the national colloquial language. In his language, extremes collide and interact to form new unities.

The Church Slavonicisms of the "democratic" styles differed from those of the high styles in being almost entirely composed of phrases which were in common use and which had thus "frozen" into lexico-semantic units. The following examples from Avvakum all appear, with minor variations, in other works of a religious content: завопил высоким гласом; воздохня из глубины сердца; убойся Бога, седящего на херувимех и призирающего в бездны; умягчил ниву сердца ее; семя словеси Божия на ниве сердца их подавлено. Particularly frequent are literal citations from Holy Writ and church books, usually with no indication of the source and with an adaptation of meaning to the context: Бог излиял фиал гнева ярости своея на русскую землю; излиял Бог на царство фиал гнева своего; Ох, горе! всяк мняйся стоя да блюдется да ся не падет; посем разумея мняйся стояти, да блюдется да ся не падет (cf. I Cor. 10:12). In this fashion Avvakum used traditional phraseology to direct the reader's consciousness to a familiar church, or biblical, context.

Also characteristic of Avvakum is that he compared church phrases and symbols to the spoken language and explained them by synonyms taken from the spoken language: *бысть же я ... приалчен*, сиречь **есть захотел**; *возвратилось солнце к востоку*, сиречь **назад отбежало**; *зело древо уханно*, еже есть **вони исполнено благой**. He explicated biblical metaphors and allegories in the same realistic, everyday fashion. For example, яко мал квас все смешение квасит (cf. I Cor. 5:7–8) is explained thus: Павел ... глаголет приводную речь, указуя не в клас, якоже в квас: от мала великая прокиснет, тако и в вас от злоб и лукавства добродетели будут непотребни. Colloquial expressions fuse with bookish formulas and give them a concrete appearance: держись за Христовы ноги; полны сети напехал Бог рыбы; само Царство Небесное валится в рот. In this fashion an ideological interaction between the church language and the everyday national language is achieved, as one and the same word vacillates between the biblical and the conversational lexicons. For example, the image of the wolf from the Evangel is clothed now in Church Slavonicisms, now in colloquial formulas: at one point it's сии бо волцы, а не пастыри, душегубцы, а не спасители; at another it's Мотаюсь ... посреде волков яко овечька или посреде псов яко заяц.

In such literary styles as these, Church Slavonic, protected from Western novelties, is not a closed sphere of archaic forms of liturgical expression, but a basic structural element of everyday speech. In narrative, epistolary, and publicistic genres it is linked to colloquialisms and adapted to their semantics, but at the same time it attracts the colloquialisms to itself. A good example of such interaction is Avvakum's use of the word бес (demon), which acquires different connotations in different contexts. Avvakum himself struggled with demons; he used the word as a synonym for the Nikonians; he used it also as a synonym for the buffoon (*skomorox*), the brawler, the thief, and the fop.

These seventeenth-century literary styles freely mixed Church Slavonic with everyday language and even with vulgarisms. Occasionally, this everyday language seemed to approach the language of the peasant, though it never fused with it. Generally, it remained in the sphere of the everyday language of various elements of the urban population. The word мужик (peasant) had a derogatory connotation for Avvakum.

II. THE SECULAR, BUSINESS LANGUAGE AND CITY COLLOQUIAL LANGUAGE

The question of the social styles of the city colloquial language and their relation to the secular language of affairs is one of the basic problems in the study of the literary language of the seventeenth and eighteenth centuries. The degree to which the national (colloquial) language participated in the development of the literary language defined the degree to which Church Slavonic was Russified. Conversely, the "literariness" of the spoken language depended on the nature of the social group's attitude toward the culture of the written word. After all, the colloquial, national language not only nourished the literary language but also was nourished, in turn, by it.

Schools and textbooks played an important role in this process—
that is, in "Slavonicizing" the speech of various social groups—since
in the seventeenth century one learned one's letters from Church
Slavonic books, by rote. Moreover, many Slavonicisms must have
passed from the Psalters and breviaries into ordinary speech.
Already in the seventeenth century such Slavonicisms as the
following were circulating in the colloquial language: возвращать,
наслаждатья, заблуждаться, смущать, рассуждать, понуждать, на-
дежда, одежда, краткий, призрак, враг, распря, разный, влажный,
мрачный, and participles with -щ-. It is enough to compare the
letters of Aleksej Mixajlovič with those of Peter the Great to see
the changes wrought in the lexicon, phraseology, and syntax of
the ordinary language of their class. Peter the Great has syntactic
Polonisms, the verb at the end of the sentence, more borrowings,
and more technical expressions. He also allowed himself jokingly
ironic mixtures of Church Slavonic and mythological images—a
feature not characteristic of the language of Aleksej Mixajlovič. This
testifies both to the considerable alteration, in as brief a time as
fifty years, of the literary norms of one and the same class, and to
an increasing rapprochement between the literary system and the
colloquial and business languages.

Particulary interesting, however, is the everyday language of those
social groups whose knowledge of Church Slavonic was limited. The
lower nobility, whose language was close to that of the peasantry,
would serve as a case in point, but also indicative is the language
of city artisans and merchants. Ludolph's grammar of 1696,
mentioned earlier, gives some idea of the speech of these people.
There *is* a reflection in his grammar of the language of the upper
classes, but in the main his dialogues reflect an intimacy with the
commercial class: for example, надобе купить только что нужно;
Отнеси бушмаки к сапожнику и вели их починит; Много я издержал
на етую работу, а жаль мне, что деньги не в мошне держал.

As already mentioned above, the entire orientation of Ludolph's
grammar was based on a hope that the Russians, like other
Europeans, would develop the resources of their own language and
begin to publish books in it. Some of Ludolph's dialogues even
reveal a certain prejudice against narrow clericalism and religiosity.
If one looks at his "idioms" one is forced to admit that—barring
some archaisms and the fact that seventeenth-century man was

pretty much steeped in Slavonicisms—on the level of conversation concerning "elevated" themes, Ludolph's language somewhat resembles that of the pre-revolutionary middle class. This fact testifies to the historical stability of the colloquial language (or at least of some of its everyday clichés) in those social classes which were untouched by Western civilization. "Завтракал ли ты?" "Я поздо ужинал вчерас, сверх тово я редко ем прежде обеда." "Изволиш с нами хлеба кушит?" "Челом бью, дело мне." "Тотчас обед готов будет, девка, стели скатерт ..."

Ludolph's indications of differences between spoken Russian and Church Slavonic are also interesting. He notes, in the colloquial language, full vocalization, **ч** instead of **щ**, **о-** instead of **е-**, and **ё** instead of **е** in the "final syllable" (*pijosch, bijosch*). And he notes some peculiarities in the morphology of the colloquial language: the locative singular in **-у** in masculine nouns; the genitive singular of the masculine-neuter adjective in **-во** instead of Slavonic **-го**; the absence of the superlative in **-ейший**; and past tense forms in **-л** instead of the aorist. There is, in fact, a total absence of aorists and imperfects in Ludolph's conversations. He also provides a series of lexical parallelisms between Slavonic and Russian: истина–правда, рекл–сказал, выну–всегда, etc. And he makes interesting observations concerning: the coexistence of dual and plural forms (своема глазама and своими глазами), with preponderance of the latter; the nominative case instead of the genitive after the higher numerals (пять попы); the preponderance of the instrumental plural case ending **-ами** (городами, древами) alongside datives and locatives in **-ом**, **-ех** (городом, древом, городех, древех); the exclusive use of Russian rather than Slavonic forms of the adjective declension; the comparative degree in **-и** (моложи, больши); and the frequent use, in the colloquial language, of hypocorisms and pejoratives.

Ludolph's grammar, unlike previous grammars such as that of Smotrickij, is empirical and free of doctrinaire attitudes. Ludolph took his examples from oral language. He noted the importance of verbal prefixes and set up a tense and mood system akin to that of school grammars of the eighteenth and nineteenth centuries. The colloquial language, the future structural base of a national literary language, appears fairly clearly on the pages of his grammar.

12. THE STYLES OF THE EVERYDAY LANGUAGE OF THE CITY

Changes in everyday life, the development of new forms of etiquette, the influence of European customs—all complicated the genres employed by the city colloquial language, and each created new conditions for differentiation. For an indication of the sharp social contrast between different styles of city colloquial and city written language, it is revealing to compare a love letter written by a scribe from Tot'ma (1688) with an amorous epistle composed by an army orderly of Colonel Cej (1698). The scribe writes in petty bourgeois colloquial with dialectisms and virtually no Church Slavonicisms; he shows only the influence of chancery style (primitive forms of conjunction, for example):

Дождись меня в бане, а я к тебе на вечер от воеводы приду из гостей рано, а домой не иду спать. А мне говорить много с тобою, а при людях нельзя, да не стану. Да послушай — добро будет. Да отпиши мне ныне скоряе, я буду. Да повидайся, друг мой, нужно мне. Ономнясь было еще хотел говорить, да позабыл, а се испугался ...

The orderly's epistle is in a totally different style. It is clearly oriented toward noble tastes and imitates rhymed verses (*virši*):

Очей моих преславному свету,
И не лестному нашему совету,
Здрава буди, душа моя, многия лета
И не забывай праведного твоего обета.

The language of the epistle shows clear bookish influences. The lexicon and phraseology vacillate from colloquial to Slavonic. Compare the following: златые; во дни мимошедшие; наипаче; as opposed to как было бы тошно; и я бы отселя полетел; животочик. In addition, there are Ukrainianisms, Polonisms, and a gallant, bookish farewell.

In these various fashions, the colloquial and the business languages increasingly evinced their pretensions to literariness.

13. THE ABSENCE OF NATIONAL PHONETIC (ORTHOEPIC) AND ORTHOGRAPHIC NORMS FOR LITERARY EXPRESSION

There were no fully established orthographic or orthoepic norms for the secular or conversational languages of the higher classes.

The traditions of pronouncing and writing Slavonic were being weakened either by the influence of other languages (such as Ukrainian) or by the strong impact of Russian dialects. The pronunciation "system" of the ruling class bore all the traits of a mixed dialect. To be sure, there was a tendency to imitate the pronunciation of the Moscow nobility and Moscow civil servants. But in the Muscovite pronunciation, although there were no sharp dialectisms in the consonant system, there were fluctuations between North Russian and South Russian norms in the vowel system. Toward the middle of the seventeenth century, the spelling of such proper names as Афанасей, Андрей, and Александр with an initial **a** instead of **o** tended to become established. This feature is connected with the increased influence of South Russian dialects, as is the clear *akan'e* seen in the letters of Aleksej Mixajlovič and Peter the Great. In Peter the Great's papers, we have examples such as великое сумнения and нижнея слова—both nominative singulars.

The language of Moscow in the seventeenth century was a mixture, since various dialects and foreign languages (both Eastern and Western) were spoken there. The upper classes thus had no "literary" norm. The issuance in 1675 of an order by Aleksej Mixajlovič, stating that a person was not to be considered dishonored if he happened to write certain phonetic dialectisms in a petition, was clear evidence for such a state of affairs.

Thus, in summary, the basic processes taking place in the literary language of the seventeenth century were: first, a disintegration of the Church Slavonic system; second, the growth of Southwestern (Ukrainian) and West European (mainly Latin and Polish) influence; and, third, a broadening of the literary functions of the living Russian language and of the business or chancery language.

2

The First Half
of the Eighteenth Century:
The Mixing of Styles

I. THE INCREASE OF WEST EUROPEAN INFLUENCES AND NEW
SOURCES OF THEM

In the Russian literary language of the beginning of the eighteenth
century, the processes which had become evident in the second half
of the preceding century continued their development. But new
phenomena occurred as well. There was increased opposition to the
ecclesiastical literary culture, in the name of living Russian speech,
and in the name of the secular language, the chancery language,
the juridical language, and technical and professional dialects.
There were also attempts to create a new national norm akin to
the norms of West European languages, attesting to a broader
influence of Western culture and civilization. Polish remained, for
some time yet, the upper-class model in various technical fields.
Many Polonisms, however, were a residue of earlier borrowings,
and, although Poland remained an intermediary for West European
concepts, the number of translations from Polish was reduced.
Before the time of Peter the Great, Polish translations were the
order of the day. During his reign they almost disappeared. Growing
knowledge of Latin and other Western languages permitted a
by-passing of Poland. Polish influence gave way to German. But
the Polish and Latin influences, which had penetrated the written
language and the speech of the upper classes quite deeply, provided
a background for continued Europeanization of the literary
language, particularly in the development of abstract concepts.

Latin played an enormous role in the elaboration of abstract scholarly, political, civil, and philosophical terminology in the eighteenth century. Word lists of the first half of the eighteenth century give ample testimony to the influence of Latin: естественность (*essentia*), чистый разум (*purus intellectus*), чувственность (*sensatio*), право естественное (*jus naturae*), провидение (*providentia*), умозрительные (*theoretica*), сущее (*ens*), философия умственная (*rationalis*), самостоятельные (*absoluta*), обоюдужительные (*amphibia*), самоволие (*spontaneitas*), приличное (*decorum*), правило (*norma*), обязательство (*obligatio*), закон естественный (*lex naturalis*), винность (*culpa*), прилог (*conditio*).

2. THE SIGNIFICANCE OF TRANSLATIONS IN THE PROCESS OF EUROPEANIZATION OF THE RUSSIAN LITERARY LANGUAGE

The increased translation activity of Peter's time, directed at sociopolitical, scholarly, and technical literature, led to a modification of Russian constructions in the direction of European ones. A new way of life, a developing technical education, and a change of ideological landmarks demanded new forms of expression. New intellectual demands led to borrowings and translations of West European concepts. At the beginning of the eighteenth century, the influence was external: instead of an independent development of a conceptual system based on West European models, there was merely a borrowing of terms or a replacement of Russian terms with foreign equivalents. Elements of the same sort of fetishism that had developed about Church Slavonic words were now carried over to West European terminology and phraseology. F. Polikarpov, for example, in one of his translations, left some Greek and Latin terms in the original, *for the sake of a better understanding;* other terms he borrowed and glossed (ангуль–угол, екватор–уравнитель).

Two tendencies were at loggerheads, however; for the process of mechanical borrowing was not compatible with the simultaneous trend to translate European terms into Russian or Slavonic. Moreover, with expanded study in all sorts of technical fields, the question of rendering scientific terms became extremely difficult. There is a story of a translator who committed suicide because he despaired of translating French horticultural terms. Even experienced translators had difficulty conquering the linguistic material. Russian did not yet have the resources to render all the abstract and technological terms. One of Peter the Great's ukases attempted to remedy the situation by ordering that specialists in certain technical fields be required to learn languages and that language specialists be required to learn a technical field.

3. THE ASSIMILATION OF WEST EUROPEAN ADMINISTRATIVE, SOCIO-POLITICAL, MILITARY, MARINE, TECHNOLOGICAL, SCHOLARLY, AND BUSINESS TERMINOLOGY

The language of the Petrine epoch was characterized by an increase in the significance and influence of the governmental language. The reorganization of administration and of military and naval affairs, and the increase of trade and manufacture, all led to the establishment of a new terminology imported from Europe. This "Europeanization" clearly bore the stamp of the government.

Most administrative terms came from Germany, such as the Table of Ranks and such words as патент, контракт, штраф, архив, асессор, факультет. One scholar calculated that a quarter of the borrowings of the period consisted of administrative terms, and aptly characterized the situation in the following manner (with borrowed nouns and words derived from them):

Появляются теперь *администратор, актуариус, аудитор, бухгалтер, герольд-мейстер, губернатор, инспектор, камергер, канцлер, ландгевдинг, министр, поли-цеймейстер, президент, префект, ратман* и другие более или менее важные особы, во главе которых стоит сам *император.* Все эти персоны в своих *ампте, архиве, гофгерихте, губернии, канцелярии, коллегиуме, комиссии, конторе, ратуше, сенате, синоде* и в других административных учреждениях, которые заменили недавние думы и приказы, *адресуют, акредитуют, апробуют, арестуют, баллотируют, конфискуют, корреспондуют, претендуют, секондируют, трактуют, экзавторуют, штрафуют* и т. д. *инкогнито* в *конвертах, пакетах* разные *акты, акциденции, амнистии, апелляции, аренды, векселя, облигации, ордера, проекты, рапорты, тарифы* и т. п.

There was a strong Latin, as well as German, influence on this administrative vocabulary, sometimes through the intermediary of Polish. Judging by the form, many nouns in **-ия** came through Poland (акциденция, инструкция, нация, etc.). The same is true of verbs in **-овать** (авторизовать, адресовать, etc.).

Many military terms were also borrowed from German (юнкер, генералитет, лозунг, вахта, лагерь, штурм, etc.), although there was also a strong French influence in this area (барьер, батальон, бастион, гарнизон, пароль, манеж, марш). In maritime terminology, Dutch and English predominated. From Dutch came such words as гавань, рейд, киль, руль, верфь, док, кабель. From English there came бот, фут, бриг, мичман. It is interesting to observe that Dutch words were borrowed in connection with ships made of metal, whereas the English terms refer to wooden ships. Only a small number of Italian, French, and German naval terms were borrowed: флот, абордаж, алярм, десант came from French; бухта, лавировать came from German; мол, авизо came from Italian. But even here there was mixture—there could be competition, for example, between German and Dutch terms.

Additional barbarisms entered the Russian language at the beginning of the eighteenth century in the areas of engineering, mining, urban architecture, agriculture, and various crafts. Here, too, the influence was predominantly Polish and German, although certain architectural terms were taken from Italian. In the fields of learning and technology (mathematics, economics, jurisprudence, political science, natural history, geography, anatomy, and other areas), there was also a great influx of foreign terminology at this time.

In addition to the borrowings which provided terms for new things and concepts, there were also some which merely replaced native Russian words: виктория was used instead of победа, for example, and резольвовать instead of решать.

The written styles of technology and bureaucracy, permeated by Europeanisms and fostered by government practice, gradually moved toward the center of the literary linguistic system. Petrine Europeanization was thus reflected in a polytechnicalization of language. Russian "Europeans" betrayed a craving for dictionaries and lexical commentaries which introduced society into the sphere of European "communal life." Antiox Kantemir, in his translation of Fontenelle's *Entretiens sur la pluralité des mondes* (1730), provided a host of translations, commentaries, and lexical juxtapositions. A few examples will suffice for our purposes: имагинация (умоначертание, или мечтание, причудение), порцелин (по-русски фарфор), вояжир (по-русски ездок, тот, что в дороге), баллон (пузырь надутый), интерес (дело, польза, корысть). Note also: предсуждение–*préjugé*, рассуждатели–*raisonneurs*.

The literary language was reorganized on the basis of this kind of political and technical reconstruction. Moreover, the old system of the secular, official language was disturbed; and the ideological and rhetorical forms worked out on the basis of religious polemical writing had to adapt themselves to new lexical material and a new semantic content.

4. THE DEVELOPMENT AND TRANSFORMATION OF PROFESSIONAL DIALECTS

In addition to the European influences discussed above, professional phraseology from the city colloquial language began to find its way into the literary language. Already in the seventeenth century, city dwellers had begun to adopt professional phraseology which emanated from the German settlement in Moscow or from Southwestern Rus' (the Ukraine and Belorussia). In the Southwest, a middle-class city social structure had formed earlier, as had various guild jargons. In the seventeenth century, therefore, when a wave of artisans came to Moscow from the Southwest, words of West European origin established themselves in the language of handicrafts. In shoemaking, we have such terms as дратва, вакса, клейстер. And in cabinetmaking and metalwork, words like бляха, бондарь, клапан, кран, винт appeared around the turn of the century. Moreover, terms which had been adopted earlier were replaced or modified: printing terms, for example, which had been adopted from Italian in the sixteenth and seventeenth centuries, now began to show the influence of German. It is interesting that the Russian terms for engraving (резать and its derivates) gave way now to градировать, based on German. At mid-century, with the rise of French influence, the latter term in turn gave way to гравировать.

5. THE EUROPEANIZATION OF THE EVERYDAY, SOCIAL—WRITTEN AND CONVERSATIONAL—LANGUAGE OF THE UPPER CLASSES

Technical and professional elements changed the general tone of the styles of the written language; but they could not attain a governing role in the "domestic" or social language of the upper classes, who were attracted to the social externals of European civilization. New words and new concepts entered the everyday language of society only as the norms of social etiquette changed. Eastern hyperbolic and self-deprecatory forms of address, for instance, disappeared from correspondence. In Tsarevich Aleksej's early letters to Peter the Great, the old formulas are required: Государю моему батюшку, царю Петру Алексеевичу сынишка твой, Алешка, благословения прося и челом бьет. But toward the end of the first decade of the eighteenth century the address is simply: Милостивейший государь батюшко! and the letter ends with всепокорнейший сын и слуга твой Алексей. The old traditions remained strong, but the new interest in "Romanic gallantry" was clearly reflected in language.

Changes in costume, social conduct, and education also led to new concepts and borrowings. Here the role of Polish, which at the beginning of the century still preserved its importance as a worldly, aristocratic language, was especially great, both as a direct source and as an intermediary one. Words such as the following established themselves in everyday speech: авантаж, аккуратный, бал, властный, грунт, деликатный, дигнитар, диспут, квит, конфузия, кошт, мода, пашквиль, публичный, рисунок, скарб, специальный, труп, факт, шельма, шоры. Not all these words came into the language in the beginning of the eighteenth century—many of them were borrowed in pre-Petrine times; but they did change their function at this time, by entering literary usage. Many such words were Polonisms only in the sense that they had come through Polish from Latin, French, or German. Other examples of this sort are авантура, автор, амбиция, визит, зала, каналья, кураж.

Many words applying to the social milieu came directly from French and German. From French, we have пассаж, экипаж, фонд, резон, приз, менаж, марьяж, лимонат, etc. From German came позумент, галстук, фурман. The interest in barbarisms also led to new "European" phraseology: for example, на голову побить неприятеля (*aufs Haupt schlagen*); паки пришел в себя (*er ist wieder zu sich gekommen*). It even led to a passion for peppering one's prose with foreign words: я не получил на оное *антвортен*; во всех своих делах сколько *фермите* и твердости показал. These phraseological examples are taken from the letters and papers of Peter the Great.

The influence of German and French was strengthened by the fact that their practical value was quickly realized by the landowner and merchant, and also by the fact that both languages were educationally important to the aristocracy. Up to the forties, however, German was of more significance than French.

6. THE FASHION FOR FOREIGN WORDS

The Westernizing tendencies of the Petrine epoch were reflected not only in the borrowing of many words for new concepts and objects, but also in the disturbance of the external forms of both the church language and the everyday language by barbarisms for which there was no real need. The use of foreign words created a special stylistic nuance of modernity. It was a means of breaking away from both the old traditions of Church Slavonic and the old-fashioned everyday colloquial language. The very phonetic novelty of the structure of borrowed words seemed to call for a reformed structure of the literary language which would correspond to the appearance of the reformed government.

The fashion went so far that some members of the nobility of the time almost lost their ability for normal, correct use of the Russian language and developed, instead, a mixed jargon. Such was the language of Prince V. I. Kurakin, the author of *Gistorija carja Petra Alekseeviča:* В то время названной Франц Яковлевич Лефорт пришел в крайнюю милость и *конфиденцию интриг амурных.* Помянутый Лефорт был человек забавной и роскошной или, назвать, *дебошан* французской. И непрестанно давал у себя в доме обеды, *супе и балы.* Peter the Great had to chastise one of his emissaries for excessive use of foreign terms: "In your reports (В реляциях твоих) you use very many Polish and other foreign words and terms. Because of this, it is impossible to understand what is at issue. Therefore, in future, all your reports (реляции) to us are to be written in the Russian language, without recourse to foreign words or terms."

But the use of barbarisms was only an external symptom of a new, Europeanized language style. What is striking in the official and publicistic language of the Petrine era is the constant use of doublets. The foreign word is immediately followed by its Russian synonym or by a new lexical definition, which is either enclosed in parentheses or simply joined by a conjunction. This technique had an educational function in a context where the government was attempting to bring large masses of people into a new political system; and it was commonly employed in laws, publicistic tracts, and technical translations from the beginning of the eighteenth century up to the 1840's. A few examples will suffice to illustrate the method: Некоторые акциденции (или доходы) получать; апелляцию или перенос до коммерц-коллегии чинить; аркибузирован (расстрелен); в такой дистанции (расстоянии); никакой рефлексии и рассуждения не имели; мир ... подтвержден ратификациями (подтверженными грамотами).

7. THE BROADENING OF THE COMPOSITION AND FUNCTIONS OF BUSINESS STYLES IN CONNECTION WITH THE PROCESS OF MIXTURE AND REGROUPING OF STYLES AND STRENGTHENING OF THE LITERARY RIGHTS OF SPOKEN RUSSIAN

The Europeanization of the scholarly, technical, publicistic, and social lexicons changed the systems of the business styles of the written language and broadened their rights and functions even more than in the seventeenth century. The adaptation of Russian to West European languages, and its mixing with them (as exemplified by the codex of correspondences between the Russian and Western conceptual systems which was worked out in translations), could be most easily carried forward in the official, publicistic, social, and everyday styles. The stylistic stratification of the written literary language (a language midway between Slavonic writings and social varieties) was extremely complex and variegated, particularly if one takes narrative styles into account. The phonetic, grammatical, and lexical fluctuations were also numerous and variegated.

In the corrections of a text of a Russian translation of the time, it is interesting to note the application of a principle of replacing simple, vulgar expressions with more elevated, bookish, Slavonic, or chancery expressions. For example, буде is corrected to ежели, поругание is changed to презрение, and хозяйкам is replaced by госпожам. Also characteristic of the style of the epoch are mixtures of vulgarisms with solemn Slavonicisms. In the language of one translator, подмески не было, не замай, and прамолвишся exist side by side with достизаю, выну, and пакирождение.

The secular literary language of Petrine times, which grew out of publicistic and official styles, was, by designation and significance, more "national" than Church Slavonic. It was closer to oral styles and less bound by the shackles of Church rhetoric. Moreover, it could respond to the program of the regime with greater flexibility. The secular literary language thus became the decisive norm of literariness. This state of affairs coincided with the social program of the regime, which brought to the fore a service and merchant class of mixed origins. The new class in turn took part in the formation of Europeanized styles of the business language.

8. THE ROLE OF THE SOUTHWESTERN LITERARY TRADITION IN THE PROCESS OF MIXTURE OF STYLES IN THE RUSSIAN LITERARY LANGUAGE

In the second half of the seventeenth century, when Russian came under the influence of the Ukrainian-Polish business language, many Ukrainianisms and Polonisms entered the language of the upper classes of the nobility and clergy. In the first third of the eighteenth century, this "mixed" composition of the Russian literary language became more complex; but the language retained, in its basic features, both its double character and its freedom to fluctuate (depending on function and social situation) between the refined rhetoric of Slavonic, the monotonous syntax of the chancery language, and the motley forms of the conversational speech of society.

The mixed forms of this kind of language may be illustrated by the epistolary style of an immigrant from the Southwest, Dimitrij, Metropolitan of Rostov (the excerpt is from a letter to students at the Rostov seminary):

Дети, слышу о вас худо: вместо учения учитеся раздражению, а неции от вас во след блудного сына пошли со свиньями конверсовать. Печалюсь зело и гневаюсь на вас; а якоже вина развращения вашего та, что всяк живет по своей воли, всяк болши, того ради ставлю вам сенеора господина Андрея Юревича, чтоб он вас мунштровал як цыганских лошадей, а кто будет противен, той пожалован будет плетью.

In this passage we have Slavonicisms (неции, печалюсь зело, яко же, etc.), Latin-Polish borrowings (конверсовать, сенеор, мунштровать), chancery phrases (а кто будет противен, той будет пожалован плетью), and colloquialisms (всяк болши, цыганских лошадей). The same sort of stylistic mixture may be found in the letters of Stefan Javorskij and Feofan Prokopovič.

9. THE INSTABILITY OF THE PHONETIC SYSTEM OF THE LITERARY LANGUAGE IN THE FIRST HALF OF THE EIGHTEENTH CENTURY

The orthoepic norms and the orthography of literary and business styles were very unstable. The general tone was dictated by Moscow upper classes. But Muscovite pronunciation itself had not yet become unified. Northern and southern features were still conflicting (e.g., various degrees of *akan'e*, fluctuations between [γ] and [g], fluctuations between the comparative endings **-яе** and **-ее**, etc.). In general, dialect forms freely existed in conversational Russian, so that the problem of normalization became acute only at mid-century. Grammatical handbooks spoke exclusively of the norms of Church Slavonic phonetics. The church pronunciation, which, in principle, strove for a comparatively exact reproduction of the graphic forms of the text (e.g., distinction between **ѣ** and **e**; preservation of stressed **e** before hard consonants; pronunciation, on the Ukrainian model, of a velar fricative [γ]; etc.), broke into the everyday language and contributed another admixture to it.

10. BREADTH AND FREEDOM OF GRAMMATICAL (MORPHOLOGICAL) FLUCTUATIONS IN THE LITERARY LANGUAGE OF THE BEGINNING OF THE EIGHTEENTH CENTURY

Phonetic variation was accompanied by grammatical fluctuations. In the literary styles which required solemnity and rhetorical expression, many archaic Slavonic forms of declension were to be found: for example, forms preserving the substitutive softening of velars (в грамматице, человеци), dative plurals in **-ом, -ем** (войском, болезнем), instrumental plurals in **-ы, -и** (с народы), locative plurals in **-ех** (походех), and archaic forms of the adjectives. There were also Slavonic conjugational forms: for example, infinitive endings in unaccented **-ти,** second person singular endings in **-ши,** the imperfect and aorist, and the adverbial participle in **-юще,** **-яще** (помышляюще).

The manner in which these archaic forms were used is an indication of the social origin of the style, since a passion for these forms in the language of the middle class or the nobility was always accompanied by errors in their use.

The grammatical rupture between such Church Slavonic archaisms and the living language was clearest in the area of verbal aspect and tense. While the high styles of the "Slavonic dialect" cultivated the archaic variants of the past tense (the aorist, imperfect, and compound past), and only dimly differentiated aspect, the living language already clearly differentiated perfective and imperfective aspects and used aspect to compensate for the loss of the former tenses. On the other hand, it was precisely in the business and narrative styles of the literary language that Muscovite and even provincial dialectal features appeared freely. Examples are: (1) South Russian colloquial forms of the nominative plural neuter in **-ы, -и** (болоты, деревьи, писании, письмы, from the letters and papers of Peter the Great. Trediakovskij wrote that "Many not only say—which is pardonable—but also write: рассуждении, повелении, instead of рассуждения, повеления."); (2) genitive plural forms in **-ей** for feminine nouns with nominative singulars in **-a** (пашей, from Peter the Great; пулей, from Pososkov; these forms became more common toward mid-century); (3) genitive plurals in **-ов, -ев** for neuter nouns (примечаниев, здоровьев, трактованиев; these endings also spread to those nouns which formed their nominative plurals in **-ья**); (4) still quite rare, but characteristic, genitive plurals in **-ов, -ев** for feminine nouns with nominative singulars in **-a** (бомбов, старых азбуков, from Peter the Great); (5) North Russian comparative degrees in **-яе**; and (6) free and frequent use of iterative verbs in **-ывать, -ивать.**

In general, the mixture of Slavonic and Russian forms was not subject to any firm grammatical regulation in any of the various literary styles. There were dim echoes of the Southwestern rhetoricians' theory of three styles; but these were lost in the commotion that arose when the old, feudal, literary language of the church collided with the fresh, unregulated languages of Russian business and conversation.

11. STYLISTIC VARIETY AND DISORDER IN THE SPHERE OF SYNTAX

There was an even greater lack of order in syntax. Here one could still find the old, primitive, conversational, coordinate constructions of the business language. These either lacked conjunctions all together or connected clauses with the conjunctions и, а, да, но; sometimes they were complicated by monotonous forms of subordination using the conjunctions понеже, дабы, чтоб, etc., or relatives such as который, кой. Thus they often formed a mechanical, associative chain. Such constructions were a mixture of archaic Slavonicisms and spoken forms, and there was no logical order to their development. In the simpler constructions, the syntactic center was the verb, surrounded by a few complements and one or two adverbs. Here is an example from the turn of the century:

А морозы были великие, многие на дорогах помирали, также и снеги были глубокие, а вода была великая на Москве, под Каменный мост под окошки подходила и с берегов дворы сносила и с хоромами и с людьми, и многих людей потопила, также церкви многие потопила ...

At the beginning of the eighteenth century there also existed more intricate syntactic structures. In their manner of linking clauses, in their phraseology, and in their complicated word order (with the verb at the end), these bore the stamp of the refined, literary, Latin-Polish or German syntax. A quotation from a ukase of Peter the Great will illustrate the style:

Господа сенат! Хотя я николи б хотел к вам писать о такой материи, о которой ныне принужден есмь, однакож понеже так Воля Божия благоволила и грехи христианские не допустили. Ибо мы в 8-й день сего месяца с турками сошлись и с самого того дня, даже до 10 часов полудня в превеликом огне не точию дни, но и ночи были, и правда никогда, как и почал служить, в такой дисперации не были, понеже не имели конницы и провианту ...

There were also "beautiful" forms of expression which, in their manner of composition and in their varieties of symmetrical disposition of words, followed the rules and contrivances of South-western (Latin-Polish) rhetoric. For example:

И тако аще обратимся к исскуству его величества в политических делех, то усмотрим, что не токмо в оных в свете так многие явные и великие дела сам показал, что может за лучшего политика почтен быти, но и многих из подданных своих (которые в том почитай не малого исскуства не имели), привел в такое состояние, что могут равняться с министры других еуропейских народов, и в негоциациях политичных и чюжестранных дел с доброю славою должность свою за высоким его величества наставлением отправляют.

Finally, among the various syntactic forms of the period, there continued to exist those Slavono-Greek constructions which derived from seventeenth-century styles with their penchant for "weaving of words."

12. PROCESSES OF STYLISTIC MIXTURE IN THE AREA OF THE LITERARY LEXICON AND PHRASEOLOGY

The lexical and phraseological composition of the secular business styles of the literary language was also variegated. It had a broad social and dialectal scope. At one extreme, it included the conversational language of the city, the language of the peasantry, and provincial dialect elements. The same was true of the colloquial language, which made wide use of synonyms and dialectal doublets. A Russian-Dutch lexicon of 1717 reveals a number of such synonymous usages in its definitions: for example, *постоялый двор* или *нослежной двор*; *ширинка* или *платок*; пень, колода, чурбан, отсечек. Tatiščev, in his *Razgovor o pol'ze nauk i učilišč*, cites a number of colloquial or rural words employed by the nobility: вот, чють, эво, это, пужаю, чорт, instead of се, едва, здесь, страшу, бес. Also interesting is the use of colloquial speech in the satires of Kantemir, as, for example, in his first satire (1729):

> ... глупо он *лепит горох в стену*
> Румяный *трожды рыгнув* Лука подпевает ...
> Когда все дружество, вся моя *ватага*
> Будет чернило, перо, песок да бумага ...
> Вот для чего я, уме, немее быть *клуши* советую
> *Плюнь ему в рожу;* скажи, что *врет околесну* ...

At the other extreme, however, these same secular business styles dipped heavily into Church Slavonic. F. Polikarpov's *Trejazyčnyj leksikon* contains much from the Slavonic "dialect," although it also has many business, conversational, and colloquial doublets: *лоно* или *пазуха*; *извнутряю* или *потрошу*; *яко же рещи—как наприклад сказать*; *зад главы* или *затылок*; *брак* или *свадба*; *постройка зри созидание*. It occasionally has living expressions without Slavonic synonyms: *брюхатая жена*; *вошливый*; *обора* зри *веревка*. But Polikarpov's passion for Slavonicisms and his insufficient inclusion of everyday expressions and foreign borrowings apparently displeased Peter the Great, since Musin-Puškin informed Polikarpov that the dictionary was not well received.

Thus, even in the lexicon of that transitional epoch there was a considerable mixture of elements from various languages and styles, as the plethora of undifferentiated synonyms makes all too clear. It is obvious that the need for a stylistic and grammatical normalization of the literary language was becoming ever more perceptible and urgent.

13. THE LANGUAGE POLICY OF THE GOVERNMENT AND THE PROCESS OF MODERNIZATION AND IDEOLOGICAL TRANSFORMATION OF THE CLERICAL LANGUAGE

The process of forming new literary styles out of a mixture of elements from European, ecclesiastical, business, and conversational languages was accelerated and regularized by government instructions. This process was a symptom of the nationalization of the Russian literary language, of its separation from the professional church language, and of its rapprochement with the everyday styles of the spoken language.

The sort of literary expression cultivated by Peter the Great and his associates was made clear in instructions to translators. V. Musin-Puškin, one of the executors of Peter's translation enterprises, asked Polikarpov to correct one of his translations, using simple Russian words and the words of the Foreign Office rather than the elevated words of Church Slavonic. The language worked out by the translators in the Foreign Office was precisely the linguistic structure from which the inventory of the national literary language was to be drawn. It was an amalgam of the colloquial language, the everyday conversational language, the business language, and the church language, as well as the lexicon, phraseology, and semantics of West European languages—particularly Latin, Polish, German, and French. It was exemplified in publicistic, narrative, diplomatic, bureaucratic, and technical styles.

The system of Church Slavonic was considered inadequate for

expressing the ideology of a reorganized society. An illustration of the tendency to restrict the sphere of use of the Slavonic "dialect" (and at the same time evidence that Church Slavonicisms were incomprehensible to the broader public) is provided by synonymic translations of Slavonicisms into Russian: ветрило–парус; клятва–божба; овн–баран; ковчег–сундук; древле–давно; дондеже–на всякое время; зде–здесь; далече–далеко; зле–худо, неладно. The simplification of the literary language and the criterion of understandability were guiding principles of the government policy, as well as a felt need of society. A translator wrote to Peter the Great concerning a translation of a book on mechanics: "I humbly implore your Highness to deign to hear this tract first and decide, with the intelligence bestowed on you from above, what value there will be in it for people. For the author of the tract wrote very concisely and obscurely, caring less for public benefit than for the subtlety of his philosophical writing." Peter the Great wrote to Ivan Zotov in the same vein: "In the book which you are now translating, you must take care to translate as clearly as possible; and one need not adhere to a word-for-word translation but, having arrived at an exact understanding, one must then write as clearly as possible."

Peter's instructions to the Synod concerning the composition of the catechism are also interesting in this connection: "... it must be written so simply that a villager can understand it. Or in two ways: simpler for the villager and more elegantly for the cities, for the delectation of the listeners—as seems most fitting to you." Here Slavonic and the colloquial language are opposed not simply as different styles of the literary language but also as social and esthetic incommensurables.

In this fashion, in the first third of the century, a sharp division was made between the Slavonic "dialect" and secular styles. Trediakovskij stated that Slavonic had become "very unclear" (очюнь темен). However, even within the style of the business language, it was not a question of a complete break with the church-book tradition but of a modernization and ideological transformation of it. It was a question of finding the living elements in it and utilizing them for the further development of a Europeanized Russian literary language. What took place within Church Slavonic, therefore, was a differentiation of liturgical and cult elements from the national, literary elements—which society then secularized. There was no exchange of one language for another, but a reorganization of a literary language which was now composed of a mixture of Russianisms, Slavonicisms, and Europeanisms. Yet the literary style of the Petrine era, despite its mixed character, never ceased to be called "Slavonic." Indeed, sometimes Russian and Slavonic were equated with each other; and sometimes the term "Slavono-Russian" was used as a designation of the new, national, Russian literary language which had not broken with the Church Slavonic tradition but had merely removed the professional, ecclesiastical elements from it.

14. CHANGES IN THE STRUCTURE OF THE CHURCH SLAVONIC LANGUAGE

The transformation of secular styles of the literary language could not but be reflected in the structure of the church language as well. A whole series of Church Slavonic genres, such as homiletic literature, underwent a still greater influence of business and publicistic styles. A process of church "specialization" and liturgical "professionalization" took place. In the church-book language, the forms which were introduced by the Southwestern tradition became dominant—with the exception that out-and-out Ukrainianisms were gradually weeded out of Russian Slavonic (although Sumarokov was still complaining of vestiges of them). But, although Ukrainianisms were removed, the influence of Southwestern rhetoric retained its force until the second half of the eighteenth century. There was a noticeable interest in rhetorical figures, though the results were often too refined and monotonous. Occasionally one locution would go on for pages. Word distribution, length of periods—often complicated by inserted phrases—reminded one of school Latin. For added beauty, foreign words were often inserted, for at that time they did not offend the ear.

Another development within Church Slavonic was a differentiation of styles, in which some styles became secularized. Prokopovič's sermons, for instance, show a strong secular tone in their mixture of Slavonic, everyday words, trivialities, and borrowings:

Когда слух пройдет, что государь кому особливую свою являет любовь, как вси возмятутся, вси к тому на двор, вси поздравляти, дарити, поклонами почитати, служити ему, и умирати за него будто бы готовы, и тот службы его исчисляет, которых не бывало, тот красоту тела описует, хотя прямая харя, тот вводит рода древность из-за тысячи лет, хотя бы был харчевник или пирожник ... А с тем, кто в такое добро вбрел, что делается, тот уже и сам себя забыв кто он, не ведомо что о себе мечтает. Между тем от зеркала не отступит, и делает экзерцицию, как бы то честно и страшно являти себе ...

On the other hand, the high, solemn styles of the language of civil affairs were, in turn, being nourished by church rhetoric, mingling it with Europeanisms and words from the business and secular languages. One may find examples in panegyrics, which used clear archaisms (archaic forms of participles, the aorist, archaic lexical items such as абие, обаче, and even forms without jotation—оружиа, etc.). There was frequent collision of high-style with conversational words: и те *русацы*, **увидя храбрость** вашу; *абие* **оружие брося сами побегут**. Alongside Slavonicisms, foreign borrowings would appear: объездя свои полки и всем *кураж* наговоря, *викторию* приял. These mixtures of Slavonic and secular-panegyric styles only deepened the contradictions between the archaic, professional aspects of Slavonic and the social, everyday base of the secular literary language.

The obsolete forms of Slavonic gradually had to be winnowed out of the literary language. Everyday Russian elements—either identical with Slavonic elements or brought into greater or lesser concordance with them—as well as Europeanisms, assumed primary importance.

15. REMNANTS OF MEDIEVAL FETISHISM IN THE SPHERE OF THE CHURCH-BOOK LANGUAGE

For a long time, up to the second half of the eighteenth century, a magical, devotional attitude toward "Holy" words and a religious-scholastical interpretation of them persisted. This attitude is what mainly distinguished the language of the clergy and of people who came from the ranks of the clergy. Trediakovskij is an instructive example. After unsuccessful attempts to reconstruct the literary language on the basis of the spoken norm of the educated classes, he returned, in the fifties and sixties, to the cult of the Slavonic language—at a time when patriotic and nationalistic attitudes were being reborn in governing circles. In addition to his European habits, he revealed a fetishistic attitude toward words which had a symbolic, religious meaning in the church.

For an understanding of the principles of the magical-theological interpretation of religious concepts which had come to characterize the clergy and people from the clergy, Trediakovskij's remarks on Sumarokov's use of words are important. Sumarokov had written Отверзлась *вечность*, все герои предстали во уме моем. Trediakovskij commented: "The author is prophesying about the past ... and it is not correct to say that *eternity* opened to him; for instead of eternity, it was *antiquity* that opened ... Eternity is a property only of God, not of heroes." Even more indicative is his subsequent scholastic interpretation of the idea of eternity: "If I were not absolutely certain that the author knows absolutely nothing about theology, I would think that he is speaking of what theologians call *aeternitas a parte ante* ... and that from this, at the end of all things, there will follow *aeternitas a parte post*."

But such a theological attitude toward the word in literature was an atavism, and characteristic mainly of the clergy. Even Trediakovskij had first fought for the secularization of the literary language and only later bowed to the majesty of the "Slavonicism" of the high style. Furthermore, his scholastic nominalism was a far cry from the word-fetishism of the Schismatics. It is symptomatic that that same Trediakovskij announced the necessity of breaking with the sources of scholastic education by opposing the exclusive role not only of Greek but also of Latin, and by calling for a deeper mastery of West European languages and culture.

16. THE REFORM OF THE ALPHABET AND ITS SIGNIFICANCE FOR THE HISTORY OF THE LITERARY LANGUAGE

The reform of the alphabet in 1708 was a sharp blow to medieval attitudes toward the Church Slavonic language. It was a clear expression of the end of the hegemony of church ideology and an external, but very significant, symbol of the break between the church-book language and the secular speech styles. The new civic alphabet approximated the model of European printed books and was a first step toward the creation of a national Russian written language. Slavonic graphics ceased to be the literary norm and was reduced to the role of the hieroglyphics of a religious cult. Moreover, the graphic change removed from the literary language such trappings of "Holy Writ" as the abbreviation signs (титла) from words which command reverence.

To be sure, the reform was not a radical one. The new alphabet differed from the Slavonic one in that, at first, the letters и, з, ω, ꙍ, ѱ, ѯ, ѕ, and ѵ were totally excluded from it, accent marks and abbreviation marks were removed, and the rest of the letters changed their form to correspond more to Latin graphics. Soon, however, concessions seemed to be made to the Slavonic alphabet: the letters ѕ, ꙍ returned, two dots were always placed over the letter **i**, and the letter ѵ gradually came back into use.

Thus, the reform of the alphabet, by not radically changing the graphic basis of Church Slavonic literature, represented a mixed, transitional state. But its significance was great, for it increased the need for a sharper delineation of the line between "church" and civic linguistic forms and categories. Trediakovskij's profound criticism of the phonetic and morphological basis of church graphics, in his *Razgovor ob ortografii*, is a case in point. He noted that the aorist, the dual number, the old adjectival forms, the dative plural in **-ом**, etc., belonged to the Slavonic language, but not to the civic one. He had a negative attitude toward the grammatical norms of Smotrickij and Polikarpov. Trediakovskij's very idea of writing and printing "according to the sound" (по звонам) reveals the felt need, in Russian society, for a national self-determination in language and an emancipation from the feudal church-book culture.

17. THE APPEARANCE OF NEW LITERARY-ARTISTIC STYLES

In the atmosphere of chaotic mixture and conflict of new and old forms—the religious and the secular, the national and the foreign—in the Russian literary language at the beginning of the eighteenth century, the seeds of new styles of narrative and lyric expression germinated and began to grow. They created an original synthesis of the national and the European literary cultures. At the same time they deepened the connection between the artistic language and folk literature. Russian poetry abandoned syllabic verse and began to imitate European and folk tonic-verse models.

Stimulated by contacts with Europeans and other foreigners from the German suburb in Moscow, a *sui generis* "European" style of expression arose in intimate lyrics. For example, the biblical concept of passion as fire now appeared in phraseological forms that were close to the images and lexicon of European lyric poetry:

> Мне же бедному достоить
> *Искры в пепел закопать* ...
> *На сто* [что] *же в них любовь искры родила*
> Иже сердце во мне *нещадно жгут.*

The phraseology of the European sentimental romance is also revealed in the image of the heart wounded by Cupid's arrows. Compare Trediakovskij, in the poem "Proščenie ljubvi":

> Покинь, Купидо, стрелы
> Уже мы все не целы,
> Но сладко уязвлены
> Любовною стрелою
> Твоею золотою.

Other commonplaces of this sentimental phraseology, which reproduced the sensibility of the West European "gallant," were the images of fetters and bondage, and of the lover melting from love. The loved one, the joys of love, and love itself were compared to a flower. Many of the images and mythological accessories of school classicism penetrated this sentimental phraseology and appeared beside images from Christian mythology. The biblical angel became an epithet for the loved one: Остаюсь, мой ангел, верный твой слуга по гроб. The same images and phraseology penetrated the genres of narrative and drama.

In this fashion, a flood of West European "gallant" phraseology entered the Russian literary language at the beginning of the century; and with it came changing manners and Europeanized forms of social intercourse.

In lexicon, grammar, and phraseology, however, these new currents still betrayed the mixtures of the Petrine era. Church Slavonicisms still formed the lexical base for both poetry and narrative; obsolete nominal forms still appeared, as did the aorist; and the language still could not get along without chancery elements (such as фортуна злая мне ничему не служит). West European barbarisms were also present, and there were many traces of Ukrainian and Polish lexical elements, particularly in the lyric poetry of the very beginning of the century.

Finally, traces of the everyday colloquial language and of folk poetry are to be found in songs and lyrics of the period. Academician V. Peretc can hardly be correct when he asserts that the lexical peculiarities of folk speech had only a weak influence. As a matter of fact, the colloquial language of the city played a significant role in the new style of gallantry and erotic languor, as evidenced in this poem:

> А я свои глаза
> Мочу слезами.
> Для чево так? Я не бывал твой враг.
> Одумайся, от сна пробудися,
> Проклятый враг, поть вон.
> Для ча мне мстишь
> И милова манишь
> Прочь отгоняешь.

18. THE PROCESS OF FORMATION OF SECULAR LITERARY STYLES OF THE NATIONAL RUSSIAN LANGUAGE

The new "Europeanized" forms of the Russian literary language which arose in narrative prose and lyric poetry were a symptom of the growth of secular national styles. The literary language approached the spoken language of educated society. New currents came from West European literature by way of translation. V. K. Trediakovskij's *Ezda v ostrov ljubvi* (a translation of Tallement's *Voyage de l'île d'Amour*) most clearly shows the need for a new language in a society undergoing Europeanization. The translator's preface announced a crisis in the church-book language and sounded the call to bring the literary language closer to the "simple Russian word, the one we use when we speak to each other" (Trediakovskij saw the literary norms as reflecting the speech of the court nobility and the educated bourgeoisie).

The translation of Tallement's novel was put forward as a creative attempt to participate in the formation of a non-Slavonic literary language suitable for the transmission of the feelings, thoughts, and concepts of a society in transition. According to Trediakovskij, the social significance of the attempt derived from three factors: "Firstly, the Slavonic language is a church language— and this is a secular book. Secondly, the Slavonic language, in our time, is very obscure and many read it without understanding—and this is a book about sweet love which, therefore, should be understandable to all. Thirdly (which may seem the least important to you but which, for me, is the most important), the Slavonic language now sounds harsh to my ear, even though until now I not only wrote in it but spoke it with everyone ..."

An analysis of the language of the translation—and of other translated and original novels of the first half of the century—shows that it contained the same sort of mixture of Slavonic, Russian, and Western elements as the lyric poetry of the time. But the Polish stream had begun to dry up, to be replaced by German and French ones (especially among the upper classes).

The language of the petty-bourgeois styles of the eighteenth century was, at the same time, more "demotic" and more archaic. It was more hobbled by the obsolescent norms of Slavonic and the chancery language. It was less "literary" from the point of view of those genres and styles which were oriented toward the upper classes. Polish-Ukrainian verses, chants, psalms, and old translated novellas continued to flourish among the middle classes during the course of the eighteenth century—at a time when the literary tastes of the upper classes had changed sharply. Notes in eighteenth-century collections of verse show that the old poetry was preserved among people of the cloth, petty bureaucrats, merchants, junior officers, and soldiers—that is, among semi-educated people. People of this milieu continued to read the manuscript collections of novellas made in the sixteenth and seventeenth centuries. Such old literary genres had their influence on petty-bourgeois styles of the literary and written language. These styles, changing and adopting elements from the "high styles," remained on the peripheries of literature almost to the end of the eighteenth century.

The Russification of the literary language took place through constant contact with the city colloquial language as well as with the language of peasants. After the rejection of Slavonic, the language of the peasantry became a natural ally of the new literary language. However, the democratic tendencies in the literary language were very restricted—these were but the first sprouts of a new, national, literary language—and Trediakovskij saw the base of the new literary language in the spoken language of the upper classes instead. He considered it imperative, in fact, to introduce the norms of this upper-class spoken language into the high style.

The task of creating a national literary language, however, even in this restricted form, was beyond the powers and status of Trediakovskij. The language of such a Europeanized, non-gentry intellectual did not correspond to the norms of the noble taste which he tried to follow. And, despite his philippics against all that was "rustic" or "base," Trediakovskij himself often stumbled into coarseness. He could not free himself of petty-bourgeois colloquialisms or of the bookish trivialities of a seminary graduate. Thus, in the works of this "professor of eloquence," there is a strange mixture of church words, vulgar colloquialisms, archaisms, barbarisms, and his own numerous neologisms. Examples may be seen in the ode "Vešnee teplo":

> **Премножество** явилось птиц,
> На ветвь с той ветви от *поспеха*,
> **Препархиваящих** певиц.
> **Вещает** *зык* от них громчайший
> Что их жжет огнь любви жарчайший ...

But what we have here is not a question of personal tastes or personal failures. Rather, it is a question of fluctuations in the styles of the literary language. And soon Trediakovskij was to follow a different path.

19. THE TENDENCY TOWARD RESTORATION OF THE CLERICAL TRADITION IN THE SECOND QUARTER OF THE EIGHTEENTH CENTURY

Reaction against the dominance of foreigners in the upper levels of government and bureaucracy and the growth of national self-consciousness in the forties had their effect on the conception of the literary functions of Church Slavonic, particularly in regard to the high style. The desire to limit enthusiasm for "Europeanisms" and to eradicate French and German distortions of the Russian language led to an overvaluation of the historical role of Church

Slavonic in the system of the Russian literary language. The question of regulating literary styles on the basis of varying mixtures of Russian and Slavonic became unusually acute. Historically valid methods were not found at once, and extreme tendencies came into being.

Trediakovsky, sensitive to the spirit of the times, soon altered his own direction, to advocate now that Slavonic be restored to its former leading role. The forties and fifties saw an intensified restoration of the literary rights of Slavonic. Protests against the dominance of European languages became louder, and, at the same time, the break between the high styles and the national Russian language base became greater. On the one hand, Trediakovskij asked: "Why are we to endure the poverty and restrictions of French when we have the lavish wealth and breadth of Slavono-Russian?" And, on the other hand, he inveighed against those who complained that his use of Slavonic words was "not Russian" by declaring that their real complaint was not that the words were foreign to Russian, but, rather, that they did not come from the marketplace or the public square. He thus opposed both a modeling of the high style on French and German and a broadening of the literary rights of the vernacular. He asserted the importance of styles organized either on a Slavonic or Slavono-Russian basis, particularly in those works which had to do with either religious or intellectual subjects.

The result, of course, was that the solemn and official styles of the literary language became archaized. An outward manifestation of this archaizing tendency was the change of the external form of the word. Trediakovskij insisted on writing and pronouncing Тилимах, and not Тилемах or Телемах; ироический, and not героический; пиима, and not поэма; etc. Republishing, in 1752, a work he had first published in 1735, Trediakovskij systematically Slavonicized it and excluded conversational and chancery elements from it. A few examples follow:

1735	*1752*
пред мои представляют очи	мысленному зрению моему представляют
не будет никаковыя отговорки	не будет отнюдь отречения
что все чрез меру	а сие все безмерно

Accusing Sumarokov of a "base" word usage, Trediakovskij averred that a chief source of Sumarokov's difficulty lay in the fact that he had not had an adequate acquaintance with church books in his youth and, therefore, did not possess either a sufficient stock of "select" words or a habit for the proper ordering of words. Sumarokov, in turn, accused Trediakovskij of ruining the literary language with excessive Slavonicisms in spite of his earlier attraction to the "vernacular dialect"; and he drew the moral that "Truth has nothing to do with any extreme."

The conquest of "extremes" could come about only through a harmonious synthesis of national Russian elements, indispensable European elements, and those elements of Slavonic which still retained their vitality. Trediakovskij, however, dashed from one extreme to another. He lacked artistic taste, "a feeling for proportion and suitability" (Puškin), and the historical breadth of a genius.

Thus, in the first decades of the century, the problems of creating a national literary norm and of achieving a structural unification of various elements were not solved. Although the contours of new, Europeanized styles had made their appearance, the roles of various social and linguistic elements were not yet clearly defined, and feudal traditions in the literary language had not yet been overcome. The achievement of synthesis and the extension of the borders of the literary language in the direction of the living language were yet to be accomplished, in different fashions, by two great eighteenth-century writers, Lomonosov and Sumarokov.

3

The Mid-Eighteenth Century: Normalization and Disintegration of the Three Styles

The broadening of the literary language in the direction of the living, national language, the mixture of styles (particularly of "high" and "low"), the stormy process of assimilating lexical borrowings, the polytechnicalization of language, the complication of the content and functions of the chancery language, the disintegration of the ideological basis of Church Slavonic (which had governed the literary system up to the seventeenth century)—all these phenomena of social and linguistic flux began to slow their tempo toward the fourth decade of the eighteenth century. Democratization and Europeanization of the language could not regulate the different stylistic varieties of the literary language. No firm system of literary styles and genres had been worked out, despite the fact that new forms of literary expression had appeared in the Petrine era.

Such stylistic contradictions and chaotic lack of system could be overcome either by a new synthesis of those same linguistic elements which had exerted a basic unifying force in the past—namely, Church Slavonic and the various styles of written and spoken Russian—or by a "Europeanization" of the Russian language which would assimilate the grammar, semantics, and stylistics of the West European languages. The former, however—a new synthesis of Church Slavonic and everyday Russian—was more

55

consonant with national and historical realities and could cooperate sooner in the democratization of the literary language. Such a synthesis, moreover, would provide a base for the gradual assimilation and nationalization of the deeper structures of West European languages, and would provide a release from external lexical borrowings (barbarisms). The West European stream in the first half of the century was still too weak to pretend to equal status with Slavonic.

2. THE HISTORICAL BASES OF THE THEORY OF THREE STYLES

The attempt at a theoretical establishment of a new system of literary styles conditioned by the interaction of Church Slavonic and national Russian elements within the literary language is connected with the name of Lomonosov—the great reformer of the Russian language and the creator of its first scientific grammar. In this attempt, Lomonosov used as a framework "the theory of three styles," which was known to ancient rhetoricians and was put forth by many Slavic rhetoricians of the sixteenth and seventeenth centuries.

The premises for Lomonosov's reform consisted of three basic propositions: First, he wished to establish that the literary functions of Church Slavonic had narrowed, that the restoration of "decrepit" systems of the church language was unrealistic and pointless, and that what was necessary was to develop and elaborate that part of the Slavonic tradition that was viable, understandable, expressive, and semantically meaningful. Second, he hoped to prove that the living structural elements of Church Slavonic were to be sought for in the Bible, in liturgical books in common use, and in popular religious works such as saints' lives—and not in the professional, polemical, or dogmatic church literature. Third, he asserted, as historical fact, that the forms of national speech were an essential, organic part of the literary language and that the composition and relationship of various literary genres were conditioned by the methods and principles of the mixing and interaction of Church Slavonicisms and Russianisms.

In his *Pis'mo o pravilax rossijskogo stixotvorstva* (1739), Lomonosov established the idea that the Russian literary language must develop "according to its national composition, but not in isolation from general human culture." He put forth three theses: that the development of a language must rest on its native properties—it must not borrow what is unnatural to it; that one must utilize and affirm what is native; and that one must not borrow what is objectionable, nor bypass what is good.

The basic ideas of Lomonosov's system of three styles were set forth and developed in his discourse *O pol'ze knig cer'kovnyx v Rossijskom jazyke* (*ca.* 1758). Here, the historical significance of Church Slavonic was seen to lie in the fact that it transmitted classical and Christian Byzantine culture and provided the literary language with many scholarly, philosophical, and abstract terms. In these respects, the development of Russian differed from that of the literary languages of Western Europe, where the formation of many national languages took place in isolation from the medieval language of church culture (Latin). Church Slavonic, in contrast, stood in a direct and close relationship to the Russian language. The Church Slavonic language, nationalized by Russian culture and serving as the "Holy" language of religion and church books, at the same time enriched and developed the national language. It was a limitless source of semantic and artistic influence on the styles of the Russian language. This relationship of Slavonic and Russian was proof positive, for Lomonosov, of the necessity of creating a literary system by a synthesis of the two. Russian society, in trying to create a national language adequate to the technical and cultural level of the age, must therefore do so, not by a general rejection of Slavonic, but in close cooperation with its living traditions.

In this historical framework, Lomonosov affirmed a close connection between the tradition of Slavonic writing and the future development of the national Russian language; he even pronounced Church Slavonic the custodian of the national unity of the Russian language. He pointed out that dialects of the Russian language, spread out over a vast territory, were mutually comprehensible, unlike the situation in Germany; and he was inclined to see the source of this unity in the influence of Church Slavonic.

Lomonosov also attributed the historical stability of the basic lexical stock of the literary language to Church Slavonic. Thus, Church Slavonic appeared not only as the source and the support of the national unity of the Russian language, but also as the structural base of the Russian literary language. From it were to flow the peculiarities of the three styles—high, middle, and low.

3. THE THREE STYLES OF THE LITERARY LANGUAGE. DIFFERENCES
IN THEIR LEXICAL AND PHRASEOLOGICAL STRUCTURE AND IN THE
AREA OF THEIR USE. LOMONOSOV'S WORK IN THE CREATION OF
A RUSSIAN SCIENTIFIC TERMINOLOGY

The structure of each style was defined by the relationship of Slavonic to Russian forms. The Slavonic forms were to be only those in general use. Lomonosov thus took most of his Slavonicisms from the books used in the divine service, namely the Psalter, The Acts of the Apostles, and the Evangel, although he also made many borrowings from Proverbs, and from prayers and hymns. Even more important was Lomonosov's attitude toward the grammatical structure of Church Slavonic. All archaic forms were to be excluded, and only the living, productive forms—those which brought the literary language into close contact with church literature—were to be used in the high style.

Lomonosov assigned strictly defined genres to each style. Heroic poems, odes, and ceremonial speeches on important themes were to be written in the high style. ("By means of this style, the Russian language, utilizing the Slavonic language of church books, has the advantage over many European languages.") The middle style was to be used for friendly verse epistles, satires, eclogues, elegies, and "all theatrical works which require the ordinary human word for a lively presentation of the action" (although the high style could be used to express heroism or elevated thoughts). In prose, the middle style was to be used to describe "memorable events and noble teachings." Comedies, humorous epigrams, songs, familiar epistles, and accounts of ordinary affairs were to be written in the low style.

The styles were differentiated grammatically, lexically, phraseologically, and even phonetically. But in his *O pol'ze knig cer'kovnyx*, Lomonosov touched only on the lexical differences between the styles. He isolated five categories of words: (1) Church Slavonicisms which were completely obsolete and unusable (рясна, овогда, etc.);

(2) Slavonicisms which were known to all literate people even though they were not used in speech (отверзаю, насажденный, взываю, etc.); (3) words common to both Russian and Slavonic (Бог, слава, рука, etc.); (4) Russian words unknown to Church Slavonic but accepted in the conversational language of cultured society; and (5) words from the language of the common people. The first category of words was banished from the literary language. The mixing of the other four categories, in various proportions, determined the three styles. In Lomonosov's opinion, the high style should consist of words from the second and third categories. The middle style should consist of words from the third category, although it could use some colloquial Russian words, provided that they were not too vulgar and "low," and it could also use a small quantity of "high" Slavonicisms, provided that great caution be taken to prevent the style from becoming pompous. The low style could not have any Church Slavonic words; it consisted of conversational and colloquial words and expressions, and even permitted, "upon consideration," words from the language of the common folk.

Such a division of the linguistic material belonged entirely to Lomonosov. Kantemir and Trediakovskij approached it, but they were not conscious of what they were doing. What is very important is that Lomonosov not only divided the Slavonic material but categorized the Russian lexicon as well; for he was aware that the juxtaposition of a vulgarism and a Slavonicism would repel the individual with a well-developed taste. Moreover, since one of Lomonosov's guiding ideas was that linguistic evolution was continuous, he was able to join the old and the new into one harmonious whole, thereby removing some of the grounds for objection by opposing camps—that is, proponents of the old and proponents of the new.

Parenthetically, it is interesting to note that Lomonosov himself used vulgarisms and dialect forms on occasion, even in the high style. Sumarokov castigated him for this failing, as did Trediakovskij, who wrote:

> Он красотой зовет, что есть языку вред:
> Или ямщичей вздор, или мужицкой бред.
> Пусть вникнет он в язык славенский наш степенный
> Престанет злобно врать и глупством быть надменный ...

Besides striving for nationalization of the church language, Lomonosov also limited the usage of European barbarisms. Even the most scholastic sermons of the seventeenth and early eighteenth centuries were filled with foreign borrowings taken from the chancery or political languages. In place of excessive borrowing in the sphere of abstract and scholarly terminology, Lomonosov introduced neologisms based on Russian or Slavonic morphemes. He also advocated changes in the semantics of already existing words, and Europeanization of the language of science by utilizing the international scholarly terminology founded largely on Greek and Latin roots. Many of the words and terms which Lomonosov created, borrowed, or semantically changed are now part of the language of science. Some examples are: воздушный насос, земная ось, равновесие тел, кислота, магнитная стрелка (neologisms); горизонтальный, диаметр, квадрат, атмософера, барометр, микроскоп, поташ (words of general international currency); опыт, движение, наблюдение, явление, частица (semantically changed native words).

4. THE PHONETIC DIFFERENCES BETWEEN THE STYLES

The differentiation of the three styles was not limited to their lexical and phraseological content. There were also, as mentioned above, phonetic, morphological, and syntactic peculiarities. Phonetic differentiation, however, occurred only between the high and the low style, and, coupled with the predominance of Slavonic morphemic shapes in the high style (lack of full vocalization, Slavonic **жд** and **щ** instead of Russian **ж**, **ч**, etc.), it contributed toward distinguishing the high style as a special variety of the literary language.

One of the major differences was the pronunciation, in the high style, of [e] in those places (under accent before a hard consonant) where native Russian had [o]. Contemporary grammarians pointed out, for example, that colloquial speech had миӧд, лиӧд, весиӧлый where learned speech had мед, лед, веселый. In his *Grammatika*, Lomonosov pointed out case and tense forms which were pronounced with a и̂о in the colloquial language: триӧх, везиӧш, огниӧм, ниӧс, виӧрст, бриӧвна. He also provided a list of words for which he recommended such a pronunciation: мед, лед, лен, пес, Петр, for example. Thus, originally, the pronunciation of an [o] was confined to the low style, and even as late as the beginning of the nineteenth century A. S. Šiškov could complain that such a pronunciation was not consonant with the "nobility and purity" of the literary language. In the middle style, the colloquial pronunciation was not canonized until Karamzin's reform at the end of the century, even though it had long been the accepted pronunciation in the language of educated society.

Another important phonetic difference between the high-style (and the church) pronunciation and that of the low style was *okan'e* (the pronunciation of unaccented, orthographic **o** as [o]). There is testimony to this feature in statements describing church pronunciation, in some of Lomonosov's statements, and elsewhere. This feature, too, persisted into the nineteenth century.

Up to about the 1760's, the high style followed the church distinction in the pronunciation of **ѣ** and **e**. Trediakovskij compared the pronunciation of **ѣ** to German and Polish pronunciation of the Latin sequence *ie* and considered its fusion with **e** "immeasurably wrong." In other words, **ѣ** was supposed to be distinguished from **e** by having a higher and narrower pronunciation. Moreover, before **ѣ** the preceding consonants were to be fully palatalized, while before **e** they were to be only "partially" palatalized. The distinction, however, which was already foreign to the colloquial language, disappeared completely in the sixties.

Still another feature which differentiated the high style from the low was the pronunciation used to render orthographic **г**. In the low style it was pronounced as a voiced velar stop, [g], while in the high style it was pronounced as a voiced velar fricative, [γ]. Trediakovskij, speaking, of course, of the literary pronunciation, stated: "We Russians all pronounce **г** like the Latin *h*." There were even suggestions that the Latin symbol *g* be introduced to render the pronunciation of words which belonged exclusively to everyday language. Lomonosov, who was of North Russian origin and favored a voiced velar stop, seemed to wish to restrict the sphere of usage of the fricative. He stated that it came from Slavonic and suggested that it be used in such words as Господь, глас, благо, and their derivatives, and in the oblique cases of Бог. Šiškov, at the beginning of the nineteenth century, still spoke of the predominance of the fricative pronunciation in the high style.

Many writers spoke of differences in stress between the high style and the low and often considered deviation from the high style reprehensible. In the absence of firm norms, colloquial and even dialectal stresses sometimes found their way into the high style. Sumarokov accused Lomonosov of using North Russian accents occasionally, and was, in turn, criticized by Trediakovskij for using accents characteristic of the conversational language of the Muscovite nobility. In 1812, a list of words in which there was a difference of stress was published, with the suggestion that the church pronunciation be followed in the high style, while the "civic" pronunciation be used in the low style and in conversation. A few examples follow:

Church pronunciation	*Civic pronunciation*
во́инствующий	войнству́ющий
де́рзнет	дерзне́т
зна́менует	знамену́ет
избра́н	и́збран
сумра́к	су́мрак
це́на	цена́

Finally, the "phonetic" system of the high style differed from that of the low by a system of special intonations and gestures.

5. THE PRINCIPLES OF GRAMMATICAL DIFFERENTIATION OF THE STYLES. MORPHOLOGICAL DISTINCTIONS

Questions concerning the grammatical differentiations of the styles were particularly important. There seemed to be an imperative need to establish the deviation of Slavono-Russian style from the church language. Grammatical categories which had disappeared from general use but were preserved in the church language (the aorist, the imperfect, and declensional forms with substitutive softening of the velars: руце, врази) were still appearing in the written language of the middle class and sometimes even in that of the nobility. Trediakovskij complained, for instance, of the survival of archaic forms in the dative and locative plural of certain nouns. What normalization of the high style required was a definition of those forms of Church Slavonic which still had literary rights.

Limitation of Church Slavonic forms opened the gates for native Russian ones.

Grammatical differences between the high style and the low are itemized below. The first fourteen items (and unidentified quotations) are from Lomonosov's *Grammatika:*

(1) In the genitive singular of masculine nouns, the predominant ending in the high style was **-a**, in the low style **-y**. "This difference in the antiquity of words and the importance of the designated objects is very perceptible and often shows itself in one and the same noun. For we say Святаго Духа, человеческаго долга, ангельскаго гласа, and not Святаго Духу, человеческаго долгу, ангельскаго гласу. In contrast, it is more natural to say розоваго духу, прошлогодняго долгу, птичья голосу, instead of розоваго духа, прошлогодняго долга, птичья голоса."

(2) In general, the same stylistic repartition applied to the prepositional singular of masculine nouns. The ending in the low, "Russian" style was **-y**; the high, Slavonic ending was **-e**. (This was particularly true after the prepositions в and на.)

(3) The low style differed from the high style in its wide use of diminutives and augmentatives.

(4) The comparative and superlative endings in **-ейший**, **-айший**, **-ший** were considered a mark of "the solemn and high style, particularly in poetry" (высочайший, превысочайший, обильнейшии). But one was warned not to use these endings on adjectives which did not occur in Slavonic or which had a "low" meaning.

(5) In the high style, ordinal numerals preserved their archaic forms (четыредесятый and not сороковой; девятьдесятый and not девяностой). Similarly, the ordinals from eleven to nineteen were to retain their archaic forms in specifying the day of the month and in those instances when the reference was to an important matter (сентября пятоенадесять число and not пятнадцатое число; Карл вторыйнадесять and not Карл двенатцатой).

(6) The collectives двое, трое, etc., "are used only with people— and then mainly with people of lowly origin; one should not say трое бояр ... but, rather, три боярина."

(7) Participial forms were declared to be a characteristic of the high, Slavonic style. Therefore, participles could be formed only from those Russian verbs which were identical with the corre-

sponding Slavonic ones, both in form and meaning. Participial constructions were only to be used in writing; in the spoken language they were to be replaced by relative clauses. Participles were not to be formed from verbs with a low meaning. Finally, in those places where participles were appropriate, the participles used were to be formed from Slavonic verbs and not from their Russian cognates (e.g., волшебствующий and not колдующий).

(8) Past passive participles from Slavonic verbs ended in **-ый**, genitive **-аго**, and were to be written with a double **-нн-**. In Russian, they ended in **-ой**, genitive **-ого** (and **-ово**), and were to be written with one **-н-**.

(9) In adverbial participles, the ending **-ючи** was declared to be more appropriate for Russian verbs and **-я** for Slavonic verbs (thus толкаючи and not толкая; дерзая and not дерзаючи).

(10) In the "simple Russian language," interjectional forms of the verb, created from imperfective past tenses, were permitted for the depiction of "rapid actions." So, from глядел one could form глядь, from брякал, бряк, from совал, сов. Compare, in V. I. Majkov's language: тут щука приплыла и уду трях.

(11) In passive constructions, the use of the reflexive verb was declared to be a property of the high style (он от нас превозносится). However, it was considered safer to use the passive participle, because фараон потоплен водою was unambiguous, whereas фараон водою потопился introduced the semantic possibility that he was drowned by his own wish.

(12) The verb есмь was rarely expressed, especially in normal style and conversation; but, in the high style, the use of the form was always possible.

(13) With the interjection O!, Slavonic used the genitive case (О чуднаго промысла!), while Russian used the nominative.

(14) In Slavonic, the use of the dative absolute was recommended, "upon due deliberation." "Perhaps, with time," said Lomonosov, "the common ear will become used to it and this lost beauty and brevity will return to the Russian language."

A. A. Barsov, who defended the literary rights of the city colloquial language in his grammar of 1771, added a number of items to this list:

(15) In the declension of nouns, the following distinctions were

to be found: (a) In the low style, the nominative plural neuter ended in **-ы, -и** (желании, селы; compare, in Deržavin's language: поученьи, отдохновеньи). (b) Neuters in **-ие** which replaced the **-и-** with **-ь-** in the colloquial language had their genitive plural in **-ев**, whereas the high style maintained **-ий** (желаньев). (c) Neuters in **-мя** declined like ordinary neuters in the low style, whereas the middle and high styles maintained the old inflection (Deržavin, for example, has such forms as: сын время; в водах и в пламе).

(16) Distinctions in the declension of adjectives were as follows: (a) In the high style, the nominative singular masculine ended in **-ый**, whether it was accented or not; in the low style it ended in **-ой**. (b) In colloquial speech, the genitive singular of the masculine-neuter adjective ended in **-ово, -ево** and **-ова, -ева** (compare, in V. I. Majkov's language: ево, тово, жаренова, нашева).

(17) In colloquial speech, it was observed that the oblique cases of сорок had fallen together into one form, сорока, although variants were possible.

Another grammarian, V. P. Svetov, pointed out a few more grammatical differences between the high style and the colloquial language:

(18) In the genitive singular feminine of the adjective, forms in **-ыя, -ия** were declared to be proper only in the high style. Some writers mixed low and high styles with respect to this feature (compare V. I. Majkov: средь склизкия дороги).

(19) Declensional forms of the type **-ие, -ия, -ием, -ию**, etc., maintained the final stem vowel in the high style, whereas the colloquial language replaced it with **-ь-** (for example, житие [not житье] Петра Великого; любовию but пылью).

(20) The same phenomenon occurred in certain verbs, where the high style maintained the vowel while the low style replaced it with **-ь-** (бию, пию, as compared with бью, пью).

(21) In the second person singular and in the infinitive with unaccented ending, the high style admitted a final **-и** (глаголати, трудишися).

The number of morphological differences between the high style and the low could be still further increased:

(22) In the colloquial language, many masculines had their nominative plural in -a, -á, -ья, -ьй, whereas the high style maintained -e, -и, -ы (Trediakovskij, for example, noted the colloquial form дворяна in place of дворяне).

(23) Forms of the comparative in -яе were gradually confined to the low style. Lomonosov, who still permitted them, nonetheless recommended -ee. Sumarokov, who defended the colloquial language, also defended forms like миляй, складняе. In noble literary styles, forms in -яе were forbidden as "folkish" toward the end of the century.

(24) In the low style, there was a broad development of iterative verbs, such as станавливалась, приезживал.

The Russian literary language gradually freed itself of Church Slavonic grammatical archaisms. The autonomy of Slavono-Russian was established. The range of use of Church Slavonic forms was reduced. The morphological system of the literary language approached that of the colloquial language and, in the low style, tended to coincide with it.

6. THE SYNTAX OF THE LITERARY LANGUAGE

Literary normalization of syntax around the middle of the eighteenth century was almost exclusively centered on the high style, and this is understandable. The high style had behind it the rich tradition of church-book rhetoric, which, with Polish and Latin influence, achieved a considerable refinement by the end of the seventeenth century. Later, the influence of German rhetoric was added. In the middle and low styles, colloquial syntax was mixed with a Latin-German syntax deriving from Church Slavonic and the chancery language. French syntax, which found its support in the spoken language of the aristocracy, was only beginning to have an influence. And writers were defending a free word order, especially in poetry. Clumsy Latin-German constructions were to be found both in the business language and in various literary styles up to the last decades of the century. For example, noun forms (especially the genitive) were separated from their attributes by other nouns with their modifiers. The following quotation (dating from 1773) may serve as an example: И мы почти ежедневно

ожидаем *подлинного о Бухарестского конгресса разрыве известия.*
Also characteristic of the prose of the period is the verb in final
position: Намерение восприять изволила оный брак в месяце маие,
при помощи Вышняго, совершить.

Parodying the syntactic style of the earlier eighteenth century,
a friend of Karamzin wrote to him in 1775: Для дополнения же
твоего исскуства писать таким слогом советую тебе читать сочинения
в стихах и в прозе Василия Тредиаковского, коего о в любви езде
остров книжицею пользуюсь переводную ныне с французского
языка и весьма ту читаю.

Word order was the burning question of the Russian literary
language of the eighteenth century. Linked to it was the question
of the composition and length of the sentence and the length of the
period. The Church Slavonic, bookish period was long, with a
confused distribution of words, with the verb at the end, and with
a multitude of conjunctions which incorporated one subordinate
clause into another and sundered the thread of the main clauses.
Lomonosov, in his *Ritorika*, tried to incorporate into this high
Slavonic style a multitude of variations in word order and a
complex, intricate syntactic symmetry. He elaborated a theory of
periods in which he distinguished three types: rounded, or moderate
(in which the syntagmas were of approximately equal length);
variable (with syntagmas of quite unequal length); and abrupt
(in which the syntagmas were short and not connected by conjunctions). An example of a variable period would be:

Смотреть на роскошь преизобилующия натуры, когда она в приятные дни
наступающего лета поля, леса и сады нежною зеленью покрывает и бесчислен-
ными родами цветов украшает, когда текущие в источниках и реках ясные воды
с тихим журчанием к морям достигают ...; слушать тонкий шум трепещущихся
листов и внимать сладкое пение птиц: есть чудное и чувства и дух восхищающее
увеселение.

An example of an abrupt period would be:

Уже врата отверзло лето,
Натура ставит общий пир,
Земля и сердце в нас нагрето.
Колеблет ветви тих зефир,
Объемлет мяхкий луг крилами,
Крутится чистый ток полями ...

Thus arose, in literary composition, a complex and whimsical system for distributing and relating periods; and a symmetrical hierarchy for subordinating elements within the period was established. Speech was transformed into solemn declamation, subject to strictly varying schemes of rhythm and melody in its intonational movement.

Within the sentence as within the period, Lomonosov did not depart from the Slavonic construction—with its odd inversions and the verb in final position—which prevailed at the end of the seventeenth century. He established strict limits only for certain constructions, holding, for example, that "the adverbial participle, with its cases, is best placed first, both in prose and in verse":

> Взирая на дела Петровы,
> На град, на флот, и на полки,
> И купно на свои оковы,
> На сильну власть чужой руки,
> Россия ревностно вздыхала.

In general, whimsy (though governed by desire for symmetry) and variation were the order of the day for the syntax of the mid-century ornamental style. Lomonosov warned against beginning every period with the same part of speech, or the same case or tense. "One must endeavor," he explained, "to have the first word be now a noun, now a verb, now a pronoun, now a participle, and so on. The same care must be taken at the end of every period."

7. THE PRINCIPLES AND METHODS OF RHETORICAL CONSTRUCTION IN THE HIGH STYLE

Lomonosov's *Ritorika* is important also for the study of the stylistic structure of the eighteenth-century high genres, which relied so heavily on biblical and ecclesiastical phraseology. It gives norms for those relationships of ideas and images which defined the lexicon and the literary composition of the high style. Moreover, it breaks with a tradition that made rhetoric the exclusive property of the clergy and the higher church schools.

In the *Ritorika*, every "theme" is divided into "terms"—for example, the *theme* "incessant labor overcomes obstacles" is composed of four *terms* (conjunctions and other auxilliary words do not count as terms)—and each term is accompanied by primary, secondary, and tertiary ideas. Each individual idea generates strings of other ideas, logically interrelated and strictly regulated by rules for connecting tropes and figures. A standard system for establishing a connection between objects is first established, resting on such categories as "the whole and its parts," "material properties," "vital properties," "name," "place," "time," "circumstances," "antithetical things," etc. Then, within, for example, the category of "vital properties" (those properties which define the conceptual structure of an animate object), there are distinguished spiritual gifts, passions, good qualities, bad qualities, etc. Finally, the principles by which the elements are related within one series are regulated, and thus, within the area of "passions," for instance, contrastive pairs are established, such as "satisfaction and despair," "hope and fear," etc. In similar fashion the modes for interpreting "names" are given. Here one finds etymology (Владимир, "ruler of the world"), homonymic play (свет, "the universe," versus свет, "the opposite of darkness"), letter and sound transpositions (Рим–мир), and characterization by historical image (Аттила–бич божий), etc.

Lomonosov does not give, in the *Ritorika*, a detailed exposition of the principles for a comprehensive linkage of primary, secondary, and tertiary ideas around a "term." He merely illustrates the process with the term "obstacle," which he takes to imply the following primary ideas: of vital properties—"fear"; of time—"winter," "war"; of place—"mountains," "deserts," "seas." In turn, "fear" is surrounded by the images of "pallidness," "shaking" —and so on.

These same rhetorical categories come into play when ideas are united into sentences "which can explain them and present them more vividly to the mind." In this event, however, the rhetorical rules no longer govern a system of word-ideas, but larger compositional wholes. In the structure of the high style of the middle of the eighteenth century, constant, stable forms of conceptual relationships were arranged in the same ways and in the same categories, with regard both to words and to phrases and idioms. One could say that it is this abundance of set phrases and idioms, which appear as whole conceptual units, that sharply sets off the high from the middle style in the first half of the century. To the end of the century, the middle style had no stable phraseological system. Examples of this property of the high style may be taken from Lomonosov. Compare these lines from his "Oda na vzjatie Xotina":

> Россия как прекрасный крин
> Цветет под Анниной державой ...

with the biblical phraseology (Isa. 35:1): Да возрадуется пустыня и процветет, яко крин. Or compare these, from "Oda na vosšestvie na prestol Petra III":

> Тебе от верной глубины
> Руками плещут воды белы;
> Ликуют западны пределы ...

with the biblical phraseology (Ps. 97:8): Реки восплещут рукою вкупе, горы возрадуются.

This grammar of ideas was subordinated, however, to the demands of "poeticalness," which produced a qualitative division between the high and "everyday" styles. An essential element of the high style was its tropes. A solemn, ornamental style based on biblical phraseology and symbolism was established, in which the Slavonicism appeared as an element of abstract ornament. The language had to be filled with pathos and poetic rapture, and the style had to be elevated and animated. All this was brought about by "ornate" expressions (conceits), in which strange, unusual, or unnatural images were linked together. Lomonosov established fourteen different varieties of conceits, following in this the practice of rhetoricians of the Kievan school of the turn of the century (although his practice was complicated by German influence as well). Examples of Lomonosov's demonstrations are:

Comparison:
> Раздранный коньми Ипполит
> Несходен сам с собой лежит

Transformation:
> Смотря на цепь свою, он сам оцепенел,
> И жалким голосом металл об нем звенел.

In this fashion, a play on words came to be characteristic of the high style; sharp and unexpected metaphors were canonized; daring epithets which disturbed logical relationships were introduced; and a whole system for linking "far-fetched ideas" was established. Slavonicisms could stand next to mythological names, scholarly terms, and personal names (in antonomasia). All such devices, however, were of a different order, and were used in a different manner, than the devices of non-belletristic language.

The high style, which, in Lomonosov's opinion, was to be used primarily for civic, heroic, governmental, or religious-philosophical themes, was thus governed by the complex devices of "conjunction of ideas."

8. CONTRADICTIONS BETWEEN THE THEORY OF THREE STYLES AND THE LINGUISTIC PRACTICE OF EDUCATED CIRCLES

The theory of three styles did not provide exhaustive criteria for the exact delimitation of words and constructions in the literary language. Lomonosov's reform renewed an old principle but left its development and elaboration to the individual taste. In everyday usage the differentiation of the styles was more complex. Defining the structural properties of the prosaic middle style was the most difficult. Here, almost to the end of the eighteenth century, there reigned a motley mixture of Slavonic and chancery constructions with forms of a neutral, everyday language.

Sumarokov wrote, in an article "K tipografskim naboršcikam": "You know that not only many translators, but also some authors, know even less of grammar than do the scribes who pride themselves on their favorite words—понеже, точию, якобы, имеет быть, не имеется, and others like them." He also reproached Lomonosov for using words from the chancery language even in the high style: "Токмо is a chancery word, and is equivalent to так как, якобы, имеется."

The literary language, however, with its complex and contradictory evolution, could not remain channeled by the theory of three styles; only the high style of Elizabeth's time appeared in these more or less clear outlines. And even here, Lomonosov's colors were to fade; for the aristocracy, submitting to the influence of French pre-revolutionary culture, was fascinated by French oratory. A language suitable for transmitting thoughts and feelings of a more everyday, simple, and, at the same time, more delicate, complex, and varied nature, was being developed. Sumarokov was not without justification in sharply and maliciously parodying, in his *Vzdornye ody*, the empty, conventional, and pompous symbolism, and the queer composition, of Lomonosov's metaphors:

Lomonosov ("Oda" IX):

> Заря багряною рукою
> От утренних спокойных вод
> Выводит с солнцем за собою
> Твоей державы новый год.

Sumarokov ("Vzdornaja oda" III):

> Трава зеленою рукою
> Покрыла многие места;
> Заря багряною ногою
> Выводит новые лета ...

Lomonosov ("Oda" XV):

> Целуйтесь громы с тишиною;
> Упейся молния росою;
> Стань ряд планет в щастливый знак —

Sumarokov ("Vzdornaja oda" I):

> Там громы в громы ударяют
> И не целуют тишины:
> Уста горящих тамо молний
> Не упиваются росою.

And so the written language of secular society developed in a different direction, along non-Slavonic lines. Lomonosov's work very quickly needed correction by his imitators. And it incited to direct opposition those writers who were trying to create styles approaching the semantic systems of West European languages.

The three styles codified by Lomonosov did not encompass literature translated from European languages. It was difficult to find phraseological equivalents in the conventionally metaphoric, church-book structure of the high style. Therefore, it was necessary either to combine Slavonicisms with barbarisms, thereby destroying the structural principles of the high style, or to create calques, thereby allowing a heterogeneous mixture of lexical categories. In either case, the limits of the style were violated, and new structural forms of the high and middle styles arose which bore little correspondence to Lomonosov's norms. Thus the theory of three styles, based on various principles and devices concerning the relationship of Slavonic and Russian (or, more accurately, on a gradual progression from "Slavonic" genres to mixed, Slavono-Russian ones, and finally to purely Russian ones), revealed both its schematism and its lack of correspondence with either the more complicated stylistic categories of the literary language or the variety of social dialects of the spoken language. The division of styles in the theory was not historical or etymological, but normative and systematizing. The reform was aimed at foreign influences. But it was precisely in this area that Lomonosov's norms for the high and middle styles were most seriously shaken.

The structure of the high style was based on the tradition of common church books, a tradition which was tending to become more and more theological and professional. But the evolution of the high style—in the direction of "secular" literary genres—pulled it away from the original church-book context and led to its organic transformation into a middle, "French" style, or into a high, "colorful" style (which also, more often than not, had its origin in French poetics and rhetoric). Thus, the high, Slavonic style could develop largely on the basis both of obsolescent church books and of theological, homiletic literature. But Russian artistic literature, which was trying to enter the cultural and historical context of West European literatures, was leaving the church culture ever farther behind. To this antinomy in the high style—which is historically connected with the dying out or transformation of a number of its genres (such as the heroic poem, the ode, and the tragedy)—there was a corresponding fluctuation and lack of norm in the middle style. It was an intermediate sphere without clear boundaries. Yet both the high style (which had submitted to the norms of French rhetoric) and the middle style were precisely what best satisfied the interests of a Europeanized, educated society.

In this connection, I. I. Dmitriev's evaluation of Sumarokov (in *Vzgljad na moju žizn'*) is very characteristic: "From the milieu of the youth of the Corps of Cadets, Sumarokov appeared on the arena and we soon heard a new euphony in the Russian language. We were overjoyed at the play of wit. We came to know odes, elegies, epigrams, comedies, and tragedies and, despite both our accustomedness to tradition and his novelty in forms, words, and expressions, we immediately felt the superiority of the young fellow-champion over the court poet, Trediakovskij, and were all charmed by his poetry. It was truly a giant step."

Moreover, the national, occasionally regional, dialectal current in everyday use even in the highest society was so broad, and so fresh, that it could not be stopped by the barriers of the low and middle styles any more than it could be stopped, at the end of the eighteenth century and the beginning of the nineteenth, by the dam of Karamzin's language. This was because the low style still had no norms whatever and reflected everyday conversation, untrammeled by salon etiquette.

9. THE COLLISION OF THE CHURCH-BOOK LINGUISTIC TRADITION WITH THE STYLISTIC CULTURE OF THE FRENCH LANGUAGE

The problem of harmonizing the Russian literary language with the semantic system of French found varying solutions. For the high, solemn genres, the task consisted of Europeanizing Church Slavonic, of fusing French semantics with church-book forms of expression. This kind of attempt became especially common during the second third of the century and was of great importance for the future development of literary Russian. For the middle styles were not worked out sufficiently to be either satisfactory or accessible to broad circles of society, and they as yet had no close connection with either West European languages or spoken Russian. (Trediakovskij had tried to achieve a synthesis with spoken Russian, but often lapsed into "coarseness.")

The demand for a synthesis of a solemn, church-book rhetoric with French oratory came from the highest circles (usually of the capital). In his *Čistoserdečnoe priznanie*, D. I. Fonvizin very colorfully showed how, in his own case, a provincial nobleman first studied Russian from church books and peasant tales, and then, having found himself in court circles in the capital, discovered that it was "impossible to live" in aristocratic circles without knowing French.

In the first version of *Nedorosl'*, which is probably to be dated in the sixties, Fonvizin clearly depicted the cultural and linguistic division in high society—the division between the old culture, based on church literature, and the new culture, with its secular, European foundation. Aksen asks Dobromyslov whether his son has yet learned his "letters." Dobromyslov doesn't know what is meant by "letters," but states that his son has learned French, German, Italian, various sciences, dancing, fencing, horseback riding, etc. And then the following dialogue ensues:

Aksen: But does he know the breviary and the Psalter by heart?

Dobromyslov: By heart, no, but he can read them.

Aksen: Don't be angry, but what good is all that science when he can't recite either the Psalter or the breviary? Then he doesn't know the rubrics of the divine service?

Dobromyslov: Why should he? That belongs to the churchmen, and what he must know is how to live in the world, be useful to society, and be a good servant of the Fatherland.

In Fonvizin's high style there is a clear tendency to synthesize French and Church Slavonic, and the language abounds in Gallicisms and Slavonicisms, as well as pure Russian terms. In this fashion, the Slavono-Russian high style, in all its features, underwent the influence of French rhetoric, which governed the linguistic tastes of the nobility. But in Fonvizin's prose middle style as well, Slavonicisms and Gallicisms were mixed with each other and with forms of the colloquial language. In various of his works, one may find the following categories of words, expressions, and turns of phrase: (1) Church Slavonicisms, often with a solemn, archaic tone (главное *рачение* мое; общий или *паче сказать* природный характер нации; *потрясли основания сего пространного здания*). His Slavonicisms are particulary archaic in the high style (*колико тяжких воздыханий восходило к небесам*), and phraseological Slavono-Gallicisms will exist beside them (*воздать природе горестную дань*). (2) Chancery expressions existing side by side with Slavonicisms (*надлежит присовокупить* к нему и развращение нравов). Characteristic also of the language of the time are such Latin-German constructions as как люди с пятью человеческими чувствами в такой нечистоте *жить могут*. (3) Gallicisms, and "Europeanisms" of various kinds, usually consisting of borrowed words and phraseological calques (*взяв свои места* [*prendre place*]; я принял смелость [*prendre l'audace*]; в самых *генеральных терминах*; *модель вкуса*; *сделать визит*). (4) Words and expressions of the everyday colloquial language (*жить в грязи по уши*; колокольня уже *не Ивану Великому чета*).

The language of Fonvizin's prose is typical of the literary styles of the third quarter of the eighteenth century, which were adapting the literary tradition of the beginning of the century to both the European system of expression and the national Russian speech.

10. THE EVERYDAY SPEECH OF RUSSIAN SOCIETY AND ITS LITERARY NORMALIZATION

Not all elements of the higher levels of society sought a synthesis of Slavonic and French, however. A great many educated people of the provinces and the capital tended rather to break with Slavonic, attempting to work out a system of literary styles that was free of excessive Slavonicisms and that combined European language culture with colloquial Russian.

The everyday language of the period did not avoid the colloquial language of the petty bourgeoisie and freely used elements from peasant language, even from dialect. In the fables of V. I. Majkov, for example, one finds: портняжка прибежал, пыхтит и, как *собака*, *рьяет*; in V. V. Kapnist's *Jabeda:* где плохо лежит, там *зетит* он далеко (with a word from criminal argot meaning "look sharp"); in Sumarokov's parables: мужик осла еще *навьютил* и на него себя и с бородою *взрютил*; in I. Bogdanovič's *Dušen'ka:* иные *хлипали*, другие громко выли.

Within the category of "folk," however, there occurred a differentiation between what was "low" and what was acceptable to higher society. Conventions were used to depict the "language of peasants." For example, V. I. Lukin, in his comedy *Ščepetil'nik*, very clearly presents the "peasant dialect" of two workers from Kostroma, Miron and Vasilij. They both pronounce [c] in place of [č] (and vice versa), [з] in place of [d'], [c] in place of [t'], [i] in place of former [ě]; and they both have *akan'e*, as well as grammatical and lexical peculiarities:

Мирон (держа в руках зрительную трубку): Васюк, смотри-ка. У нас в экие дудки играют; а здесь в них один глаз прищуря, не веть цаво-то смотрят ... у них мне-ка стыда-та совсем кажется ниту. Да посмотрець было и мне. Нет, малец, боюсь праховую испорцить.

Василий: Кинь ее, Мироха. А как испорцишь, так сороми-то за провальную не оберешься. Но я цаю, в нее и подуцеть можно, и колиб она не ченна была, так бы я сабе купил, и пришедши домой, скривя шапку, захазил с нею ...

But such attempts at delimiting "folk" elements became inadequate in the second half of the century. The process of achieving a rapprochement between the everyday language and French led to a reevaluation of the function and components of the "folk" language. As a result, the "low" elements were rejected, and new forms were sought for nationalizing and Europeanizing the language.

These new social efforts could not but have their effect on the attitude toward Slavonic. The decline of the social role of Church Slavonic was evidenced by the fact that Russian, not Slavonic, was placed at the base of education (in the army cadet corps and in foundling homes, for example). I. I. Beckij made some interesting observations on the role of Slavonic in his "General'nyj plan vospitatel'nogo doma": "We adopted a laughable habit of teaching children their letters in school according to Slavonic books and the Slavonic alphabet and keeping them at this study for several years ... Children must be taught from primers printed in the language now in use before Slavonic is begun ... It is well known that every man in society must know the full force and breadth of the language of his Fatherland."

It is obvious that, in such a social and cultural situation, the high style had to disintegrate and change, moving closer to the spoken language; and the middle styles would have to acquire a greater significance in the national literary language. An example of this trend, in the history of the three styles, was the linguistic activity of the great poet and dramatist A. P. Sumarokov.

11. DEFORMATION OF THE HIGH AND LOW STYLES BROUGHT ABOUT BY RUSSIAN EVERYDAY SPEECH AND FRENCH LITERARY STYLES

Using the everyday written and spoken language of the educated milieu of Moscow as his base, Sumarokov announced a campaign against Lomonosov's high style in the name of simplicity of expression and "naturalness." According to Sumarokov, the "pomposity" and "logorrhea of weighty words" of the high style were not consonant either with oratory or with the expressive simplicity of the ordinary language. "Natural expression is the best of all." He berated poets who "give us words which no one ever speaks anywhere." He condemned the artificiality of the oratory of the clergy. And the church-book rhetoric of the high style, which was based on the substitution of conventional metaphors and periphrases for simple designations, he termed "loquacity"—a trait "characteristic of poverty of intellect."

The extent to which the artificial, rhetorical phraseology of the church-book language had become foreign to the Russian intellectuals is illustrated both by Sumarokov's *Vzdornye ody* (a parody of Lomonosov's high style) and by his stylistic commentary on Lomonosov's poetry. For example, in reference to these lines of Lomonosov:

> Возлюбленная тишина,
> Блаженство сел, градов ограда ...

Sumarokov commented:

> *Градов ограда* сказать не можно. Можно молвить *селения ограда; град* от того и имя свое имеет, что он огражден. Я не знаю сверх того, что за *ограда града* тишина. Я думаю, что *ограда града* войско и оружие, а не тишина.

Sumarokov did not have as subtle a knowledge of Church Slavonic as Lomonosov and Trediakovskij. Therefore, when he made one of his heroes speak Church Slavonic, he made mistakes. Trediakovskij was quite ready to correct him, noting in one case that "There are five errors in two and one-half lines." Sumarokov had written: Подаждь ми перо, и абие положу знамение преславнаго моего имени, его же не всяк язык изрещи может. And Trediakovskij corrected this to read: Даждь ми трость, да абие положу знамение преславнаго моего имене, еже не всяк язык изрещи может.

The mixing of Russian and Slavonic forms and the colloquial distortions of Slavonic grammar evident in Sumarokov's writing show that Slavonic was becoming a foreign language to the Russian intellectual. Trediakovskij found many errors in Sumarokov's use of Slavonic. But the norm for the writer was beginning to be "general usage," not Church Slavonic. When Trediakovskij informed Sumarokov that it was impossible to use the word опять in the high style instead of паки, Sumarokov replied: "Is it really fitting to put паки among the tender words in the mouth of a seventeen-year-old maiden when she is talking, in extreme emotion, with her beloved? But опять is an absolutely usable word, and if one is not to write опять instead of паки, then we have to abandon который, которая, которое and make a laughing-stock of ourselves by using the no longer usable words иже, яже, еже, which sound fine in our church books, but which will be in bad taste not only in amorous but also in heroic dialogues." Thus, by mixing Russian and Slavonic forms, a middle style of the literary language was created which was closer to the spoken language of the educated.

In coming forward, however, as an opponent of "extremes," Sumarokov also rejected an identification or fusion of the literary language with the colloquial one. "Why not write as we speak? Such freedom will be limitlessly great and, in the end, there won't be a trace of our ancient language. We will abolish the old dialect in conversation, after having abolished it in writing, then we will fill our language with foreign words and, finally, might forget Russian entirely. That would be very sad. Not a single nation has committed such a murder of its native language, although our language is now being threatened by such a final annihilation."

The spoken language of the educated came closer to the literary language of its own accord; and in doing so it assimilated Church Slavonic expressions. Forms of the high, middle, and even low styles mixed in the literary language, freely combining Slavonic morphemes with conversational word-forming elements, and creating stylistic variants and synonyms for the Slavonicisms. At the same time the literary language selected, from the existing synonyms, those which were less archaic and closer to living speech.

Simultaneously, there was a reevaluation of the literary rights of folk expressions in the second half of the eighteenth century—particularly when they had been accepted into the everyday language of the nobility. Sumarokov, however, rejected the regional and "village" elements he found in Lomonosov's language, and thus avoided both archaic expressions and provincialisms at the same time. He based his own language on Muscovite usage, calling for a general national language, but limiting its content and structure to the norms of the linguistic tastes of the nobility. Relying on general usage, Sumarokov used neuter plurals in -ы, -и even in the high style (in his tragedies, for example, we have forms like озеры, воздыхании, железы, действии). He had neuter nouns taking the genitive plural in -ев (подозрениев, следствиев, нещастиев). He also freely used forms with -ь- instead of -и- in the high style (молнья, божьему, отомщенье, instead of молния, божиему, отомщение). When Trediakovskij rejected such forms as being base,

Sumarokov objected: "Everyone uses them; he should rather have said that they were incorrect, not that they were base usage."

The granting of literary rights to colloquial speech was accompanied, for Sumarokov, by a struggle against lexical barbarisms. He was not a lexical conservative, for he himself introduced new words and new meanings. But he was horrified at the linguistic Gallomania of fops who larded their speech with French (and occasionally German) words, and saw in this macaronic jargon a danger of losing the national identity of the Russian language.

Sumarokov also waged war against the influence of the chancery language—an influence which had been particularly widespread since the time of Peter the Great. In the dedication of his eclogues to the "beautiful ... feminine sex," he wrote: "What is more honorable, to compose eclogues filled with amorous passion and written with good syntax or to compose the litigational letters of slanderers, filled with knavery and written with niggardly syntax? Scribes ... don't use periods and commas ... so that the syntax will be more obscure—for it's easier to catch fish in troubled waters."

Thus, Sumarokov limited the use of Slavonicisms and adapted them to the conversational language of educated society; he decisively rejected the bureaucratic language of the scribes; and he oriented his language toward that of the educated nobility, which was close, in some of its peculiarities, to the folk language (the language of the peasants, for example).

But the language of the upper strata of society was not uniform. One variant of it, most strongly opposed to chancery language, was that of the salon. It was a language ironically dubbed "the present-day foppish dialect of females." Some of the writers of the Sumarokov school, submitting to the demands of the upper levels of society, began to adapt the literary language to that of the salon.

Limitation of the functions of Slavonic and the bureaucratic language was connected with a syntactic reorganization of the literary language. Gradually disappearing from usage were such constructions as the dative absolute, the accusative with infinitive (не считающую в мыслях его ничего к ней почтительного быти), and the nominative with infinitive (Хотя день солнцем освещен, но мнит он быть средь темной ночи). But the influence of the bureaucratic and Slavonic languages on the literary language

was still very strong. One may observe it even in the language
of such light poetry as Bogdanovič's *Dušen'ka:*

> С улыбкою на всех кидая взор приятно,
> Сама *рядила путь* во остров свой обратно
> И для *отличности* такого торжества,
> Явила тут себя во славе божества ...
> Богиня, *учредив* старинный свой парад ...

Thus, in the Russian language of the eighteenth century, there
took place a gradual deformation of the high and middle styles.
Church Slavonic and chancery forms were either excluded or
stylistically transformed. Europeanization and the disintegration
of feudal culture led inevitably to the destruction of high-style norms
based on the tradition of church-book rhetoric. And spoken Russian
announced its rights to an enlargement of its literary functions.
The national bases of the Russian literary language were being
strengthened.

12. INTRUSION OF THE COLLOQUIAL LANGUAGE INTO THE MIDDLE AND HIGH STYLES. THE LANGUAGE OF DERŽAVIN

The question of redistribution of functions between the high Slavonic
style and living speech (which sometimes shifted into peasant
dialect) had an original solution in the language of a great poet of
the end of the eighteenth century, G. R. Deržavin. In his language,
one may note a number of grammatical devices which clearly
"simplify" and "lower" the high style. They are a far cry from the
refinements of the fashionable, noble salon.

In the first place, Deržavin used reflexive forms of verbs which,
according to Lomonosov's theory, should not have them. Lomonosov
preferred that reflexive forms be restricted to Slavonic verbs;
Deržavin used them with conversational verbs which had a concrete,
everyday meaning (Сколько с нею ни *делюсь* [instead of разделен];
Лель упорством *рассердился*). He used the colloquial form of the
present adverbial participle even with verbs from the high and
middle styles (блистаючи, побеждаючи). He formed adverbial participles in **-я, -а** not only from prefixed verbs in **-ить**, but also from
verbs of other categories, regardless of whether they were Russian
or Slavonic (разлиясь, низвержась). He also had a mixture of forms,
of various stylistic coloring, in his participles. Alongside archaic

Slavonic participles like творяй, создавый, седящ, ядущий, one finds participial formations from conversational verbs. Deržavin frequently used colloquial declensional forms of neuter nouns of the type время (в водах и в *пламе*; жниц с *знамем* идущих). He employed genitive plurals in **-ев, -ов** from feminine and neuter nouns (зданиев, стихиев, кикиморов). And he used such colloquial numerical constructions as На сорок двух столпах and пребудут в тысячи веках. In regard to conjunctions, it is sufficient to point out the causative use of что, as in these lines from "Na smert' Bibikova":

> Он верно любит добродетель,
> Что пишет ей свои стихи.

Even more striking is the mixture of Slavonicisms and colloquial terms in Deržavin's lexicon. Alongside expressions like На карты нам плевать пора, one finds Slavonicisms like дщерь, сих утех, предстань. This kind of mixture of high and low style was observed by Gogol': "His style is outstanding as is that of none of our poets; if you open it with a scalpel, you will see that this comes about because of an unusual combination of the very highest words with the very lowest and simplest:

> И смерть как гостью ожидает,
> Крутя задумавшись усы.

Who, besides Deržavin, would dare to connect such a matter as expectation of death with such a paltry act as the twirling of one's moustache?"

In Deržavin's language, the colloquial appears in all its everyday, familiar impudence; a good example may be found in the poem "Želanie zimy":

> На кабаке Борея
> Эол ударил в нюни:
> От вяхи той бледнея,
> Бог хлада слякоть, слюни
> Из глотки источил,
> Всю землю замочил.
> Узря ту Осень шутку,
> Их в правду драться нудит,
> Подняв пред нами юбку,
> Дожди, как реки, прудит,
> Плеща им в рожи грязь,
> Как дуракам смеясь ...

Deržavin also combined Slavonic and Russian expressions in parodistic antithesis; he provided humorous examples of intimate dialogue; and he occasionally used terms from regional dialects.

An interesting characterization of Deržavin's language is provided by V. G. Belinskij:

In Deržavin's poetry one already hears and feels the sounds and pictures of Russian nature—but mixed with some sort of Greek mythology distorted in the French manner. For example, let us take the beautiful ode "Osen' vo vremja osady Očakova." What a strange picture of purely Russian nature with Lord knows what kind of nature, of charming poetry with incomprehensible rhetoric:

> Спустил седой Эол Борея
> С цепей чугунных из пещер;
> Ужасные крыле расширя,
> Махнул по свету богатырь;
> Погнал стадами воздух синий,
> Сгустил туманы в облака,
> Давнул — и облака расселись.
> Спустился дождь и восшумел.

What are Aeolus, and Boreas, and caverns, and cast-iron chains doing here? Don't ask: why were powder, beauty-spots, and farthingales necessary? Because, in those days, you couldn't show your face without them. And how that Russian word "bogatyr'" clashes with that foreigner "Boreas"!

The living language, before Puškin, did not directly submit to organic unification with the literary language. It was not organized, not adapted to the expression of abstract ideas. It could not, in its raw state, become the semantic center of a complexly structured literary language. Moreover, the everyday colloquial language seemed too low and coarse for the society of the salon. The upper levels of society, toward the end of the eighteenth century, thus came to the conclusion that the bonding element which would unite national Russian speech and unavoidable Slavonicisms into a literary language would be French—the leading language of European civilization.

13. RADIŠČEV'S LANGUAGE

A new synthesis of living Russian speech with church-book emotional elements, through the intermediary of West European languages and revolutionary ideology, is observable in those prose works of the eighteenth century which reflected progressive tendencies. These were daring (though linguistically not fully successful) attempts to break with the old tradition of various styles in the name of a single national literary language. Radiščev's language is the clearest expression of these tendencies—which were not to see their fruition until the twenties and thirties of the nineteenth century, when Puškin, with a different ideology and different stylistic methods, was to accomplish the task.

Radiščev followed Lomonosov and Fonvizin in using Church Slavonic words and phraseology (often very archaic), but he gave them a coloration of civic pathos. He also gave the Slavonicisms a new emotional and social content by transferring them to the plane of sentimentalism. There are many examples in his *Putešestvie iz Peterburga v Moskvu:* О природа! объяв человека в пелены скорби при рождении его, влача его по строгим хребтам боязни, скуки и печали чрез весь его век, дала ты ему в отраду сон ("Sofija"); ведаешь ли, что в первенственном уложении, в сердце каждого написано ("Ljubani"); В толико жестоком отчаянии, лежащу мне над бездыханным телом моей возлюбленной, один из искренних моих друзей прибежав ко мне ("Spasskaja polest'"); да будет им творяй благостыню, их рассудок. Воссядите, и внемлите моему слову, еже пребывати во внутренности душ ваших долженствует ("Krest'cy"). Note also the following word formations: сочетование, воспоминовение, произречение.

Radiščev did not shrink from overburdening his style with very archaic words and constructions, such as the dative absolute, Church Slavonic particles and conjunctions, archaic noun endings, and Slavonic participial forms. Yet his Church Slavonic, despite its archaic outward appearance, has no trace of church ideology in it. As G. A. Gukovskij observed: "It was important to Radiščev to create the verbal principle of an 'important,' ideologically significant language. He wanted to reproduce, in the Russian language, ... the oratorical animation, the emotional tensions of the declamations of Rousseau and Raynal, the language of Mirabeau ... Radiščev uses a language traditionally surrounded by the aureole of sermonizing pathos and higher levels of thought."

Characteristic of his style are new phraseological constructions, formed from elements of the church language but of West European type (Спокойствие упреждает нахмуренность грусти, расположая *образы радости в зерцалах воображения*; извощик *извлек* меня *из задумчивости*). He also has lexical borrowings which give his prose a philosophical ponderousness (если точных несниму *портретов*, то доволен буду их *силуетами*), though he did try to avoid excessive use of barbarisms.

His syntax, however, is full of Gallicisms and reflections of the German language. Among his Gallicisms are non-agreement of the adverbial participle (Лежа в кибитке, мысли мои обращены были в неизмеримость мира), and absolute participial constructions (носимые валами, внезапу судно наше остановилось). Among his Germanisms are such turns of phrase as намерение мое при сем было то, чтобы сделать его чистосердечным and such lexical neologisms as самонедоверение, бредоумствование, времяточие.

Radiščev's Slavonicisms appear freely, and without any stylistic motivation, alongside Russianisms, forms from the speech of the educated class, and expressions from folk speech and peasant folklore. Compare examples such as: *дерет с мужиков кожу*; *плюнул почти ему в рожу*; *я волосы драл с досады*; неуспел выговорить, как *шасть* курьер в двери; я долг отдал естеству, и *рот разинув* до ушей, *зевнул во всю мочь*; *нейокнет* ли у вас *сердечко*; но любезный читатель я с тобою *закалякался*.

Radiščev also differentiates the conversational language of his personages, so that the merchant, seminarian, poet, landowner, and peasant all speak different languages. In this respect, he differs completely from Karamzin.

One should not exaggerate the number or quality of colloquial elements in Radiščev. He was a "European" to the marrow of his bones—in convictions, education, and in his whole manner of thought—who, at the same time, turned to the language and creativity of the folk. But, on the plane of literature, this tendency was only in its infancy, and Radiščev was only the first stage in a process that saw its culmination in Puškin. It was for this reason that Radiščev and his followers turned to Deržavin, in whom the "folk" element found a clearer expression than in any of the rest of the aristocratic literature of the eighteenth century.

In the epoch of the triumph of aristocratic culture, however, the basic line of development of the literary language took a different road than the revolutionary one traveled by Radiščev.

4

The Second Half
of the Eighteenth Century:
The Salon Literary Styles

I. DECLINE OF THE OLD LANGUAGE CULTURE IN THE UPPER STRATA OF RUSSIAN SOCIETY

In the second half of the eighteenth century, against the background of the political, social, and economic hegemony of the nobility, a rich culture developed which bore the clear stamp of imitation of things French. The Petersburg court strove to emulate Versailles, and this emulation found its reflection, in one form or another, in the tastes, thought, and everyday life of the aristocracy. One of the notable writers of the turn of the century, G. Dobrynin, ironically depicted the Europeanized appearance of the landowner's country seat, in which all objects had exchanged their Russian names for French ones: Вместо подсвечников–*шандалы;* вместо занавесок–*гар-дины;* вместо зеркал и паникадил–*люстра;* вместо утвари–*мебель;* вместо приборов–*куверты;* вместо всего хорошего и превосходного–*требиен* и *сюперб.* Везде вместо размера–*симметрия,* вместо серебра–*аплике,* и слуг зовут *лаке.*

This process of Europeanization led not only to a wide currency of French in "better society" (as the contemporary term had it), but also to changes in the everyday language and literary styles. The language of the aristocratic salon waged war against the church-book tradition. In 1803, in his *Rassuždenie o starom i novom sloge rossijskogo jazyka,* A. S. Šiškov explained the social causes of the decline of the old literary culture. He pointed out that the

86

children of the nobility were in the hands of Frenchmen from their early childhood and, therefore, never received training in their native language. They acquired their native language by hearing and imitation; without formal training, however, they could not achieve fluency in the literary or scholarly languages.

In his comedy *Brigadir*, Fonvizin depicted the linguistic stratification of the Russian nobility with comic exaggeration. The language of most of the characters is modeled on some one of the current conversational styles. For example, the speech of the counselor is a mixture of Church Slavonic and chancery, and the speech of the brigadier's wife is completely submerged in the atmosphere of the provincial country-seat and folk language. According to Fonvizin's depiction, the languages of the different linguistic strata were so disparate that people could not understand each other. Thus the brigadier's wife cannot comprehend the conventional Church Slavonic metaphors in the speech of the counselor, and she endows them with an everyday content:

Советник: Нет, дорогой зять! Как мы, так и жены наши, все в руце Создателя: у Него власы главы нашея изочтены суть.

Бригадирша: Ведь вот, Игнатий Андреевич! ты меня часто ругаешь, что я то и дело деньги да деньги считаю. Как же это? сам Господь волоски наши считать изволит, а мы, рабы Его, и деньги считать ленимся ...

After another such scene the brigadier's wife admits that she hears the language of the church as rarely as she hears French. The language of Frenchified fops is contrasted with the colloquial language of the nobility of the older generation, with the same comical intent:

Сын: Mon père! не горячитесь.

Бригадир: Что не горячитесь?

Сын: Mon père! Я говорю: не горячитесь.

Бригадир: Да первого-то слова, чорт те знает, я не разумею.

Eighteenth-century satire and comedy reflected this mixture of languages very clearly, though with distortions. Writers particularly enjoyed depicting the perversions of the salon styles—the Russo-French jargon of fops and women of fashion. In literary parody, however, this language was impoverished; for, in actual fact, in its full form, the Russo-French salon style must have been close to the literary language which was just being formed.

2. THE PROCESS OF ADAPTATION OF THE RUSSIAN LITERARY
LANGUAGE TO THE EXPRESSION OF WEST EUROPEAN CONCEPTS

Translated literature, and the creation of native linguistic forms closely connected with the semantic systems of West European languages, were the literary forces which aided in solving everyday problems. Translations are of enormous interest for the history of the literary language. In the middle of the eighteenth century, the process of Europeanization deepened. Morphological and semantic correspondences to West European expressions came into being; lexical borrowings became fewer. The occasional borrowing of words and concepts thus gave way to a general convergence of the semantic structure of Russian with the conceptual structure of West European languages.

To be sure, there still was a flow of borrowings, even of such words as already had their equivalents in Russian or Slavonic. In the *Zapiski* of S. Porošin, for example, we find constant use of borrowings which would be somewhat rarer toward the beginning of the nineteenth century: она танцует без *кадансу;* генерал-адмирал *президировал;* прямой был *конфиянс.*

Toward the middle of the century, however, there began to be opposition to mechanical borrowing, in the name of national forms of expression. The task of the writer or translator became one of solving the problem of the internal relationship between Russian and West European languages. Interesting material for understanding the ways in which Russian literature tried to accomplish this task may be found in Trediakovskij's translation work—particularly the work of the last period of his life. His *Sokraščenie filosofii kanclera Bakona* (a 1760 translation of a French tract on Bacon) shows how difficult was the process of finding Russian and Church Slavonic equivalents for French words, and how unstable and undeveloped were the means for expressing abstract ideas in the Russian literary language. There are many instances in which one concept may be translated by several different words (which sometimes have nothing to do with each other), and in which different concepts are rendered by the same word. The word *harmonie* is rendered as согласие, сличное сочетание, сличие; *manie* is translated неистовство, шалость, сумасбродство. On the other hand, *symphonie* and *harmonie* are not distinguished and are represented by one word, согласие; and *révolution* and *revers* are both translated as преобразование.

The transmittal of West European concepts was accomplished with three basic devices. The first was to describe and define the French word in those instances where Russian lacked the corresponding word and concept: thus *geste* became телесное мановение; *concert*–щебетание согласное; *ressource*–обилие в способах; *cabinet*–уединенная хижина; *police*–политическое учреждение. It is interesting that the major portion of these definitions were accompanied by calques; that is, a Russian calque became part of the descriptive formula: *abstraction*–отвлечение от вещества; *acteur*–действующее лицо на театре; *organisation*–членовое составление. The second device was the production of calques—the lexeme-by-lexeme translation of the French word with corresponding Russian lexemes: *indifférence*–неразнственность; *réflexion*–восклонение; *influence*–натечение; *préjugé*–предрассуждение.Trediakovskij also, characteristically, used Church Slavonic lexemes: *dissolution*–разрежение; *revers*–преобращение. Also interesting is the adaptation to general "European" concepts (derived from Greek): *sympathie*–сострастие. The third device was the adaptation of a well-known Russian word for the transmission of the foreign word: *charlatanerie*–цыганство; *idole*–богинька; *nerf*–становая жила; *réputation*–слава; *sculpture*–резьба. But far more common, in the fifties and sixties, was the use of Church Slavonic lexemes in this role: *intrigue*–ухищрение; *lustre*–паникадило; *tendresse*–благоутробие, благосердие.

3. THE SPREAD OF GALLICISMS IN SYNTAX AND SEMANTICS

The adaptation of the literary and conversational systems of expression to the transmission of West European concepts led, of course, to a change in the relationship between Russian and Church Slavonic elements in the literary language. The influence of French was connected with a limitation of the functions of Church Slavonic. Particularly significant was the role of artistic literature in the second half of the century. Writers, undergoing the influence of the West, forsook the church-book culture and took French literature as a model for their work in developing the Russian literary language.

It was thus in the area of artistic literature that a convergence took place between French and those styles which were close to the social language of the educated class.

The work of A. P. Sumarokov can serve as an illustration. In both syntax and lexicon, Sumarokov's language tried to combine living Russian forms with "Europeanisms." In syntax, Sumarokov reduced the freedom of word order, on the model of French. Trediakovskij, who used a completely free word order in his poetry and wrote in a style resembling that of an intricate, pettifogging, chancery document, was the target of Sumarokov's attacks in this regard. To such attacks Trediakovskij replied: "The esteemed author deigns to laugh at those who occasionally transpose words in poetry, as if our language were controlled by the same laws as French or German." To be sure, Sumarokov was occasionally forced, in his poetry, to depart from the "European" word order he considered normal, but generally the "correct" word order was triumphant. Sumarokov's constructions sometimes, in fact, contained pure Gallicisms:

> О, Боже, *восхотев* прославить
> Императрицу ради нас ...
> Тебе судьбы суть все подвластны ...

Commenting on these lines, Trediakovskij declared: "The adverbial participle восхотев, instead of the participle восхотевый or восхотевший, is wrong, as is evident to all those who know." Lomonosov also objected to the use of non-agreeing adverbial participles, asserting that "the adverbial participle must agree, in subject, with the principal finite verb ..."

Quite apart from these occasional violations of an established syntactic system, however, the writers of the Sumarokov school strove to bring the structure of the Russian literary language nearer both to French syntax and to the constructions of the conversational language (which mitigated the role of French syntax). They tried to create a phrase which would be as short and unforced as possible, and they avoided not only the conventional, solemn, Slavonic turns of phrase but also poetic inversion. From the point of view of the guardians of the high-style tradition, Sumarokov had not studied "periodology," had not heard of the "variety of periods" or of their "essential parts," and, in Trediakovskij's words, had not constructed "up until now a single correct period."

More vivid examples of French influence are to be found in Sumarokov's semantics. Some of his semantic Gallicisms were exposed and commented on by Trediakovskij. For example, the construction

> Дела, что небеса *пронзают*
> Леса и гордые валы.

did not please Trediakovskij, who pointed out that пронзать meant the same thing as пробадать and that it did not make sense for "affairs" to "perforate" the sky, the forest, and the proud wave. He suggested that Sumarokov had used his verbs on the model of French *percer* and that it would be better to use проникать, on the model of French *pénétrer*.

All of this shows clearly enough the struggle of Russian society for a Europeanized literary language. The Russian writer of the upper classes, from mid-century onwards, always was oriented to one degree or another toward West European languages and cultures. We need only recall the linguistic activity of Fonvizin. The growth of the educated class in cultural and social importance speeded up the process of Europeanization and hastened the convergence of the literary and conversational languages. The area in which Slavonic forms could be utilized was gradually narrowed. And toward the end of the eighteenth century the process of Europeanization of the literary language, which took place mainly through the mediation of French literature, reached a high level of development. The leader of the new literary current, N. M. Karamzin, admitted to G. P. Kamenev that, when he was elaborating "the new style of the Russian language" (новый слог Российского языка), he had in mind certain foreign authors, and that at first he imitated them, but later he began to write in a style all his own.

4. THE ROLE OF THE ARISTOCRATIC SALON IN ESTABLISHING THE NORMS OF "WORLDLY" STYLES OF THE RUSSIAN LITERARY LANGUAGE OF THE SECOND HALF OF THE EIGHTEENTH CENTURY

The social laboratory in which the norms of a new, Europeanized, fashionable style were worked out was the salon of the nobility.

K. N. Batjuškov characterized the relationship of the literary styles to the fashionable salon at the turn of the century in this way:

A major portion of the writers ... spent their lives in the noble spheres of Catherine's era—an era which was so hospitable to science and literature; there they acquired that humanity, politeness, and that nobleness whose reflection we see in their writings; in the best society they learned how to guess that secret play of passion, to observe morals, to preserve all fashionable conditions and relations, and to speak clearly, easily, and pleasantly.

P. Makarov, one of Karamzin's followers, stated that,

As early as Catherine's reign ... we borrowed sciences, arts, customs, amusements, and manners from foreigners; we began to think like other nations (for the more nations are enlightened, the more they are similar)—and Lomonosov's language became just as inadequate as Russian education under Elizabeth was inadequate for Catherine's glorious age.

These social causes produced an alienation, on the part of "high" Russian society, from the old Slavonic literary system. Karamzin sketched out a program for creating a new literary language which would satisfy a developed linguistic taste and would correspond to the spirit and style of European civilization. "A Russian candidate for the role of writer, dissatisfied with books," he suggested, "must close them and listen to conversation around him in order to learn the language better." The writer must then, in Karamzin's view, depend upon his own taste, culture, and knowledge of European languages (particularly French), and himself create the norms of such a literary language as would be capable of fusing with the spoken language and enriching it with new forms of expression. For, he complained, "the French write as they speak, and Russians have yet to speak about many things the way a man of talent would write about them." "What is the author to do? He must contrive and construct expressions. He is to guess the best selection of words. He is to give old words some new meaning, present them in new contexts—but so artfully as to fool the readers and hide from them the unusualness of the expression." The necessity of a creative reformation of the literary language thus became an axiom for writers at the end of the eighteenth and the beginning of the nineteenth centuries.

Karamzin persistently emphasized the necessity of bringing the

Russian literary language into the European community of languages:

Peter the Great transformed our Fatherland with a mighty hand; he made us be like other Europeans. Complaints are useless. The connection between the minds of older and newer Russians was broken forever. We don't want to imitate foreigners, but we write as they do because we live as they live. The particular beauties which constitute the *national* literary character are giving way to *common* beauties. The former change; the latter are eternal. It is good to write for all Russians—it is still better to write for all people.

This West European orientation of high society equated Europeanisms in general with French. The nobility introduced European expressions into both the literary language and the everyday language of their milieu. And, in 1801, G. P. Kamenev wrote: "Karamzin uses very many French words. For every ten Russian words there will surely be one French word ..."

At the same time, however (during the second half of the eighteenth century), even such a Westernizing society as this came to feel a need to substitute Russian words for Gallicisms. Changes in later editions of Karamzin's *Pis'ma russkogo putešestvennika* are symptomatic: *вояж* became путешествие; *визитация*–осмотр; *партия за партиею*–толпа за толпой; *интересный*–занимательный; *мина*–выражение; *фрагмент*–отрывок; *энтузиазм*–жар. The most varied groups of intellectuals opposed Gallicisms, in the name of national originality. M. Popov, for example, prefaced one of his poetic translations with the announcement that he had resolved to replace certain barbarisms with native Russian words. His preface was followed by a list of "newly translated words." He refused to translate one portion of a longer work because he found material in it which had no Russian equivalents, and he wished neither to create artificial words nor to leave words untranslated. M. Čulkov, in a 1769 issue of his journal *I to i sio*, published a little lexicon of Russian equivalents for certain barbarisms. Such patriotic protests against excessive borrowing continued into the nineteenth century.

5. METHODS AND PRINCIPLES OF MIXING THE RUSSIAN LANGUAGE WITH FRENCH

The increasing tendency to reincarnate West European concepts in national Russian forms testifies that the process of Europeanization

of Russian, toward the end of the eighteenth century, had penetrated even deeper into the grammatical and lexical structure of
Russian. "Instead of depicting our thoughts with the concepts and
rules accepted since the old days, we depict them according to
the concepts and rules of a foreign language," wrote Šiškov. In
this mixture of French and Russian, it is necessary to differentiate
several phenomena:

(1) As West European ideas were adopted and translated into
Russian, there occurred a semantic adaptation of Russian words
to the corresponding French ones. This led to a fusion of the semantic
range of the Russian word with that of the French word. New
abstract and transferred meanings developed which proceeded, not
from the semantic system of Russian, but from that of French.
Упиться, for example, came to have the semantic range of *s'enivrer*,
and then упоение, упоительный followed; and плоский came to
mean *plat*, in the sense of "banal." Šiškov, commenting on the
broadening of the semantics of вкус, claimed that

... the French, because of their linguistic poverty, use *goût* everywhere. They can
apply it to anything—to food, clothing, poetry, shoes, music, the sciences, and
love. But is it fitting for us ... to write ... : украшенный с тонким вкусом?
When I read тонкой, верной вкус, then am I not supposed to assume that
there also exist толстой and неверной вкус? Normally, the answer to this
is "How is one to write, or say *un goût délicat, un goût fin?*" I again repeat, that if
we ... start to think only of how to translate one or another French expression ...
in a word, if we ... don't stop thinking in French, then, in our own language,
all we will ever do is jabber, jabber, jabber ... What need do we have to say,
instead of она его любит or он ей нравится, *она имеет к нему вкус,* except for
the fact that the French say *elle a du goût pour lui.*

But at the beginning of the nineteenth century the new meaning
of вкус and the phraseology attached to it had penetrated so deeply
into Russian that even defenders of church-book antiquities had to
prove its national originality. E. Stanevič announced that "we ...
had our вкус for hundreds of years before that вкус which we got
as a Gallicism, although our forefathers, when they talked of things
related to that concept, used чувство. But this change took place
in the language itself, just as many other words have changed their
meaning." He used the same kind of argument for блистательный
(cf. French *brillant*).

The word тонкий adapted itself to French *fin* (cf. тонкий вкус,

тонкий ум, тонкий человек, тонкая бестия, cf. the words утончен-
ность, утонченный [*raffiné*]). The word живой adapted itself to *vif*
(cf. живой ум, живое воображение, живые глаза, etc.). One could
produce many other examples of the semantic "crossing" of Russian
and French words. It would be difficult to calculate the number
of Russian words which changed their meaning under French
influence at that time, but it is very great.

(2) Correspondences for foreign words had already been created
in the first half of the eighteenth century by means of calques (exact
morpheme-by-morpheme translations of the foreign words). But
during the first part of the century these calques were often made
using Church Slavonic morphemes. Now there occurred an intensive
process of selecting, transforming, and complementing such words.
Church Slavonic formations were abandoned and replaced by more
"secular" synonyms. At the same time, the calques acquired a more
abstract semantic coloring (влияние instead of натечение). Some
examples are: расположение, сосредоточить, трогательный, пись-
менность, впечатление, насекомое, переворот, обстоятельство, рас-
сеянный, for *disposition, concentrer, touchant, littérature, impression, insecte,
révolution, circonstance, distrait.*

(3) Phraseological calques appeared along with the lexical
calques. The new phrases did not arise out of the Russian linguistic
system, but were merely copies of the French constructions. In a
1768 French grammar of Russian, we have phraseological equivalents such as the following: *prendre résolution*–принять решение;
prendre part–принять, брать участие; *avec le temps*–со временем. In
Fonvizin's *Brigadir* there are similar examples: остатки дней наших–
les restes de nos jours; от всего сердца–*de tout mon cœur.*

Many such Russian translations of common French idioms and
phrases have survived into modern Russian: чорт побери, игра
не стоит свеч, проглотить пилюлю, жечь свечу с двух концов, рог
изобилия, хороший тон, с птичьего полета, рука руку моет, не в
своей тарелке, ловить рыбу в темной воде are calques, respectively,
of French *diable m'emport, le jeu n'en vaut pas la chandelle, avaler la
pilule, brûler la chandelle par les deux bouts, corne d'abondance, bon ton,
à vol d'oiseau, une main lave l'autre, ne pas être dans son assiette, pêcher
en eau trouble.*

It would be wrong, however, to reduce all the phraseological
creation of the second half of the eighteenth century and the

beginning of the nineteenth century to such simple phrases. The Russo-French phraseology of the time had other peculiarities. It bore the stamp of the mannered, periphrastic, rhetorically ornate, metaphoric language of French society and French poetry of the period. Instead of using the word солнце, Russians would say светило дня, дневное светило; instead of глаза, they would say зеркала, зерцала души or рай души; and the simple рубашка was replaced by вечная подруга мертвых и живых. These expressions were, respectively, copies of French *le flambeau du jour, les miroirs de l'âme* or *le paradis de l'âme*, and *la compagne perpétuelle des morts et des vivantes.* The adherents of the "old style" censured this inability to call a spade a spade. Šiškov provided interesting parallels between the new style and the "old" (with examples for the new style taken from Karamzin):

Old Style	*New Style*
Как приятно смотреть на твою молодость!	Коль наставительно взирать на тебя в раскрывающейся весне твоей!
Деревенским девкам навстречу идут цыганки.	Пестрые толпы сельских ореад сретаются с смуглыми ватагами пресмыкающихся фараонит.
Жалкая старушка, у который на лице были написаны уныние и горесть.	Трогательный предмет сострадания, которого уныло задумчивая физиономия означала гипохондрию.
Когда я любил путешествовать	Когда путешествие сделалось потребностью души моей

Compare also the following examples from Karamzin's *Pis'ma russkogo putešestvennika:* магазин человеческой памяти; Не знают сего прекрасного средства убивать времени (простите мне этот галлицизм); печальный флер зимы лежал на природе; нимфы радости (prostitutes).

Šiškov persistently emphasized the "excessive fuzziness of thought" in the language of the "Europeans." "The more briefly a thought can be expressed," he declared, "the better. Excess verbosity, without adding any emphasis, expands and disfigures the style."

On the basis of this Russo-French phraseological system, a new literary style developed with unusual metaphors and with specific conventional types of periphrasis. It was a style amenable neither to direct etymologizing nor to direct reference to fact. This stable,

conventional, luxuriant system of literary phraseology was characteristic of the rhetorical style of the salon. It replaced simple
reference to ideas and things and thereby made otiose any recourse
to Church Slavonic, whose strength had been in its rich rhetorical
phraseology, systematized by the Lomonosov school.

(4) French influence changed syntactic government. The connection between the etymological structure of words and their
syntactic properties was broken. Šiškov, in his *Rassuždenie o starom
i novom sloge*, gives an example of such a change: "... people translate
влияние, and despite the fact that the verb ... requires the preposition в (вливать вино в бочку, вливать в сердце ей любовь), they use
the newly concocted word according to French grammar, placing
it ... with the preposition на: *faire l'influence sur les esprits*–делать
влияние на разумы."

Syntactic changes also led to the appearance of case governance
by nouns which had formerly taken no complement. For example,
there was a broad expansion of the use of the genitive complement.
The noun предмет, taking on the meaning of French *objet*, began
to be used in such constructions as предмет кровопролития, предмет
ссор, предмет любви. The noun чувство, under the influence of
French *sentiment* in the meaning "sense," "sensibility" (*sentiment du
ridicule*), began to appear in such constructions as чувство изящного,
чувство истины, чувство целого. Occasionally, such usages could
lead to ambiguity of meaning, as when Karamzin used the collo-
cution мученики христианства ("martyrs of Christianity").

French influence also led to changes in verbal constructions, as
when French *précédé* led to the formation of a passive participle
from an intransitive verb: предшествуемый. Compare also, in the
language of Puškin: стихотворений, знаемых всеми наизусть и столь
неудачно поминутно подражаемых (*imitées*); механизму стиха г-на
Катенина, слишком пренебрегаемому (*négligé*) лучшими нашими
стихотворцами.

At the same time, French influence contributed to the headlong
development of analytical constructions in both verbal and nominal
syntagmas.

(5) Under the influence of West European languages (first
French and then, at the beginning of the nineteenth century,
English), a word order came to be established which corresponded
to tendencies present in the Russian language itself. Karamzin

played a fundamental role in this syntactic reform of the literary language. The following norms were established for word order: the subject must come before the predicate and its complements; the adjective must come before the noun, the adverb before the verb; adjectival and adverbial phrases should be put in the same position as adjectives and adverbs; in complex sentences, the governing elements must be placed next to those they govern; the dative, or instrumental, complement of the verb must precede the accusative complement; words describing the circumstance surrounding an action should be placed before the verb—if they depend on the predicate, they follow the predicate; all appositives must follow their main ideas; and defining words must always stand after the word defined (e.g., житель лесов, кот в сапогах) and not before it. Such a word order was considered normal for the system of the literary language. To evaluate the significance of the reform, one need only juxtapose a Latin period and a German period of Lomonosov with the new period of Karamzin, as follows:

Уже мы, римляне, Кателину, столь дерзновенно насильствовавшего, на злодеяния покушавшегося, погибелью отечеству угрожавшего, из града нашего изгнали.

Благополучна Россия, что единым языком едину веру исповедует, и единою благочестивейшею самодержицею управляется, великий в ней пример к утверждению в православии видит.

Юная кровь, разгоряченная ночными сновидениями, красила нежные щеки ее алейшим румянцем; солнечные лучи играли на белом ее лице и проницая сквозь черные пушистые ресницы, сияли в глазах ее светлее, нежели на золоте.

This type of word order did not violate the spirit of the Russian language. Rather, it was in agreement with its own evolutionary tendencies. The influence of West European languages (particularly French) merely furthered the understanding of these tendencies and the inclusion of them in strictly defined norms.

Stylistically motivated deviations from the norms, aimed at creating expressive variation, were of course permitted. In emotional discourse the logical word order was complicated to achieve a heightened effect. Furthermore, the requirements of euphony and rhythmic cadence played a large role. Excessive use of rhythmic prose, however, was forbidden.

(6) In the syntax of the sentence there occurred, above all, the disintegration of the complex period (sentence) which was founded

on the one hand, on the Latin-German model and, on the other hand, on the model of chancery style. We have the following statements from a handbook of the time: "... in the old days, the intervals between one period and another were very great, so that very often it was not possible to read a sentence aloud in one breath; but now, for the most part, short sentences are used, because it is hard to understand long ones. Eight, ten, fifteen, words in a sentence—and that is enough." The exclusion of a number of particles and conjunctions also changed the logic of the syntactic progression. A journal of the time announced that

> Понеже, в силу, поелику
> Творят довольно в свете зла.

Under the influence of French, a coordinate construction consisting of a participle or adjective and a relative clause became established; note the following example from Karamzin: потом ввели нас всех в богатую залу, обитую черным сукном, *и в которой* окна были затворены.

Occasionally, old conjunctions acquired new meanings under West European influence. For example, the conjunction чтобы came to be used with the infinitive, after an interrogative, on the model of French *pour* (И кто же ты, чтоб петлей мне грозить— Žukovskij), and after the adverb слишком, on the model of French *trop ... pour* (Сильвио был *слишком* умен и опытен, *чтобы* этого не заметить—Puškin). It also came to be used with the subjunctive after the verbs слушать, думать, допустить, etc., to serve the function of French *que* (не мог равнодушно слушать, *чтобы* говорили о ... картинах—Karamzin). Furthermore, it could be used to form a periphrastic descriptive construction in place of a dependent infinitive phrase (Пошел он к королю и приказал, *чтобы* о нем немедля доложили—Žukovskij; compare the German: *und befahl, dass man ihn unverzüglich anmelden solle*).

The reduction of the number of conjunctions was compensated for by complex forms of syntactic symmetry. Constructions came to have a playful variability and unexpected collocations. The salon styles demanded that the author produce unexpected analogies and play with ideas. Gogol' aptly characterized these late eighteenth-century changes in the style of the literary language: "When our poetry left the church, it suddenly found itself at a ball ... The

Russian language acquired a freedom and an adroitness at flying from subject to subject—an adroitness unknown to Deržavin."

6. THE STYLISTIC NORMS OF THE SPEECH OF THE LITERARY SALON

The language of the French salon of the pre-revolutionary period, of the period of Louis XIV, was the ideal of the Russian aristocracy. Books were published for people of fashion; they originated in salons and were communicated to the salon public before they were released to the general public. All writers had to be a part of salon society, whatever their specialty might be. Everyone was interested in questions of style. Mathematicians, naturalists, lawyers, and psychologists published tracts and books on style and the art of writing. Good taste and fashionable usage were the literary norm. The lexicon was purified of excessive heaviness by the exclusion of technical terms, Latin and Greek terms, and the like. Dialectal, provincial, domestic, and folk terms were also excluded from the vocabulary—in short, everything that might shock a "fashionable lady." These puristic tendencies attracted the Europeanized Russian aristocrat.

The living language entered this refined atmosphere only in negligible quantity and after strict selection. "Bare simplicity" of expression was considered unesthetic and even "indecent." The evaluation of the literary quality of a word was conditioned by the entire social and everyday context of its use. The "tone" of a word, as Karamzin put it, was important. The norm for literary expression was to be on the level of the ideal image of a sensitive, gallant, and enlightened man. The language of the salon and the literary styles which developed in this setting thus had no sympathy for everyday speech. A book review of the time complained that "The translator tried very hard to conform to the language used in normal conversation. But he should have imitated people who speak well, and not those who speak badly. Folk expressions should not serve as the norm for the writer." Another review castigated a writer for comparing the heart of an unhappy man with a heated frying pan: "The frying pan is very useful and indispensable in the kitchen, but in literature, particularly in comparisons and similes, one can get along without it."

Chancery expressions and Slavonic "bookish" words were banished with the same persistence and zeal. Karamzin stated that the locution в следствие чего, дабы was "too much like the chancery, and very repulsive in the mouth of a woman who ... was more beautiful than Venus." The ideological and mythological system of Slavonic was foreign to the courtiers. Apart from the biblical phraseology, which was common to all of Europe, it seemed to them to be a mechanical series of archaically worded images and expressions. They wished, therefore, to put some of these expressions to rest and to adapt others to the requirements of the language of the salon. Karamzin's parodistic selection of "obsolete" Slavonicisms, in his ridicule of the големые претолковники, иже отревают все, еже есть русское, и блещаются блаженне сиянием славеномудрия, gives an indication of how a basic element of Church Slavonic appeared to the Westernizers. Lomonosov's principle of mixing Slavonic with the language of the folk was being rejected.

At the same time, the very semantics of Church Slavonicisms were being changed. Torn out of their context, Slavonic words were projected upon the semantic system of the everyday language and "etymologized" in *that* context. In the process, according to Šiškov, "some went into complete oblivion; others, despite the wealth of their semantic content, grew strange and wild to unaccustomed ears; others changed their meanings completely and are being used not in the sense they were formerly used." Šiškov provided many examples of such usage. In the line В безмолвной куще сосн густых, he pointed out that куща could only mean a hut or cabin, and what a куща сосн could be he would not dare to guess. It is interesting that Karamzin made precisely this error in one of his poems and, later, under the influence of Šiškov's criticism, corrected it.

Selection and prohibition were only the initial stage in the handling of Slavonicisms. The next stage was one of phraseological adaptation and redefinition. An example of the way the salon "conquered" Church Slavonicisms is the punning use of biblical symbols in one of Karamzin's letters: Как можно вымарать стихи свои? Они для меня всех дороже. Воля твоя: Я *воскрешу* их, *сниму с креста или крест с них.*

Thus the Church Slavonic lexicon, selected and adapted for the various styles and genres of the language of high society, was torn from the context of church ideology. In this "cleansed" form, it entered into various combinations with everyday phraseology, with the spoken language of the educated, and with French. Šiškov complained: "The Slavonic language is despised, no one studies it, and even the clergy, drawn by the powerful hand of habit, is beginning to abandon it." A whole series of genres in the high and even the middle style of Slavonic was doomed to die.

The task of the Europeanized aristocrats was to create the forms of a social "eloquence" which would be very different from the chancery and Slavonic styles and would have no trace of "folkishness." It would be oriented toward the French language and the rhetoric of the "noble" bourgeois and aristocratic circles. The different styles of this salon literary language were to be determined by the degree of rhetorical refinement. "The high style must be distinguished, not by words and phrases, but by the content, thoughts, feelings, pictures, and colors of poetry," wrote one of Karamzin's adherents.

7. THE SIGNIFICANCE OF KARAMZIN IN THE HISTORY OF THE RUSSIAN LITERARY LANGUAGE

The creation of a "new style" which was supposed to organically unite national Russian and general European forms of expression and break decisively with the Church Slavonic tradition is linked with the name of N. M. Karamzin. In all genres, Karamzin tried to bring the literary language close to the spoken language of educated society. However, since he considered the everyday social language insufficiently developed, he hoped to raise its cultural level and strengthen its capacity for literary expression with the aid of West European linguistic culture. He called upon writers to borrow foreign words and expressions or else create corresponding Russian ones for the expression of new ideas. In his own literary activity, he provided clear and, more often than not, successful examples of word formation (влюбленность, промышленность, будущность, общественность, человечный, общеполезный, достижимый, усовершенствовать, for example). In trying to implant in the Russian language the abstract concepts and subtle nuances of thought and feeling which had been elaborated by West European culture, Karamzin broadened the range of meaning of the corresponding Russian, or Russified Slavonic, words (as in потребность, развитие, тонкости, отношения, положения). In freeing the Russian literary language of the excess weight of Church Slavonicisms and chancery words, Karamzin had as his goal the formation of a *single* language which would be accessible to a wide range of readers—one language "for books and for society, so that people will write as they speak, and speak as they write."

But the new style he created was not sufficiently democratic. It did not encompass the broad, and fresh, current of the folk language, and it greatly limited the literary functions of the everyday colloquial language. Having taken its start from the norm of the tastes of the aristocratic salon, it was somewhat mincing and mannered, and excessively elegant. Yet the work accomplished by Karamzin in the area of phraseology and syntax was indeed monumental. He gave the Russian literary language a new direction—a direction which would be followed by such significant Russian writers as Batjuškov, Žukovskij, Vjazemskij, and Baratynskij. Even Puškin's language owes much to Karamzin.

Basically, Karamzin produced a new grammatical reform in the Russian language by abrogating the obsolete norms of Lomonosov's grammar of three styles. He declared war on the cumbersome, complicated, dull or pathetically oratorical, declamatory constructions which had been inherited partly from Church Slavonic and partly from Latin-German learned styles. The principle of a pronounceable language, the principle of easy reading of a literary text, the principle of transmuting poetry and prose into speech without the artificial intonations of the high style—all these lie at the base of the new stylistics. The basic aims of Karamzin's syntactic reform were an easy, logical division of speech and a natural sequence and connection of ideas. Archaic conjunctions were rejected, and those which remained received new meanings. The method of subordination changed. The length and content of the sentence were reduced.

Karamzin elaborated complex and figured, but easily scannable, forms of various syntactic figures within the sentence. The structure of large syntactic units was based on the principle of uniting homogeneous clauses. The phrase was condensed and shortened. Restriction in the use of conjunctions was compensated for by a variety of expression, a play of intonation. Only coordinate conjunctions were preserved almost in their entirety. The ones most used were и, или, а, and но—and, very rarely, ибо. Of subordinating conjunctions, only the following remained: что, чтобы, когда, как, пока ог покамест, между тем как, едва, лишь, потому что, затем что, для того что, есть ли (если) and, very rarely, ежели, and the forms of relative subordination который, кой, где, etc. The elimination of obsolete conjunctions gave the new style an elegant simplicity. Incorporation of one clause within another was forbidden. Coordination had preference over subordination. The conceptual variety of concatenations without a conjunction increased. The device of unexpected and witty associations became established. Curtailment of the number of conjunctions with literary rights led to the complication of the formations of those which remained, and these developed subtle distinctions of meaning. The break with the old bookish tradition was accomplished.

Karamzin's language, which itself underwent a complex evolution from *Pis'ma russkogo putešestvennika* and *Bednaja Liza* to the final volumes of *Istorija Gosudarstva Rossijskogo*, was the basis of the new grammatical normalization.

8. GRAMMATICAL NORMALIZATION OF THE RUSSIAN LITERARY LANGUAGE AT THE BEGINNING OF THE NINETEENTH CENTURY

The regrouping of styles, the destruction of the high, Slavonic style, and the limitation of the literary functions of the colloquial language could not come about without a restructuring of the morphological system of the literary language. Some of the forms previously allowed in the low style were rejected. Some of the morphological peculiarities of the high style were consigned to the historical archives, while others were incorporated into those styles which were now the literary norm. All these factors led, at the beginning of the nineteenth century, to the establishment of a stable grammatical system, which, in its basic outlines, would be adopted by the styles of the latter part of the century.

The following traits of the low style were declared incorrect and began to decrease in number:

(1) Neuter nominative plurals in **-и, -ы** were rejected except for

diminutives in **-це, -ко** (such as зеркальцы, местечки). Attitudes varied, however. Forms like имении, желании (which were fairly frequent in the language of Sumarokov, Fonvizin, Radiščev, and other eighteenth-century writers) were categorically forbidden. But forms like леты, селы, etc., were not removed definitively from literature until the next grammatical standardization, at mid-century.

(2) The endings **-ев, -ов** in the genitive plural of neuter and feminine nouns were declared non-literary, except for "certain nouns ending in **-ье** in common use in the colloquial language: кушанье–кушаньев, поместье–поместьев." A noun like крыло could have the genitive plural крыл or крыльев but not крылиев.

(3) The instrumental plural in **-ы, -и** for masculine and neuter nouns was forbidden. It had been frequently used by continuers of the Lomonosov tradition, but had already begun to die out in the second half of the eighteenth century.

(4) Instrumental plural forms in **-ми**, such as избавительми, победительми (Fonvizin), коньми, рыцарьми (Deržavin), were banned. However, they continued to serve as doublets during the first half of the century, gradually narrowing in scope and becoming transformed into a closed group of individual cases.

(5) Censured, but still appearing in the written language, were feminine dative and locative forms of the type шинеле, при мысле, на кровате, and genitive singular forms in **-e** from feminine nouns in **-a** (e.g., у колонне).

(6) Comparative endings in **-яе** were rejected. The ending became **-ее** regardless of accent.

The grammatical normalization reduced the number of morphological dialectisms in the literary language. A complex differentiation took place within the grammar of the low style. A whole series of morphological categories which had once been characteristic of the low style was now admitted into the literary language without any particular stylistic assignment:

(1) Genitive and locative singular forms in **-y** for masculine nouns were no longer considered colloquial. Their number was reduced and they were more strictly defined in semantic terms: for example, this genitive ending was reserved for masculine nouns denoting abstract, material, or collective concepts. But application

of such definitions was not consistent, since the spoken language employed these endings more broadly and freely.

(2) Whether declensional forms of the type **-ие, -ия, -ию** retained the penultimate vowel or replaced it with **-ь-** was left to the individual writer. However, N. I. Greč, in his *Praktičeskaja russkaja grammatika* (1834), recommended, probably on artificial grounds, that the forms without the vowel be used if the stem ended in a hushing sibilant (помощью, ночью).

(3) Masculine nominative plurals in **-a** achieved a wide currency in the literary language and even came to include animate nouns.

(4) Masculine nominative plurals in **-ья** (листья, друзья, крючья, брусья), which had still been considered colloquial by the Academy grammar of 1809, were now considered literary. Semantic differences were now established between pairs such as листы–листья, мужи–мужья, зубы–зубья.

(5) In the instrumental singular of feminine nouns, the endings **-ою, -ой**, and **-ею, -ей** were given equal literary rights, but in adjectives the endings **-ой, -ей** were considered colloquial.

(6) Nominative singular masculine adjective forms in **-ой, -ей** (instead of **-ый, -ий**) and genitive singular masculine and neuter adjective forms in **-ова, -ева, -ово, -ево** ceased to be attributes of the low style, since they were recognized to be merely orthographic reflections of standard literary pronunciation. The spellings **-аго, -яго** were considered a sign of church pronunciation.

However, the adoption of certain features of the low style into the general literary language and the complete banishment of others did not mean that the concept of an all-national colloquial language had died out. This language was grammatically opposed to regional varieties and was considered a variety of the "general" language, close to the literary one. Iterative verbs, for example, were considered colloquial. The particles **-ко, -то, -от** (давай-ко, солдатка-то, отец-то вышел) were assigned to colloquial speech, as were the adverbial participles in **-ючи, -ши**.

The many examples of stylistic regrouping listed above show quite clearly that a "neutral" grammatical system was already being developed in the literary language. This sytem was also supposed to regulate the conversational language of the intelligentsia.

The rapprochement between the literary and conversational

languages was accompanied by a reverse current in the direction of the bookish language. Certain forms of the high style were adopted for general literary use and thereby neutralized. Those morphological categories which did not bear the stamp of archaism or of church language now came to be considered acceptable. This happened to comparatives and superlatives in **-ейший, -айший**, and to participles and adverbial participles. It is interesting to compare the attitudes of the Academy grammar and of Greč toward the last two categories. Whereas the Academy grammar still considered participles to be an appurtenance of the high style, and thus discouraged their formation from everyday verbs, Greč's grammar silently permitted such formations and considered participles a property of the general literary language. In fact, Greč made a plea for the use of participles in the spoken language. But the plea was of no avail, and they remained a literary phenomenon even though their formation was extended to all verbs.

At the turn of the century, there was clear evidence that participles were increasing their adjectival properties. This tendency is demonstrated by wide use of adjectives in **-мый** in the meaning of "capability" or "adaptability" (corresponding to the French suffix *-able:* e.g., непроницаемый, неутомимый, достижимый). Past passive participles also increased their descriptive properties (смущенный взор, удивленное выражение лица). Karamzin even tried to introduce degrees of comparison in participles, but without success. An increase in adjectival qualities in participles led to changes in the syntactic function of their tenses. For example, confusion in the use of past and present active imperfective participles with the past tense of the finite verb began at that time. In Karamzin's *Bednaja Liza,* we have such contrasting constructions as Остановилась над Лизой, *лежавшей* на земле and Видались под тенью дубов, *осеняющих* глубокий, чистый пруд.

The above transformation of participles was organically connected with an increase in the ability of the adjectival system to express properties. French, with its well-developed system of abstract concepts and descriptive adjectives, was again of assistance. Adjectives were now formed to take the place of noun plus preposition (e.g., бестрепетный, замогильный). The development of descriptive adjectives was accompanied by limitation of possessive adjectives. On the model, again, of European languages, the genitive of the noun was preferred: for example, приход льва was now preferred to the львов приход which had reigned to the end of the eighteenth century. The formation of verbs on adjectival stems (улегчить, облегчить) was widely practiced. Some writers often used adjectives as nouns, as in these examples from Žukovskij: так живо *близкое, далекое* так ясно; иль оплакивать *бывалое* слез *бывалых* дайте мне.

In this fashion, the limits and functions of grammatical categories changed, partly under European influence. The "old style" gave way to a new, "neutral" style, which entered into active relations with the spoken language of various social groups. Archaic Church Slavonic forms were evaluated from the point of view of their social utility, and many were rejected. There was strong opposition to unaccented infinitive endings in **-ти,** to second person singular endings in **-ши,** and to feminine adjective genitive singular endings in **-ыя, -ия.** There was a characteristic tendency to define the range of the Church Slavonic verbal alternation **-т-, -щ-** vis-à-vis the native Russian alternation **-т-, -ч-.** Greč allowed the Slavonic type of alternation in verbs in **-ить** and in a few other verbs which had been borrowed from Slavonic, such as клеветать, роптать, трепетать.

9. THE PHONETIC SYSTEM OF THE RUSSIAN LITERARY LANGUAGE AT THE BEGINNING OF THE NINETEENTH CENTURY

The phonetic system of the literary language also began to be stabilized at the beginning of the century. The phonetic system of a "general" literary language, based on the neutral norms of Moscow, began to be opposed to local varieties. Echoes of North and South Russian pronunciations were judged to be non-literary. The rules and norms of *akan'e* were more clearly delineated. But, most important, Russian phonetic peculiarities were opposed to Slavonic ones. Currency was achieved for [o] instead of [e] under accent before a hard consonant or in final position. (Karamzin had introduced the letter ё to designate this pronunciation in *Aonidy,* Book 2, in 1797). Exceptions were made only for Church Slavonicisms which were not used in ordinary conversation. The sphere of use of the velar fricative [γ] was restricted. Greč limited it to the position before a vowel in words of Slavonic origin, and, in other positions, to a few other religious words such as Бор [box]. In this fashion, the secularization of Slavonic forms was accompanied by a Russification of their pronunciation. A full-fledged Slavonic pronunciation was restricted to the "reading of church books."

The phonetic system set up at the beginning of the nineteenth century has remained, without serious alterations, up to the present.

10. THE HISTORICAL SIGNIFICANCE OF THE STYLES OF THE ARISTOCRATIC SALON

The literary styles of the end of the eighteenth century and the first quarter of the nineteenth outlined the basic structure of a national Russian literary language in the areas of phonetics, morphology, and syntax. The basic trends in the development of the literary language of the nineteenth century were begun. But the lexical content, the semantic system, and the ideology of the literary styles of the eighteenth century were very narrow and socially limited. They could not, therefore, satisfy all levels of Russian society—to which they were recommended as a strictly closed system of literary expression.

5 The Early Nineteenth Century: Stylistic Contradictions

1. THE IDEOLOGICAL LIMITATIONS OF THE LITERARY STYLES OF
THE END OF THE EIGHTEENTH CENTURY AND THE BEGINNING
OF THE NINETEENTH CENTURY

The literary styles which were being formed in the second half of the eighteenth century, and which were finally realized in the first decades of the nineteenth, were viewed by Russian society, in the first quarter of the nineteenth century, as the semantic center of the national Russian language. Though recognizing both the merits and the faults of the reform connected with Karamzin's name, the general opinion was that Karamzin had responded to the needs of a new educated class which had neither the refinement of the courtier nor the scholasticism of Slavono-Greco-Latin training. At the same time, it was noted that the tastes of that educated middle class were not the same as Karamzin's and that, in certain respects, he remained a part of eighteenth-century literature. Writers of both noble and non-noble origin adopted and mastered the external forms of the new style, but they felt, at the same time, its ideological deficiency.

As the thirties approached, an acknowledgment of the conceptual monotony, intellectual poverty, social and stylistic limitations, and incomplete "nationality" of the salon language which Karamzin symbolized became a commonplace. It was even denied, by some, that Karamzin was a reformer of Russian prose, because of the paucity of ideas in his work. V. K. Kjuxel'beker complained that the rich Russian language had been reduced to the polite language of a few, *"un petit jargon de coterie."* There were attacks on the excessive Gallicisms in the language of the salon.

In his "Literaturnye mečtanija," Belinskij wrote:

That was an age of phrase-making. They strove to find the right word, but they cared for meaning only to the extent that they avoided nonsense. Karamzin was by nature endowed with a reliable musical ear for language and an ability to express himself smoothly and beautifully—consequently, it was not hard for him to transform the language. They say that he made our language a copy of French, just as Lomonosov made it a copy of Latin. That is only partly true. It is probable that Karamzin tried to write as one speaks. In that event, his error consisted in the fact that he despised the idioms of the Russian language, he did not listen to the language of the simple folk, and he did not study native sources at all.

2. THE SOCIAL, EVERYDAY, AND POLITICAL REASONS FOR THE
TENACITY OF CHURCH-BOOK LINGUISTIC TRADITIONS

Since the "new" style was opposed to the "old," and since Church Slavonic was one of the main structural elements of the old style, it was natural that the new style should encounter violent opposition from those social groups whose ideology found its literary expression in the language of church books. These groups consisted of the clergy, bureaucratic circles, broad segments of the city bourgeoisie, the merchant class, and a part of the nobility. To be sure, some of the clergy (particularly people in the capital and at the court) were "Europeanized"; but they were the exception.

The bureaucratic milieu preserved many vestiges of Church Slavonic, insofar as Church Slavonic seemed to be so close to the archaic chancery language, and because it was utilized for the composition of forms of official rhetoric, such as manifestoes. The Psalter, the church book, and the sermon remained the property and the reading matter of the merchants, people of the "third estate," scribes, and the like. Conservative circles of the nobility also defended the Church Slavonic linguistic culture. On the one hand, the provincial, petty gentry had not yet freed itself from the tradition of learning its letters from the Psalter and the breviary. On the other hand, various levels of the noble bureaucracy and aristocracy saw in Church Slavonic and its ideology a protective, national element counteracting the bad influence of French and the bourgeois-liberal, materialistic, and even revolutionary ideology connected with French. Šiškov wondered: "Isn't the desire of certain new writers to equate the written language with the spoken one, that is, to make it the same for all manner of written compositions, rather like the desire of those new wise men who have decided to make all human estates equal?"

In this connection, it is important to recall Paul's decree of 1797 regarding "withdrawal from use of certain words and the replacement of them by others":

Words withdrawn:	*In place of them, it is ordered that the following be used:*
сержант	унтер-офицер (хотя и прежде отставлен)
общество	этого слова совсем не писать
граждане	жители или обыватели
отечество	государство
приверженность	привязанность или усердие

Even more light is thrown on the social and political situation by the parallels drawn by G. Dobrynin, in his *Zapiski*, between the "classical" high style and the new, romantic style based on French post-revolutionary, bourgeois semantics. As he put it:

I like to say what is understandable, and I like to hear what is clear and useful.

I understand, for example:	*But the following is not to my taste:*
восстановить и утвердить порядок правления	поставить здание на незыблемых столбах политических
I can write: падение государства и его законов	*But I will not write:* потеря тяжести, равновесия политических постановлений. Anyone who writes like this is, to my way of thinking, like a druggist who mashes history and mechanics together in one mortar.
I can say that: Духовенство могло бы произвести споры за веру, проклятия и казни	*But I won't say that:* духовенство зажгло бы религиозную войну
I understand: исступление народа во время всеобщего мятежа	*But the following is revolting:* энтузиазм народа в сию эпоху революционной бури

At this time, there was also opposition to the spread of French ideas and to the extension of knowledge of the French language.

3. THE CAMPAIGN OF REACTIONARY GROUPS OF RUSSIAN SOCIETY FOR THE CHURCH-BOOK LANGUAGE CULTURE

The conservatives defended Church Slavonic as the national, historical base of the Russian literary language and as the source of both its unity and its rhetorical beauties. A. S. Šiškov was the leader of these "Slavophiles," who opposed the bourgeois, revolutionary ideas which French influence brought with it. According to Šiškov, Church Slavonic preserved primordial ideas in a pristine form. Slavonicisms were clear, rich in meaning, and laconic. Both Slavonic and Russian went back to the same roots. The only differences between them were stylistic. Those writers who, under the influence of French, tried to create one single salon style did not understand this deep stylistic difference and could not perceive the comic absurdity of such a sequence as несомый быстрыми конями рыцарь низвергся с колесницы и расквасил себе рожу. Forgetting the internal correspondences of the styles, such writers mechanically adapted the Russian language to the semantic system of French, which was too impoverished to make a distinction between он разодрал себе платье and он растерзал свою одежду, because in both instances it would use the verb *déchirer*.

Šiškov defended Lomonosov's styles and their principles. He contended that their internal unity was threatened by the intrusion of foreign borrowings and foreign semantic associations. He also defended the distribution of genres by styles, arguing that the conversational language was not adequate for all purposes: "The poet, the preacher, the philosopher, the compiler of a natural history, and writers like them need, not only the conversational language, but the entire literary language in all its breadth. Sometimes even it is insufficient; they are compelled themselves to create, to fashion words for the expression of their thoughts."

In imitation of Lomonosov, Šiškov distinguished three types in Russian literature. The first was the old Church Slavonic literature; the second was a Russian literature; the third was a young literature, borrowed from abroad. The third type was, in fact, the literature of the middle style. Šiškov did not deny its right to existence, but he deplored the thoughtless path it had taken and its imitation of French.

Thus, in the "Slavophile" conception of literature and the literary language, the emphasis was on book culture, on the Church Slavonic language. And Church Slavonic, together with the living, spoken language, was viewed as the organic base of the national Russian language. The proponents of this view were not, in general, "archaists," but nationalistic, church-book men.

The problem of social and stylistic differentiation in the spoken language was not elaborated by Šiškov, because he rejected any firm norms in the spoken language, and because he refused to see any different "styles" in it. For him it was a unity constructed on principles totally different from those of the language of literature. Its stylistic indivisibility was a result of its social and material existence. It was regulated by hearing and usage—norms to which the literary language was not subject. (Hence followed Šiškov's broader tolerance for "simple" and even "low" expressions.) And, since the norms of the language of the salon were still spoken norms, the "Slavophiles" refused to recognize their validity for the written language and even considered them inimical to the principles of literary thinking. Šiškov wrote: "The written language is so different from the conversational language that, if we imagined a man who had spent his entire life in the best society but had never read even one important book, we would find that he would not be able to understand an elevated and profound work."

4. THE SOCIAL AND POLITICAL REASONS FOR THE DEFENSE OF CHURCH SLAVONIC BY LIBERAL AND REVOLUTIONARY GROUPS OF THE INTELLIGENTSIA OF THE FIRST THIRD OF THE NINETEENTH CENTURY

The patriotically oriented liberal and revolutionary intelligentsia differed sharply from Šiškov in its social and political views, although it developed ideas similar to his concerning the literary role of Church Slavonic. P. A. Katenin, for example, like Šiškov, placed a high value on the role of church books, and on Lomonosov's reform. Following Lomonosov and Šiškov, he also considered Church Slavonic the organizing nucleus for a division of the literary language into three styles, each with its own genres. V. K. Kjuxel'beker developed similar patriotic ideas in his opposition to the salon style, complaining of the proponents of that style that, "From the powerful and rich Russian language ... they mercilessly drive out ... all the Slavonic words and images, and 'enrich' it with ... Germanisms, Gallicisms, and barbarisms. Even in prose, they try to replace participles and adverbial participles with endless pronouns and conjunctions."

The social reasons for this inclination toward Church Slavonic, on the part of those groups connected with the Decembrists, were revolutionary patriotism and democractic nationalism. Proponents of the latter usually associated the concepts of nation and folk with church literature. These groups were oriented toward folk literature and toward the high, rhetorical genres of civic poetry, historically connected, in Russian artistic literature, with the solemn pathos of Church Slavonic. It would be possible to cite many examples of Slavonic archaisms in patriotic verse composed in the high style:

> Но вящий дар от щедрых нам богов
> Священное, чудесное то древо,
> Его же вдруг земли родило чрево,
> А Зевс и дщерь его под свой прияли кров.

> Katenin, "Sofokl"

> Далече страх я отженя
> Во сретенье исшел: меня
> Он проклял идолми своими.

> A. S. Griboedov, "David"

Moreover, the poet-tribune, poet-revolutionary could find in Church Slavonic the vivid colors for a symbolically generalized, but easily understood, expression of revolutionary ideology:

> Настанет век борений бурных
> Неправды с правдою святой

> K. Ryleev, "Videnie"

> Свирепствуй, грозный день! ... Да страшною грозою
> Промчится не в возврат невинных скорбь и стон,
> Да адские дела померкнут адской тьмою ...
> И в бездну упадет железной злобы трон!

> V. Raevskij, "Èlegija 2"

6. THE COMPOSITION AND FUNCTION OF THE COLLOQUIAL AND
FOLK LANGUAGES IN THE EVERYDAY SPOKEN LANGUAGE OF
DIFFERENT SOCIAL STRATA*

Alongside the social contradictions engendered by the views of
different groups concerning the role of Church Slavonic, there were
deep divisions between literature and everyday life in regard to
the spoken language. Despite the aristocratic tendency to make the
literary language conform to the speech of the best society, there
was a sharp conflict between the refined literary styles and the
everyday speech styles of various social strata. One of the basic
components of the ordinary speech of large segments of society was
the peasant, "folk" element. It was this element that was attacked
by the Karamzin school and limited in the literary styles.

The conversational language of the petty-noble landowner was,
in general, close to the peasant language. M. A. Dmitriev noted
that "The landowner's wife and daughters were almost illiterate.
Of upbringing in the proper sense of the word there was hardly
any conception, because even the word 'upbringing' was understood
in a different sense. One landowner's wife used to say: 'I can state
that our dear father brought us up well; the only thing we didn't
have more than enough of was honey.' "

A combination of the French language with everyday, often
folkish, expressions was characteristic of the language of the aristocracy of the capital and of the wealthy (and sometimes middle)
landowning nobility. A satirical journal of the time parodied the
style in the form of a fictitious diary of a society lady: Ане такия
люди што книясь *porte la tête haute*, а та стучит ходя о пол. У графа
М. кафтан счит сновыми *boutons d'acier*, и оченна харашо, толко
сам собою он гадак.

The comic tradition very clearly reveals the occasionally very
regional, dialectal base of the colloquial language of high society,
which was at a far remove from the European salon style. In 1794,
A. Kop'ev published a one-act comedy, *Čto naše, tovo nam i ne
nada*, in which there is "phonetic" notation of the speech of the
actors. (The speech of one of the actors, the princess, is characterized by a mannered sibilance.)

*[Section 5 of this chapter has been omitted. L.L.T.]

Причудин: Ба! ба! ба! Павесин! — аткуда ты взялся? Здраствуй, братец! сматри, пажалуй *(осматривает его кругом)*, да ты в мундире, адет парядошно, куды девалась то время, как ты носил по три жилета, и чуть не надел три кафтана? ты не напеваешь арий, гаваришь па-русски, уж полна ты ли это?

Повесин: Чево братец! ат дурных сочинителей скоро некуды будет деватца; я принужден был все наряды маи бросить от глупой комедии.

· · · · · ·

Machmère: Мавруша ... падвинь ка мне столик, мать мая, загадать бала апять *(надевает очки)*. Давеча эта праклятая гран пасьянс меня замучила, таперь уж другим манером, на четыре кучки.

Княгиня (перестав писать, сердитая, сидя на софе, вяжет жилет, спускает петли и кусает себе ногти с досады) : Мавруся ... Мавруся ...

Мавруша (вяло) : Што, *ma cousine?*

Княгиня (испугавшись) : Ах, матуська! Сьто йта, паскари ... ай! Муха! ...

Machmère: Ах, мать ма! штойта за беда? Ну, правались ана акаянна! Ат тебя я эту пракляту девятку залажила, Бог знает куды, да что у вас там?

I. S. Aksakov characterized very clearly the mixture of French and peasant language in the speech of the nobility of the time:

At the end of the eighteenth century and at the very beginning of the nineteenth, the Russian literary language was ... still the property of only the "lovers of letters" and, actually, was not yet adapted and elaborated sufficiently for the expression of all the needs of the social modes and knowledge borrowed from Europe ... Many Russian men of state, who could superbly express their ideas in French, wrote Russian in the most clumsy, barbaric manner, as if they had suddenly left the beaten path for the hard clods of a newly plowed field. But often, simultaneously with the purest French jargon ... you could hear from the same lips a living, almost folkish, idiomatic speech—more folkish, in any event, than our present literary or conversational speech. To be sure, such an oral language usually served for communication with the serf domestic and with lower strata of society. But, nonetheless, that gross contrast, that harsh everyday feature, along with a faithfulness to everyday, Orthodox tradition, explains much, very much, in the history of our literature and our national self-consciousness.

Finally, a clear artistic reflection of the speech of the Muscovite nobility may be found in Griboedov's famous comedy *Gore ot uma*. If one ignores the individual peculiarities of the actors' speech, the flow of its dramatic language will contain (besides a neutral, literary stream) the following four currents: (1) a church-book or, rather, high, Slavono-Russian current (перст указательный; ум алчущий познаний; чужевластье); (2) a French current (с дражайшей половиной [*moitié*]; два дня терпение возьми [*prendre patience*]); (3) an everyday conversational current, which includes the familiar (как

пить дадут; она не ставит в грош его; да полно вздор молоть); and
(4) a folk, peasant current (больно не хитер; вдругорядь; покудова).

A close connection and interaction was thus established, within
the spoken language of the early nineteenth century, between the
colloquial speech of educated society and the speech of the peasant.

7. THE LITERARY LANGUAGE OF THE BEGINNING OF THE NINE-TEENTH CENTURY AND PEASANT DIALECTS

The lexicographical tradition and the literary stylistics of the second
half of the eighteenth century and the first half of the nineteenth
established a sharp stylistic and dialectological boundary between
the colloquial language and the folk language. The concept of
"folk" language was applied to the everyday language of the village
population (in its general, not specifically local, forms)—in general,
to the everyday language of the great masses which were untouched
by "enlightenment" and which had not absorbed the mannerisms
of the vulgar, bookish language. Elements of the folk language were
very common even in the colloquial speech of educated society.
Here are a few examples from the *Slovar' Akademii Rossijskoj* (1805–
1822): брюхатая, бывальщина, верховье реки, дуралей, краснобай,
портняга, по свойски, прибаутки, сволочь, тороторить. In a manuscript dictionary of the Academy of Sciences of the second half of
the eighteenth century, such words as the following are considered
to belong to the folk: штукарь, чушь, раздолье (prosperity),
припьян, приглух.

As is obvious from inspection of the above expressions, many
such words entered the general city conversational language during
the nineteenth century. Increased gathering of dialect materials and
a literary reclassification of peasant dialectisms were a symptom
of the literary attitude of the first quarter of the century—a sign
that it was becoming less restrictive in regard to the "folk" dialect.
Dictionary projects recognized the literary rights of some provincial
words. The tradition of excluding dialectisms did not cease, but
now there were protests. It was pointed out that old Russian
chronicles, deeds, songs, and legends contained dialectisms. It was

also pointed out that many dialectisms had formerly enjoyed perfect legitimacy. A romantically oriented society found exoticism and the charm of "primordial" freshness in dialectisms.

In connection with this literary reevaluation of folk language, an interest was shown in professional and regional glossaries, which were published in large numbers in journals and literary miscellanies. The idea arose of composing a dictionary of folk language. Individuals and literary societies more insistently and more often issued appeals for the study of the Russian language, its dialects, its etymology, its sayings, proverbs, and the like. Greč hoped that the provincial clergy and nobility would direct their efforts toward collecting dialect materials.

In this fashion, the folk, and even local, element came forward more and more decisively as valuable and significant material for the creation of a national Russian literary language. It was a symptom of the beginning of a radical "democratization" of the literary language, or, in any event, of a clear striving for the expansion of its social boundaries.

All strata of society were united in their positive attitudes toward the colloquial, especially peasant, languages. There were, of course, differences in outlook. Šiškov called for a national language "cleansed somewhat of its coarseness, rejuvenated, and adapted to our present literature." Seminarians, merchants, the petty bureaucracy, and domestics considered peasant dialects worthy of literary canonization only within strong limitations. Many members of the intelligentsia of the twenties and thirties forbade regional expressions on the grounds that they undermined the unity of the national literary language.

During the romantic period, however, the "aboriginalness," force, and colorfulness of folk expressions, which seemed to express the quintessence of the "national spirit," seemed fresh, sharp, and nationally significant, and a special attention was paid to "folk literature." Thus a blow was delivered against the European, salon styles through the intermediary of the living national language, although, to be sure, the process of giving literary rights to the folk language took place very slowly and met with great stylistic obstacles and ideological difficulties at the hands of various social groups.

8. THE COLLOQUIAL STYLES OF VARIOUS SOCIAL GROUPS

The deep social contradictions which affected the literary evaluation of the folk language had to do with the content, composition, and usage of various styles of the everyday colloquial language. The colloquial language consisted of a variety of dialects ranging from the everyday speech of the nobility (not connected with the salon) to styles which bordered on the peasant language. The lexico-graphical tradition of the eighteenth and early nineteenth centuries very clearly differentiated professional dialects from the colloquial language; but it did not make sociological differentiations within the colloquial language itself. Yet it is enough to ponder the critical judgments of contemporaries to see the social variety and even mutual hostility of the various styles of the colloquial language. For writers of the Karamzin school, many colloquialisms were "low" or "common," whereas, for writers of the intelligentsia (of differing social orientations) who did not fear "folkishness" (P. A. Vjazemskij, for one), the range of literary use of colloquial language was very broad.

In the Academy dictionaries of the time, colloquial expressions were characterized by phonetic, morphological, and, above all, lexical and semantic traits. At the same time, the concept "collo-quial" seems to have been generic and to have comprised within it stylistic variations which were expressed by terms such as "low colloquial," "low style," "low word," "simple usage," "simple dialect," and the like. Examples from the *Slovar' Akademii Rossijskoj* (1789–1794) will illustrate this broad range within the colloquial language: "приказная строка—is said in low colloquial and is equivalent to ябедник, крючкотворец"; "хапаю—a verb used in the low style and signifying хватаю, беру"; "хабар—a low word, meaning прибыль, прибыток, барыш"; "мастероват—a word used in the colloquial language: довольно искусный." Sometimes the colloquial language was fused with the peasant language; but also, and fairly often, the meanings of a word were differentiated into colloquial and folk: "варганю—used in the third person in the colloquial language and means кипит с шумом ... [but] in folk usage it means немножко на каком орудии играю."

One may find interesting material for the study of the social divisions of the colloquial language in the critical opinion expressed by representatives of different social groups concerning the language and style of literary works. For example, Bulgarin censured the language of Zagoskin's novel *Jurij Miloslavskij* as "coarse," "folkish," and "tasteless." Puškin, on the other hand, was not upset by the folkishness of the novel's style, but by the fact that the novel was infected by the language of "bad society"—that is, the speech of the semi-intelligentsia of the city, the vulgar bookishness of the wordly-wise members of half-educated spheres of the merchant class, bureaucracy, and city bourgeoisie.

The materials presented by Bestužev-Marlinskij in his sketch "Novyj russkij jazyk" are interesting for the light they throw on the social bases of the pretentious language of bad society. Bestužev-Marlinskij first comments:

Every calling has its own dialect. The upper circles imitate the *jargon de Paris*. Landowners have their own word for everything. Judges have not yet abandoned понеже and поелику. The journalists have thieves' Latin. The romanticists have their own dictionary of foggy expressions. Even scribes and soldiers have their holiday language. Every class and every calling has a different gibberish. No one can immediately understand anyone else—and hence that effort to make others think without thinking one's self. But the merchants are the worst of all. They like to talk in an elevated fashion, that is, put together a pile of words without connection or logic.

Then Bestužev-Marlinskij gives an example of a conversation between the author and two merchants at a railway station. The elder merchant's speech is illustrated as follows:

Вот, батюшка, была в двенадцатом-то году кампания, так уж кампания-с! Уж много сказать, что *богатель*. Французские все армии, да и войски уничтожительно истреблены с двунадесятью язык, и по делам супостату-с. Вся антирель теперь в Москве лежит: пушек-с — как моркови. Позвольте, к слову стало, узнать-с, достохвальный и знаменитый генерал Кульнев в конном или в кавалерицком полку служительство производить быть имел?

It was on the basis of this unique "vulgar" literariness that the semi-intelligent developed their contempt for the "folk" or "peasant" language—and this language of "bad society" was not differentiated, in the dictionaries, from the general categories of the colloquial language.

Elements of the bookish language which had ceased to be used in the language of the educated continued to exist for a long time in the milieu of the semi-intelligent, who normally drew their linguistic material not only from the folk, but also from the archaic tradition and even from the exfoliations of European letters. The solemn oral and written language of literate merchants, burghers, and manor servants was generally inclined towards a unique vulgar-bookish rhetoric. It often had a touch of the church and chancery, and avoided "low," folk words even though it could not free itself of them. It allowed constant, comic transitions from a bookish language to vulgar colloquial and to regional dialectisms. The language of this petty-bourgeois literature changed in its composition as it was submitted to complicated and varied influences of folklore and literature.

These oral and written petty-bourgeois styles were exceedingly variegated. They were considered to lie beyond the bounds of *belles lettres* in the artistic culture of the eighteenth century. It was only in the first third of the nineteenth century that they penetrated deeply into the system of the literary language and transformed it—thus entering into collision and synthesis with reigning literary styles.

9. THE COLLOQUIAL LANGUAGE AS BASIS OF THE LITERARY LANGUAGE IN I. A. KRYLOV'S FABLES

At the beginning of the nineteenth century, the language of Krylov's fables elevated the living conversational language, in its various social strata and styles, to the point where it could serve as a foundation for a national language. Krylov's copious infusion of the colloquial language into literature created the conditions for the formation of an independent, national, literary language accessible to broad masses of people. His great merits in this function were immediately recognized by people of such divergent views as Belinskij, Bestužev-Marlinskij, Bulgarin, and Nadeždin.

Krylov accelerated three processes of displacement within the system of literary styles. First, he opened the road to literature for the folk language, for types of city colloquial language (excepting those with a clear professional tinge), for the conversational bureaucratic dialect (in both its official and its familiar aspects), and for folk poetry and dialect. In this connection, Krylov's literary activity (limited, to be sure, to the fable), by violating the reigning norms of the aristocratic literary culture, corresponded to the needs and tasks of a profound nationalization and democratization of the literary language. The following examples will serve in illustration:

Коль в доме станут воровать,
    А нет *прилики* вору,
То берегись *клепать*
Или наказывать всех *сплошь* и без разбору.

"Xozjain i myši"

Разбойник мужика, *как липку, ободрал.*

"Krest'janin i razbojnik"

Бедняжка — *нищенький под оконьем таскался.*

"Fortuna i niščij"

Пошли у бедняков *дела другой статьей.*

"Fortuna v gostjax"

Не *принимать никак резонов* от овцы:
Понеже хоронить концы,
Все плуты, *ведомо,* искусны.

"Krest'janin i ovca"

Secondly, Krylov freely introduced the syntactic forms of the spoken language, with their ellipses, their innuendos, and their idiomatic peculiarities, into the structure of his literary (author's) narrative. In this fashion, Krylov opposed the expressive laconism and colorful idioms of the living language to the symmetrical monotony of the syntactic systems of Europeanized salon styles:

С лакеем в два кнута тиранит с двух сторон;
А легче нет ...

"Muxa i dorožnye"

Послушать — кажется одна у них душа,
А только кинь и кость, так что твои собаки,

"Sobač'ja družba"

Велеть молчать : так власти нет.
Просил : так просьба не берет.

"Otkupščik i sapožnik"

Потоплено скота, что и не счесть.

"Krest'jane i reka"

Он к ней, она вперед : он шагу прибавлять.
Она туда ж ; он, наконец, бежать,

"Ten' i čelovek"

Но в дружбе что за счет? Котел горой за свата,
Горшок с котлом за панибрата.

"Kotel i goršok"

Krylov's third contribution is that he mixed, with unusual artistry, archaic and bookish expressions with conversational and colloquial ones. In his work, the literary phraseology and lexicon (even in their poetic and conventional variations) mixed with the system of the conversational colloquial language. The style varied depending on theme, plot, and the expressive tone of the narration.

В каком-то *капище* был деревянный бог:
И стал он говорить *пророчески ответы* ...

"Orakul"

Тучегонитель оплошал ...
Что мой ушастый *Геркулес* ...

"Osel"

Ребенок, черепком наметя в голубка —
Сей возраст жалости не знает —
Швырнул и раскроил висок у бедняка.

"Dva goluba"

Младая лань, своих лишась любезных чад,
Еще *сосцы млеком имея отягченны,*
Нашла в лесу двух малых волченят
И стала выполнять *долг матери священный,*
Своим питая их *млеком.*

"Lan' i derviš"

Krylov's dialogue achieves extreme laconism, dramatic swiftness, and realistic naturalness. It adapts itself to the social position of the character in the fable:

"Смотри-ка, квакушка, что, буду ль я с него?"
Подруге говорит. — "Нет, кумушка, далеко!"
"Гляди же, как теперь раздуюсь я широко.
         Ну, каково?
Пополнилась ли я?" — "Почти что ничего."
"Ну, как теперь?" — Все то ж:

The retorts of his characters have the form of unrestrained, coarse, everyday familiarity far removed from all the niceties of the salon. It is the conversation of the "marketplace," in which the social differences between the speech of different segments of society are leveled out.

Many proverbs, sayings, and aphorisms passed from Krylov's language into literary currency: Если голова пуста, то голове ума не придадут места; Наделала синица славы, а моря не зажгла; А философ без огурцов; Услужливый дурак опаснее врага; Слона-то я не приметил; От ворон она отстала, а к павам не пристала.

In the language of his fables, Krylov demonstrated new ways to synthesize the literary tradition with the living Russian spoken language. He created artistic images with a profound and generalized realism and laid the groundwork for Puškin's road to the folk.

10. THE LITERARY LANGUAGE OF THE NOBILITY AND PROFESSIONAL DIALECTS

In the second half of the eighteenth century and the beginning of the nineteenth, the artistic styles of the literary language avoided words with a professional tinge. Therefore, up to the thirties of the nineteenth century, when the predominant role was played by belletristic styles (both prose and verse), professional dialects and jargons remained almost totally outside the literary language. (The styles of the language of officialdom were not considered professional, for they had a general political significance.) The use of professional words was restricted and, in the salon styles, completely prohibited. Only a limited number of words from the argot of card-playing, from forestry, from fishing, etc., are to be encountered.

Undoubtedly, those jargons that had to do with social life, the military profession, and card-playing were the most important in the city colloquial language. The dictionaries of the period give a selection of professional words which is very characteristic for the style of the age. They present terms from, above all, the chancery jargon, then from maritime and military usage, and card-playing— jargons which have to do with the business relationships and social occupations of the nobility and bourgeoisie. These are followed by words from those professional dialects which have a relationship to landowning, to the peasantry, or to the economics of the (noble) home: terms from hunting, brewing, carpentry, diamond-cutting, masonry, tailoring, shoemaking, pottery, cabinetmaking, baking, selling, and the like.

As a consequence, a great number of the dialectal varieties of the speech of the city—e.g., the language of petty bureaucrats, petty merchants, workers, etc.—found no reflection in the dictionaries and did not achieve even partial literary canonization until the thirties and forties. Thus, in this respect, too, the literary styles of the turn of the century revealed their social narrowness and were subjected to the pressure of new linguistic strata which were rising to the level of the literary language along with the cultural and political rise of "lower" social circles.

11. THE INFLUENCE OF SALON STYLES ON THE LITERARY LANGUAGE OF BROAD CIRCLES OF SOCIETY

Despite the opposition to salon styles, their normative role was great. They established themselves in the national literary language as one of the socially limited varieties of literary expression. From the twenties to the forties, probably the greatest portion of belletristic literature oriented itself, to one degree or another, toward the literary norms of the Karamzin school. Puškin could be ironic about the "high-society" tone of writers who revealed the affectedness and primness of someone who lived in the provinces and who, upon arriving in town on a visit, constantly would encounter expressions unfit for the ears of ladies. But, on the other hand, a commoner, N. A. Polevoj, would say, "It is the duty of the author to express himself in the language of good society ..." and would reject the "naked simplicity of the native language."

However, although they had a regulatory function for certain future styles, these bookish, mannered styles gradually became conservative and were transformed into a closed literary "dialect." The progressive literature of the first third of the nineteenth century strove to elaborate a general national literary language which would, insofar as possible, unite the greater portion of the literary and conversational styles. In this connection, the literary and linguistic activity of the great poet A. S. Puškin has particular significance.

6

The Language of Puškin

The entire preceding culture of the Russian artistic word not only achieved its fullest flowering but also underwent a decisive transformation in the language of Puškin. That language, which reflected directly or indirectly the entire history of the literary language from the seventeenth century to Puškin's day, at the same time determined many of the directions in which the literary language would develop in the future. It served then and would continue to serve as a vital source and an unsurpassed model of artistic expression.

In trying to concentrate the living forces of the national Russian language, Puškin first of all provided an original synthesis of those elements which had played an historical role in the literary language and which, up to the nineteenth century, had existed in contradictory and antagonistic relationships and mixtures. These were, of course: those Church Slavonicisms which were not simply archaic remnants but had been adapted to the expression of complex ideas in various literary genres; Europeanisms (largely in their French mold); and elements of the living Russian language, which freely flowed into Puškin's style beginning in the mid-twenties. To be sure, Puškin limited somewhat the literary rights of the colloquial and folk languages (particularly in their dialectal aspect) and of professional jargons. He viewed these elements from the point of view of his own concepts of "historical character" and "nationality" and subordinated them to an ideal conception of a generally understandable language of "good society." In Puškin's understanding, "good society" was not fearful of the "strangeness" of the folk

127

language (mainly the peasant language) or of naked simplicity of expression—expression, that is, freed of all "foppishness," bourgeois primness, and provincial affectedness.

Puškin thus strove to create a national literary language by synthesizing the literary culture and Russian speech. In this respect, his evaluation of Krylov's language is of profound historical and social interest. When Prince Vjazemskij, because of his aristocratic point of view, rejected Krylov as a representative of the nation, Puškin objected: "Your criticism of Krylov is laughable in the extreme; be quiet, I know that myself, for that rat is my crony." Puškin, with great wit and freedom from aristocratic prejudice, was here quoting from Krylov's fable "Sovet myšej," in which several mice who believe that the individual with the longest tail is the wisest hold a council. When a tailless rat appears, the following dialogue takes place between two of the mice:

> By what chance
> Does a tailless one sit down here with us?
> And what's become of our law? ...
> And can she be of any use to us
> When she has not even preserved her own tail?
> She'll destroy not only us but the whole underground.
> And the mouse answered—"Be quiet, I know that myself,
> For that rat is my crony."

In alluding to this fable, Puškin revealed Krylov as the tailless "crony" of his own style and thereby demonstrated his departure from a narrowly aristocratic culture of the literary word. Popular poetry was, for Puškin, the clearest expression of the "spirit" of the Russian language, and of its basic features. "The study of old songs, tales, etc.," he believed, "is essential for a perfect knowledge of the properties of the Russian language."

The synthesis of various linguistic elements—elements which had been strictly delimited by the Lomonosov-Šiškov theory of three styles, and which had been decisively reevaluated and further delimited by the stylistic canons of the Russian "Europeans" (especially by the Karamzin school and its offshoots)—formed the basis for the limitless expressive capacity of Puškin's style. Puškin definitively destroyed the traditional division of the Russian literary language into three styles, establishing instead a variety of styles within one single national literary language.

This process was inseparable from a reform of literary semantics and syntax, by which those word meanings which had formerly been delimited and which belonged to different styles, dialects, and jargons of the written language or everyday speech were combined by Puškin into a new unity. This stylistic versatility of the word was first made possible by a shifting of the old boundary between literature and life, so that gradually a realistic rapprochment between the two spheres was achieved. In Puškin's work, this process began in the twenties and became particularly clear in the mid-twenties, when he was working on *Evgenij Onegin, Cygany,* and *Boris Godunov.*

2. THE LINGUISTIC DEPENDENCE OF THE EARLY PUŠKIN ON THE STYLES OF THE KARAMZIN SCHOOL

Puškin entered the linguistic conflict of his time in the role of a "Frenchman," that is, as an advocate of the European culture of the artistic word. But he understood the conflict in his own way. At first he viewed it in the light of romantic, philosophical attitudes toward the historical process; but gradually it changed its purpose and content for him, so that, after he took the path of national linguistic realism, he attached a broad democratic character to the conflict.

For the preceding generation of Russian "Europeans" (the Karamzinians), the central literary policy had been to limit the content and forms of the literary language and to achieve a partial rapprochement between the literary language and the spoken language of educated society. One of the methods used in this reform was the translation of European (largely French) words into native Russian forms. The aristocratic salon assumed the role of arbiter of artistic taste. The salon was a woman's kingdom. The ideal image of a woman reader and esthetic lawgiver defined the stylistic structure, semantic content, and expression of the mannered, affected, worldly style of the Karamzin school. According to Puškin's definition, it was a "delicate and fastidious language." And, up to the twenties, his own language followed these "Western" traditions of the Karamzin school. His use of Slavonicisms was limited, and the national current was still not very deep.

3. THE LIBERATION OF PUŠKIN'S LANGUAGE FROM THE PHONETIC
AND MORPHOLOGICAL ARCHAISMS OF THE CHURCH-BOOK LAN-
GUAGE

Without completely rejecting the Church Slavonic heritage, with
its resources for poetic expression, Puškin gradually freed the literary
language from superfluous Slavonicisms. By the beginning of the
twenties, for instance, such obsolete Slavonic words as the following
disappeared totally, or almost totally, from Puškin's language:
вседержитель, сретать, воитель, куща, расточить (in the meaning
"rout"), поносный (meaning "shameful"), and влиять (in its direct
meaning, "pour into").

The exclusion of Slavonic archaisms was accompanied by circum-
scription and elimination of those phonetic and morphological
features of the church-book language which were typical of the
"high" Slavonic style. For example, by the beginning of the twenties,
the use of an accented, Slavonic e in a number of grammatical
categories where Russian has ё either disappeared from Puškin's
verse or remained only in isolated instances. The ending of the
third person singular non-past is one such instance; Puškin's last
use of the Slavonic vocalism in a rhyme occurred in 1821, in the
poem "Napoleon":

> Исчез властитель осужденный
> Могучий баловень *побед* :
> И для изгнанника вселенной
> Уже потомство *настает*.

Similarly, with the exception of one example in the high-style
Poltava (вознесен–измен), the year 1817 witnessed the last use of
the masculine short-form past passive participle in its Slavonic
vocalism: such rhymes as Лафонтен–побежден ("Gorodok," 1814)
were replaced by Russian rhymes like удивлен–он (*Evgenij Onegin*,
VI, 8). In contrast to Batjuškov, Puškin only occasionally used
instrumental case rhymes of the type чешуею–над нею (in *Gavriiliada*).
Puškin's gradual avoidance of morphological archaisms may be
illustrated by his use of the church-book genitive singular feminine
adjective endings **-ыя, -ия**. After 1820, only isolated examples of
them occurred, and when they did there was always stylistic

motivation: for example, зеленыя in "Skazka o mertvoj carevne" (1833), and жало мудрыя змеи in the biblical "Prorok."

Thus, with certain limitations, the principle of making the phonetic and morphological structure of the literary language correspond to that of the conversational language of educated society triumphed in Puškin's usage.

4. THE CULTURAL HERITAGE OF CHURCH SLAVONIC IN PUŠKIN'S LANGUAGE

Up to the beginning of the twenties, Puškin shared Karamzin's view that it was necessary to bring the literary language into accord with the spoken language of the educated. Consequently, he opposed the language culture of the church.

In Puškin's early poems, church and biblical expressions and images are mixed with conventional reflections of classical mythology:

> Тогда, клянусь богами ...
> Я с сельскими попами
> Молебен отслужу ...
>
> "Gorodok" (1814)

> В Меркурии архангела избрал ...
>
> Gavriiliada (1821)

Not only are Slavonicisms reduced in number and deprived of their biblical coloring, they are also used in a punning fashion, with irony:

> Чтоб в Академии почтенной
> Воскресли члены ото сна ...
> Но да не будет воскресенья
> Усопшей прозы и стихов ...
>
> "Xristos voskres, pitomec Feba" (1816)

The use of Church Slavonicisms in transferred meaning is accompanied by a "secular" reevaluation of them, as in Апостол неги и прохлад ... ("Pirujuščie studenty," 1814), and Он сочинял любовные псалмы ... (Gavriiliada, 1821). In adapting Slavonicisms to the styles of artistic literature and to the everyday language, Puškin infused them with a new semantic content. Sometimes it was free-thinking or atheistic. The poem *Gavriiliada* abounds in atheistically distorted church expressions:

> И ты пылал, о Боже, как и мы.
> *Создателью* постыло все *творенье*,
> Наскучило *небесное моленье*,
> Он сочинял *любовные псалмы*
> И громко пел: Люблю, люблю Марию,
> В унынии *бессмертие влачу* ...
> *Где крылия?* К Марии полечу
> И на груди красавицы *почию!*

This resistance to Church Slavonic culture on the part of an atheistically oriented Voltairian was also expressed by a mixture of, and a morphological and semantic interaction of, Slavonicisms with Russian expressions. For example, in *Ruslan i Ljudmila*, we have:

> Как ястреб, богатырь летит
> *С подъятой грозною десницей*,
> И в щеку тяжкой рукавицей
> С размаху голову разит.

Although contemporary criticism constantly reproached the poet for such inappropriate mixtures of Slavonicisms with everyday Russian words, this assimilative tendency persisted in Puškin's language to the end.

In the twenties, however, Puškin's attitude toward Church Slavonic began to change. The causes are complex. There was the influence of Slavophile tendencies coming from groups of the progressive intelligentsia—groups which included, among others, Decembrists and such people close to them as V. K. Kjuxel'beker and P. A. Katenin. Puškin saw in the Church Slavonic tradition a support for his opposition to the dominance of French styles. Moreover, he considered the Slavonic tradition to be more democratic and national, closer to the roots of the national Russian language; and he believed the fusion of Slavonic with the folk language to be the basic creative principle of Russian literature. "The folk dialect," he claimed, "necessarily had to depart from the literary; but subsequently they came together, and this is the material which has been given to us for the communication of our thoughts." Puškin did not value the Christian morality or religious mythology of Church Slavonic; he valued rather its simplicity, brevity, pristine freshness, and its freedom from European affectedness. Thus, in a letter to Vjazemskij, in 1823, he wrote: "I would like to have the Russian language retain a certain biblical bawdiness. I don't like to see, in our primeval language, the traces of European affectedness and French refinement. Coarseness and simplicity are more becoming to it." This return to the Church Slavonic tradition gave a certain archaic quality to Puškin's language and to some of his styles. And, in the thirties, the tendency grew stronger in certain genres.

While continuing to work the "inexhaustible mine of the Slavonic language," Puškin nonetheless freed the literary language from the bonds of church ideology. He resurrected old expressions which had a clear national character; he mixed Slavonicisms with Russian; and, through such a fusion, he created an astonishing variety of literary styles and genres. But he always drew a clear line between the broad possibilities of artistic or rhetorical usage of Slavonicisms and the narrow possibilities of their everyday usage. He pointed out that, although many Slavonicisms were successfully borrowed into the literary language, it still did not follow that one should write да лобжет мя лобзанием instead of цалуй меня.

5. THE METHODS AND PRINCIPLES OF PUŠKIN'S USE OF CHURCH SLAVONICISMS

All the peculiarities of Puškin's use of Church Slavonicisms, beginning with the mid-twenties, can be divided into three groups of phenomena. First of all, a romantic interest in the Russian Middle Ages made Puškin realize the significance of Church Slavonic as the basic literary language of that period. Hence the complex methods of using Slavonic as a means of reproducing the culture, way of life, and outlook of the time in *Boris Godunov* and *Poltava*. The poet's high evaluation of the historical role of Church Slavonic led him to carry its forms over from historical narration into the general system of the contemporary literary language. At the same time, his historicism helped him to extract the nationally characteristic and artistically valuable content from the museum of the old book culture.

Archaic Slavonicisms and expressions from the Old Russian chronicle and chancery languages penetrated into his civic poetry:

> Но *днесь,* когда мы вновь со славой
> К Стамбулу грозно *притекли* ...
>
> "Olegov ščit" (1829)

We also find, in this same poem, such Old Russian expressions as славянская дружина, победы стяг, во славу Руси ратной, строптиву греку в стыд и страх, щит булатный, etc. Other good examples may be found in "Borodinskaja godovščina" (1831):

> И Польша, как бегущий полк
> *Во прах* бросает **стяг кровавый...**
> Но вы, *мутители* палат,
> *Легкоязычные витии* ...

In addition, Puškin's romantic attraction to the "motley Eastern style" (as seen in "Podražanija Koranu," and in his imitations of the Song of Songs) led him to recognize the artistic beauties of biblical language.

In dealing with the second category of phenomena connected with Puškin's use of Church Slavonicisms, we must turn our attention to the emotional, solemn styles of his language. Here, Church Slavonic separated into three basic currents: it formed the main stock of religious lyrics; it was the source of civic rhetoric and lyric pathos; and it provided the material both for "high" epic pictures and for the literary stylization of folk poetry. It is sufficient to cite a few of the more archaic examples from the various genres. Examples from religious lyrics include the following: сердцем возлетать во области заочны; владыко дней моих; дух праздности ... любоначалия ... и празднословия ("Otcy pustynniki i ženy neporočny," 1836); даль указуя перстом; я оком стал глядеть болезненно-отверстым ("Strannik," 1835). From narrative poetry, we have: творить возлиянья, вещать благовещие речи; да сподобят нас чистой душою правду блюсти ("podražanija drevnim," 1833); се ярый мученик; древеса; исторженные пни ("Iz A. Šen'e," 1835). From "Pesni zapadnyx slavjan" (1834), we have: грех велик христианское имя нарещи такой поганой твари, etc.

In his prose language, particularly his artistic prose, Puškin used fewer Slavonic expressions, although he did not completely avoid them. He used the conjunctions дабы, ибо, the adverb токмо, and the pronouns кой, сей, оный. He also had recourse to biblical phraseology: положить ... непреодолимую преграду ("Metel'"); кто не почитает их извергами человеческого рода ("Stancionnyj smotritel'"); сие да будет сказано не в суд и не во осуждение ("Baryšnja-krest'janka"), etc., etc. Puškin's "metaphysical," abstract, and publicistic language has a more archaic phraseology and lexicon: поэзия ... *кольми паче* не должна унижаться; писателей, подвизающихся во мраке; наскуча звуками кимвала звенящего.

In the second half of the twenties, Puškin's style began to reveal tendencies toward a synthesis of the most varied forms of expression. The basic core of the system of the national Russian poetic language seemed, to Puškin, to be more or less established. Now he tried to widen the circle of literary styles. He combined "extremes"; he resurrected expressions and filled them with new artistic content. All literary barriers were removed for those elements of Russian which could pretend to a national significance and which could aid in the development of individualized artistic compositions. Old images acquired the stamp of the living national language. In "Rodoslovnaja moego geroja" (1836), one is amazed by the devices for transforming Church Slavonicisms, old chronicle formulae, Old Russian words, historical terms, and poetic images into a familiar, national style glittering with the carefreeness and simplicity of an everyday tale:

> При Калке
> Один из них был схвачен в свалке,
> А там раздавлен как комар,
> Задами тяжкими татар.
> Зато со славой хоть с уроном,
> Другой Езерский Елизар
> Упился кровию татар,
> Между Непрядвою и Доном,
> Ударя с тыла в табор их
> С дружиной суздальцев своих.
> В века старинной нашей славы,
> Как и в худые времена,
> Крамол и смут во дни кровавы
> Блестят Езерских имена.

The third category of stylistic peculiarities in Puškin's use of Church Slavonicisms is occasioned by his basic tendency to mix

Slavonicisms with Russian literary and everyday expressions, causing them to interact. Slavonicisms collide with Russian words, acquire "secular," transferred meanings, are replaced by Russian synonyms, fuse with them, and transfer their meanings to them. This process, which led to a great deal of misunderstanding on the part of the poet's contemporaries, may be illustrated by the following examples of stylistic transformation and transferred usage (from *Evgenij Onegin*):

> В том совести, в том смысла нет;
> На всех различные *вериги* ...

> Мальчишки разогнали псов,
> *Взяв* барышню *под свой покров* ...

> Старушка очень полюбила
> *Совет разумный и благой* ...

> Как *утеснительного сана*
> Приемы скоро приняла ...

> И Страсбурга пирог *нетленный* ...

> *Высокопарный*, но голодный
> Для виду прейскурант висит ...

Occasionally, Russian words acquired the meanings of semantically or etymologically related Slavonicisms. Thus, one encounters the following usage of the verb зевать, which arose on the basis of an etymological equation with зиять:

> И всех вас гроб зевая ждет,
> Зевай и ты.
>> "Scena iz Fausta" (1828)

Also interesting is the use of Church Slavonicisms in a colloquial meaning or the equation of them with colloquial doublets. We have the following parallelism of forms in *Mednyj vsadnik:* обуянный силой черной and спасать и страхом обуялый и дома тонущий народ.

6. "EUROPEANISMS" IN THE LEXICON, PHRASEOLOGY, AND SEMANTICS OF PUŠKIN'S LANGUAGE AND THEIR NATIONAL JUSTIFICATION

Puškin's methods of reflecting the lexical and phraseological "Europeanisms" in the literary language were extremely variable.

Puškin rejected, as early as the twenties, the Karamzin method of copying European phraseology. He opposed the commonplace periphrases and empty metaphors of the Russo-French styles of the turn of the century. However, he always recognized French as a model in the sphere of abstract concepts. He considered the Russian metaphysical language insufficiently developed and hoped that it would be formed on the pattern of French. For this reason, Puškin often defined Russian words with French ones; he considered the Russian terms to be semantically too fluid and unstable and tried to make their meanings more precise: семейная неприкосновенность, for example, he defined as *inviolabilité de la famille;* чрезвычайная известность, as *extrême popularité;* во всех отношениях самый народный, as *le plus national et le plus populaire.* When he wished to designate the precise meaning of самобытность in "Baryšnja-krest'janka," he added *individualité* in parentheses.

But, as he enriched the semantics of the Russian literary language with new concepts which had already been developed in West European languages, Puškin rejected, following Šiškov, the method of loan translation which had established itself in the Russian Westernizing tradition of the eighteenth century. "Many words and expressions," he claimed, "forcibly introduced into use, have remained and become established in our language, for example, трогательный, from the word *touchant* (see Šiškov's correct reasoning in this matter) ... *Dans son assiette ordinaire. Assiette* means положение, from the word *assoir,* but we translated it with a pun, в своей тарелке ..." In this fashion, Puškin set substantial limitations on the mixing of Russian and French. The principle of semantic association of "Europeanisms" with Russian everyday spheres of meaning, the principle of a necessary correspondence of West European concepts and forms and their expression to the style of the national language (and, as a consequence, a strict selection of "Gallicisms" on the basis of their harmony with the native semantic and lexical structure), and, finally, a limitation of borrowings in favor of a search for corresponding concepts in Church Slavonic and the native language—all these were the restrictive norms which Puškin gradually came to employ with regard to Gallicisms.

In those instances, however, where a corresponding expression could not be found for a foreign object or concept, Puškin allowed borrowings:

Но панталоны, фрак, жилет,
Всех этих слов на русском нет,

Evgenij Onegin (xxvi, 1)

Similarly, Puškin, unlike the Slavophiles, sanctioned those "European" meanings of Russian words as well as those simpler phrases and idioms which had already established themselves in Russian by way of translation (largely from French): носить отпечаток–*porter l'empreinte;* во цвете лет–*dans la fleur de jour;* etc. While trying to bring the general thought structure of the Russian language into closer harmony with West European languages, Puškin nonetheless resisted those phraseological forms which were either calques of mannered French metaphors or reflections of French periphrastic expressions. He constructed parallels contrasting long and flabby expressions with short and simple designations:

Дружба, сие священное чувство, коего благородный   попросту: дружба
пламень и пр.

Едва первые лучи восходящего солнца озарили во-   вместо: рано по утру
сточные края лазурного неба

It was for this reason that periphrases like Небес сокрылся вечный житель (i.e., the sun; "Kol'na," 1814) disappeared from Puškin's language toward the beginning of the twenties.

One can see the process of nationalization, or "Russification," of those images which came from French by juxtaposing such early and later Puškin passages as the following:

В последний раз, на груди снежной
Упьюсь отрадой юных дней ...

"Moe zaveščanie" (1815)

Упиваясь неприятно
Хмелем светской суеты,
Позабуду вероятно,
Ваши милые черты.

"Pod"jezžaja pod Ižory" (1829)

A no less clear example of metaphoric justification and, consequently, of semantic reshaping of a traditional lyrical periphrasis may be seen in the following expression for "spring" in *Evgenij Onegin* (vii, 1):

С улыбкою ясною природа
Сквозь сон встречает *утро года.*

Here, the "morning of the year" is associated with the image of a sleeping nature; the periphrasis becomes a metaphorical neologism. Compare the use of this periphrasis to mean "youth" in Puškin's earlier poetry:

> Погиб на утре лет,
> Как ранний на поляне цвет.
>
> "K Del'vigu" (1817)

Also characteristic is the justification of a French meaning in a Russian word, as, for example, the metaphorical meaning of *essaim* as "crowd" or "throng" in the following quotation from *Evgenij Onegin:*

> Толпа в гостиную валит.
> Так пчел из лакомого улья
> На ниву шумный *рой* летит.

But, of course, this national assimilation of European semantic elements was achieved, first of all and above all, by introducing into the literary language those words and expressions from the everyday and folk languages which were denounced as "low," "simple," and "non-literary" by the salon styles established by Karamzin and his followers.

7. REMNANTS OF SYNTACTIC GALLICISMS IN PUŠKIN'S LANGUAGE.
THEIR GRADUAL DYING OUT

In the sphere of syntax, Puškin's language contains a comparatively small number of the sort of Gallicisms which contradicted the grammatical norms of Russian. Among them are, first of all, violations of the governance of certain words, as in the following imitations of the governance of French *venger, refuser* in *Poltava; joindre à* in *Kamennyj gost';* and *fixer regards, ses yeux sur* in *Ruslan i Ljudmila:*

> *Отмстить* поруганную *дочь* ...
>
> Не он ли *помощь* Станиславу
> С негодованьем *отказал* ...
>
> Я прошу
> И вас свой голос *к ним соединить* ...
>
> И старец беспокойный взгляд
> *Вперил на витязя* в молчанье ...

Similarly, one finds occasional instances of noun plus descriptive genitive of another noun, in imitation of French, instead of the usual adjective plus noun: девы веселья (*filles de joie*), дева красоты, дева неги и любви, сабля мести, язва чести, жизни цветы, etc.

Of particular interest is Puškin's use of an analytical construction employing a preposition in a situation which would normally call for direct governance. Compare the following instances of imitation of French *pour* and *en, dans* in "K Čaadaevu" and *Pikovaja dama*, respectively: Пока сердца *для* чести живы; Молодые люди, расчетливые *в* ветреном своем тщеславии ...

Puškin's language also still shows instances of the influence of French syntax in its use of turns of phrase which are independent and not in agreement, functioning as introductory syntagmas or isolated participles and adjectives:

> Тошней идиллии и холодней, чем ода,
> От злости мизантроп, от глупости поэт,
> Как страшно над тобой забавилась природа ...
>
> > "Èpigramma" (1815)

> Бежал от радостей, бежал от милых муз
> И слезы на глазах—со славою прощался ...
>
> > "K nej" (1817)

Compare also the following sentence from *Dubrovskij:* Маша не обратила никакого внимания на молодого француза, воспитанная в аристократических предрассудках, учитель был для нее род слуги или мастерового.

But these few syntactic Gallicisms were mere relics of the kind of Europeanism which was characteristic of aristocratic language culture in the eighteenth century. Puškin's significance lies precisely in the fact that, although he retained some French (and English) constructions, he established a harmonious syntactical system which was justified *on a national basis*. He thus brought Karamzinian syntax to a point of unusual logical clarity by endowing it with masculine tension and a rapidity of narrative movement.

8. THE ORIGINALITY OF PUŠKIN'S POSITION IN REGARD TO SYNTAX

Although Western stylistic devices had a great influence on Puškin, they were subjected to decisive transformation on the basis of the

Russian language. In Puškin's verse, and particularly in his prose, word order follows those "European" syntactic principles which were "Russified" or justified by everyday Russian usage: descriptive adjective before noun, subject before predicate, objects after the verb. All of these are exemplified in the following citation from "Vystrel":

Это было на рассвете. Я стоял на назначенном месте с моими тремя секундантами. С неизъяснимым нетерпением ожидал я моего противника. Весеннее солнце взошло, и жар уже наспевал. Я увидел его издали. Он шел пешком, с мундиром на сабле, сопровождаемый одним секундантом. Мы пошли к нему навстречу. Он приблизился, держа фуражку, наполненную черешнями. Секунданты отмерили нам двенадцать шагов.

Prosper Mérimée, who translated *Pikovaja dama* into French, wrote to Puškin's friend Sobolevskij: "I find that Puškin's sentence sounds completely French. I have in mind, of course, the French of the eighteenth century. Sometimes I ask myself whether all of you—boyars—don't think in French before you write Russian." It is interesting to compare Puškin's prose with Mérimée's translation:

Две неподвижнные идеи не могут вместе существовать в нравственной природе, так же, как два тела не могут в физическом мире занимать одно и то же место. Тройка, семерка, туз — скоро заслонили в воображении Германна образ мертвой старухи. Тройка, семерка, туз — не выходили из его головы и шевелились на его губах.

Deux idées fixes ne peuvent exister à la fois dans le monde moral—de même que dans le monde physique deux corps ne peuvent occuper à la fois la même place. Trois—sept—as—effacèrent bientôt dans l'imagination de Hermann le souvenir des derniers moments de la vieille comtesse. Trois —sept—as—ne lui sortaient plus de la tête et venaient à chaque instant sur ses lèvres.

While recognizing French, and later English as well, as his syntactic models, Puškin nonetheless did not introduce syntactic norms into Russian which were foreign to it. Rather, he brought the syntax of the literary language into greater and greater accord with that of the spoken language. He opposed the dominance of the qualitative and emotional categories (forms of adjectives, participles, adverbs, relative clauses, and periphrastic expressions) which were characteristic of Karamzin's followers. His syntactic reform—based on a recognition of the dominance of the verb and the noun, on changes of tense forms, and on changes in the devices for syntactic linkage—led to a complete renewal of the narrative style of prose and verse. In this respect, there was a rapprochement between Puškin's views and those of the opponents of Europeanism, the Slavophiles. Their leader, Šiškov, also defended the verb against the dominance of descriptive words in the style of the "Europeans." However, Puškin's conjunctive devices and rhythmic forms of writing syntactic units within the sentence bore the clear stamp of Europeanism and made Puškin's language similar to that of French turn-of-the-century traditions.

The fundamental constructive function of the verb is particularly clear in the language of Puškin's prose. A very good example may be found in *Pikovaja dama:*

Часы пробили первый и второй час утра, — и он услышал дальний стук кареты. Невольное волнение овладело им. Карета подъехала и остановилась. Он услышал стук опускаемой подножки. В доме засуетились. Люди побежали, раздались голоса, и дом осветился. В спальню вбежали три старые горничные, и графиня, чуть живая, вошла и опустилась в вольтеровы кресла. Германн глядел в щелку: Лизавета Ивановна прошла мимо его. Германн услышал ее торопливые шаги по сгупеням ее лестницы. В сердце его отозвалось нечто похожее на угрызение совести, и снова умолкло. Он окаменел.

A word count of *Pikovaja dama* has shown that it has 40 per cent verbs, 44 per cent nouns, and 16 per cent epithets. A word count of the significant words in "Metel'" yielded 28.7 per cent verbs, 9.8 per cent adjectives, and 5.3 per cent adverbs. Compare Gogol''s language in *Mertvye duši*, which has 50 per cent nouns, 31 per cent verbs, and 19 per cent epithets.

Puškin's verse narrative style is richer in adjectives, but the verb still plays a governing role. There are almost no extended, linked dependencies (as, for example, the descriptive genitive) in nouns. The nouns themselves, in governing cases, preserve verbal properties. Puškin wrote услужливый угодник *Царю небес* and not Царя небес. Generally, the noun is only modified by one adjective, so that it is not the organizational center of a complex syntactic construction. B. Tomaševskij, in studying the language of *Gavriiliada*, correctly noted that even the epithet seems to have the verbal component predominating: besides adjectives with the suffix **-ливый** (заботливый, услужливый, послушливый, шутливый, нетерпеливый), there are many epithets with the suffix **-тельный** (внимательный, пленительный), and various deverbative, largely participial, forms of the passive voice (забытый, необозримый, благословенный, усталый).

Thus, Puškin constructed syntactic groups on the model of French and English word order but, at the same time, in full harmony with the "spirit" of the Russian language. He made the verb the center of the construction and made all other members dependent on it. The absence of various degrees of subordination within the simplest syntactic group gave the literary language a logical clarity.

9. THE RHYTHM OF PUŠKIN'S PROSE

The rhythmic movement of syntactic groups in the language of Puškin's prose is subordinated to a symmetrical principle. Syntactic units—that is, the simplest semantic and intonational grammatical entities (syntagmas)—normally contain from six to twelve syllables. Most often they range from seven to nine syllables, and, in rare cases, they reach fifteen to eighteen syllables. Often the sentence contains only one syntagma; occasionally it contains two to four syntagmas; and normally it does not exceed seven to eight syntagmas. A complex syntactic whole also does not normally exceed eight to ten syntagmas. An example may be taken from *Kapitanskaja dočka* (with the number of syllables given in brackets):

Я выглянул из кибитки [8]; все было мрак и вихорь [7]. Ветер выл с такой свирепой выразительностью [14], что казался одушевленным [9]; снег засыпал меня и Савельича [11]; лошади шли шагом [6], и скоро стали [6].

A study of Puškin's methods in making a précis of I. I. Golikov's *Dejanija Petra Velikogo* showed that Puškin consistently replaced complex sentences with short phrases. Often, Puškin's sentence consists of just two elements:

Golikov	*Puškin*
Грозили ему силою, но г. Шипов ответствовал, что он умеет обороняться.	Шипов упорствовал. Ему угрожали. Он остался тверд.

In reality, this rhythmic constructive system was a *particular* embodiment of the general rule which was formulated in the following fashion in Karamzinian prose theory: "Words, expressions, and punctuation marks are to be so distributed as to make reading easy and pleasant."

10. THE LOGICAL CLARITY OF COMPLEX SYNTACTIC CONSTRUCTIONS IN PUŠKIN'S LANGUAGE

The methods of syntactic coordination and subordination utilized in Puškin's prose also serve the cause of logical clarity and grammatical compactness. Paratactic constructions, or coordinate constructions with the conjunctions и, а, но predominate. Subordinate constructions are very limited. Besides relative and subordinate clauses with the conjunction что, characteristic for Puškin's language are temporal clauses with the conjunctions когда, как, едва, лишь (in prose, occasionally, как скоро), conditionals with the conjunctions если, но если, clauses of purpose with the conjunctions чтобы (чтоб), дабы, and causatives introduced by для того что, затем что, потому что, ибо.

This logical clarity in syntactic form, close to the French and English type, was achieved not by doing violence to Russian word order but by originality in selection of native resources.

11. THE RAPPROCHEMENT AND MIXTURE OF LITERARY SYNTAX WITH THE SYNTAX OF THE SPOKEN LANGUAGE IN PUŠKIN'S POETRY

In the last period of his creative work, beginning at the end of the twenties, Puškin freed the language of poetry from the unwieldy constructions of the old Slavono-Russian style. He produced a synthesis of the literary and spoken syntactic forms, using the criteria of realistic clarity and national acceptability. As a consequence, everyday "prose" invaded the poetic language, transforming it and bringing it close to the unforced syntax of oral narrative. The language of *Mednyj vsadnik* provides ample illustration:

> Прошла неделя, месяц, — он
> К себе домой не возвращался.
> Его пустынный уголок
> Отдал в наймы, как вышел срок,
> Хозяин бедному поэту.
> Евгений за своим добром
> Не приходил. Он скоро свету
> Стал чужд. Весь день бродил пешком,
> А спал на пристани; питался
> В окошко поданным куском.

The attempt to bring various literary styles closer to the spoken language is reflected in syntactic condensation, in a limitation of the length of syntagmas and sentences. The short, strictly organized sentences are arranged in a symmetrical chain. This laconic, but semantically rich, language produced an impression of fragmentariness on the writers of the Karamzin school, who were accustomed to a complex, configurated syntax, full of parallelisms, antitheses, and correspondences. It is interesting that Žukovskij changed the final lines of Puškin's verse "Kto iz bogov mne vozvratil ..." (from "Iz Goracija"). Puškin had:

> Как дикий Скиф хочу я пить.
> Я с другом праздную свиданье.
> Я рад рассудок утопить.

and Žukovskij united the sentences into a period which corresponded to his own stylistic rules:

> Как дикий Скиф хочу я пить
> И с другом празднуя свиданье,
> В вине рассудок утопить.

As it approached the rapid flow of an oral tale, Puškin's poetic syntax often was reduced to simple sentences consisting only of principal members:

> Дети спят, хозяйка дремлет,
> На полатях муж лежит,
> Буря воет; вдруг он внемлет:
> Кто-то там в окно стучит.
>
> "Utoplennik" (1828)

His poetic language also reproduced the freedom of the spoken language, with its rapid transitions and ellipses:

> Повсюду я готов. Поедем ... но, друзья,
> Скажите: в странствиях умрет ли страсть моя?
>
> "Poedem, ja gotov ..." (1829)

From the end of the twenties, Puškin freely and widely used conversational constructions in various genres and styles of his lyric language:

> Но чорт его несет судить о свете,
> Попробуй он судить о сапогах.
>
> "Sapožnik" (1836)

Меня зовут аристократом.
Смотри, пожалуй, вздор какой.

"Moja rodoslovnaja" (1830)

С ней речь хотел он завести
И — и не мог. Она спросила,
Давно ль здесь, откуда он
И не из их ли уж сторон.

Evgenij Onegin (VIII, 19)

The rapid change of different speech levels and the identification of the narration with the consciousness of different characters in the novel varies and deepens the oral element in the syntax of *Evgenij Onegin:*

Приехал ротный командир;
Вошел ... Ах, новость, да какая!
Музыка будет полковая!
Полковник сам ее послал.
Какая радость: будет бал!
Девчонки прыгают заране;
Но кушать подали.

(V, 28)

Вперил Онегин зоркий взгляд:
Где, где смятенье, состраданье?
Где пятна слез? ... Их нет, их нет.
На сем лице лишь гнева след.

(VIII, 33)

The syntax of the spoken language appears even more clearly when the author's exposition is mingled with the speech of others:

Поздно ночью из похода
Воротился воевода.
Он слугам велит молчать;
В спальню кинулся к постеле;
Дернул полог ... В самом деле!
Никого; пуста кровать.

"Voevoda" (1833)

Puškin's mixing of the syntax of the literary language with that of colloquial Russian is also typical of this period:

Улыбка на устах увянувших видна;
Могильной пропасти она не слышит зева;
Играет на лице еще багровый цвет. —
Она жива сегодня, завтра нет.

"Osen'" (1833)

The very presence of conversational syntax in literary constructions added an unusual simplicity and an intimate significance to "philosophical language"—the language of profound and abstract ideas. Such syntax may be found in the poem "Iz Pindemonti" (1836).

Mixture of styles led to new forms of lyric composition. The expressive force of speech is different in the literary language from what it is in the conversational language. Sharp emotional contradictions arise in the semantic structure of the poem. The poem "Pora, moj drug, pora" (1834?) provides an excellent example of this effect of syntactic mixture. Into the lyric movement of phrases almost completely bereft of any trace of conversation there suddenly bursts an intimate, conversational syntax which even includes the colloquial interjection глядь, the conversational adverb как раз, the characteristically colloquial disjunctive conjunction а, and especially the conjunctive и: предполагаем жить—*и глядь—как раз умрем*. It even seems as if poetic euphony has been sacrificed in favor of the principles of the conversational language, with its predilection for short words. After these lines, the phraseology and syntax of the literary language begin again. Such alternations of literary and conversational syntax create a unique, "tonal," dichotomy of lyric perception, through the conjoining of intimate, simple, profoundly personal, and artless conversation with the solemn symbolism of the lyric monologue.

Thus the insurmountable boundary between the poetic language and everyday prose was erased—and prose began to glitter with the bright colors of the poetic language.

12. PUŠKIN'S ROUTE TO A DEMOCRATIC REFORM OF THE RUSSIAN LITERARY LANGUAGE

Up to the end of the second decade of the century, Puškin's language contained very few words or expressions which could be labeled, according to the standards of the time, "low," unliterary, colloquial, or peasant. Хват ("Kazak," 1814), детина ("Gorodok," 1814), ерошить волосы ("Moemu Aristarxu," 1815), закадышный друг ("Mansurovu," 1819), and a few other such words, do not go beyond the bounds of the norms of the everyday colloquial language of the nobility. One may easily find parallels in the previous Karamzinian tradition. Only an occasional item will lead in the direction of D. Davydov's language. A deviation in the direction of folk and colloquial language, somewhat greater than that allowed by Karamzinian norms, is first noticed only in *Ruslan i Ljudmila* (1820). In any event, the heroes of the poem do not talk and act according to the rules of salon etiquette. They are somewhat stylized along the lines of "olden times" and fairytale folkishness:

> Княжна с постели соскочила ...
> Дрожащий занесла кулак,
> И в страхе завизжала так,
> Что всех арапов заглушила.

The language of the heroes is direct and coarse, as may be seen from the following words of Ruslan:

> Молчи, пустая голова!
> Я еду, еду, не свищу,
> А как наеду, не спущу!

Thus, by the beginning of the twenties, Puškin rid himself of the stylistic fetters of the Karamzin school and began a stubborn struggle against conventional salon language in the name of a democratic, national, Russian literary language. It is completely natural that literary conservatives of the time should have accused Puškin of excessive democracy and of using a non-literary language.

The concept of *bonne société* was put forth by Puškin as the norm for defining the boundaries and the structure of the new literary language. It was immeasurably broader than the Karamzinian concept of "high society" and did not contradict the linguistic tastes of the democratic strata of the intelligentsia. It was, to put it briefly, adaptable for the creation of a synthetic literary linguistic system. But one first had to know and evaluate the social and linguistic divisions present in the Russian language. Puškin did not approve of, and in general avoided, ethnographic provincialisms. From local dialects and professional jargons, he only introduced that which was generally known and which could achieve national recognition. Puškin rejected the superficial layer of bourgeois imitations of the salon and copiously utilized the most characteristic features of the living national language. He ridiculed Karamzin's epigones, who, in his words, "every moment consider one expression a barge-hauler's expression, another a peasant's expression, a third unpleasant for ladies' ears, etc.," and who "shun the simple language and replace it with simple thinking." "If *Nedorosl'*—this unique monument of national satire—" he continued, "if *Nedorosl'*, by which Catherine and her entire glittering court were once carried away, were to appear in our time, then, in our journals ... they would note with horror that Prostakova scolds Palaška with [the terms] каналья and собачья дочь, and compares herself to a—сука! 'What will the ladies say,' the critic would exclaim, 'after all, this comedy could fall into their hands.' What a tender and fastidious language these gentlemen have to use with ladies!"

Puškin, on the contrary, emphasized the connection between "society" and the "folk," both in life and in literature. "The frank and original expressions of simple folk," he believed, "are repeated in high society without offending the ear." For Puškin, the process of democratization was a sign of a "mature literature." "In a mature literature, there comes a time when minds, bored by monotonous works of art limited by the bounds of a conventional, select language, turn to fresh national inventions and the 'strange' colloquial language ..." He noted, however, with bitter irony, that "the charm of naked simplicity is incomprehensible to us." Nonetheless, Puškin strove to bring literature closer to the language of the "simple folk": "The conversational language of the simple folk (who don't read foreign books and, thank God, don't express their thoughts in French, as we do) is also worthy of the most profound investigation ... It wouldn't hurt us to listen, occasionally, to the women who bake communion bread in Moscow. They speak an amazingly pure and correct language."

Puškin's many references to the language of various kinds of "simple" folk show that he was defending the literary rights of folk poetry, of the peasant language, and of those stylistic layers of the city colloquial language which were close to the peasant language. Thus, where the problem of broadening the limits of the literary language had once centered on the everyday language of high society, Puškin shifted that center to the language of city and country "folk." In his "Zametki o Borise Godunove," Puškin even used the adjective "marketplace" in speaking of this element in his language: "There are coarse jokes and folk scenes. A poet doesn't have to be marketplace of his own free will if he can avoid such scenes; but, if not, then he doesn't have to try to replace such scenes with something else."

"Folk" and "nationality" were collective names for all those genres of literature which, at the beginning of the nineteenth century, served almost the whole nation. This broad category of nationality also included those monuments of Old Russian literature which bore little likeness to the then-current concept of literature. This national literature represented, for Puškin, not just a synthesis of national and European culture, but also the quintessence of "historical nationality." P. A. Vjazemskij used the concept when he neatly characterized the relationship of Puškin's language to folkishness: "What appeared more clearly in Puškin was historical nationality ... Puškin would say, somewhat paradoxically, that one must study the Russian language among flour dealers and bakers of communion bread, but, most likely, he didn't listen to them very much and, in his own speech, rarely imitated the folk." This means that Puškin evaluated the everyday colloquial language from the point of view of its characteristic social functions. The lexicon and stylistic features of the colloquial language were tested against oral folk literature and were co-opted into literature on the basis of their national, historical typicalness.

Puškin contrasted the folk speech with the speech of "bad society," that is, the language of the half-educated, whose epitome he saw in the language of N. Polevoj and the *Moskovskij telegraf*. In this light, the folkishness of Puškin's language has a noticeable tinge of folk poetry and peasantry (most clearly reflected in his letters). Puškin, valuing the folkishness of his narrative poem *Brat'ja razbojniki*, suggested that Bestužev-Marlinskij print fragments of the poem in *Poljarnaja zvezda*, "if the national sounds харчевня, кнут, острог don't frighten the delicate ears of the lady readers." On the other hand, the thirties' critics noted that "the bandit from the simple folk occasionally speaks a bookish language; consequently there is untruthfulness and inaccuracy in the local color." Be that as it may, the assimilation of the colloquial and the folkish into Puškin's language is very clear in the mid-twenties.

13. THE BROADENING OF THE BOUNDARIES AND FUNCTIONS OF THE COLLOQUIAL AND FOLK ELEMENTS IN PUŠKIN'S LANGUAGE

The colloquial element in Puškin's language began to increase during the twenties, bringing with it its own semantic system. The polished affectation of the abstract metaphors of the French style was disrupted by simple words closely connected with everyday life. Colloquial words and idioms bear a clear imprint of the social milieu, the speaking subject, and his means of expression. Colloquialisms also bring with them the syntax of the spoken language. For example:

> Как загасить вонючую лучинку?
> Как уморить Курилку моего?
> Дай мне совет — Да ... *плюнуть на него* ...
>
> "Živ, živ Kurilka" (1825)

> Я сам служивый: мне домой
> Пора убраться на покой ...
>
> "Otvet Kateninu" (1828)

Moreover, words closely connected with the objects they designate create a realistic depiction. Objects and designations which were ignored by the literary tradition of the nobility now entered the middle style, the author's narration, and the effect may be seen in the following lines from *Domik v Kolomne* (1830):

> При ней варилась гречневая каша.
> Бывало, мать давным-давно храпела,
> А дочка — на луну еще смотрела ...

Colloquial and even folk speech appeared even more freely in the tale and in dialogue. Here, the mode of expression and the terms of address became free and unconstrained even when the actors were depicted in noble surroundings. In *Evgenij Onegin* (IV, 32), a stern critic addresses the authors of elegies in the following manner:

> ... "да перестаньте плакать
> И *все одно и то же квакать*."

In the poem "Rumjanyj kritik moj" (1830), the author himself speaks to the critic in the free and easy, familiar terms of the colloquial language:

> Поди-ка ты сюда, присядь-ка ты со мной,
> Попробуй, сладим ли с проклятою хандрой ...

In "Moja rodoslovnaja" (1830), the author's monologue includes "folk" expressions:

> И не *якшаюсь* с новой знатью,
> И крови спесь *угомонил* ...
> *Я сам большой, я мещанин.*

The author's poetic style now even accepts such coarse words as сволочь:

> А вы ребята, подлецы,
> Вперед! Всю вашу *сволочь* буду
> Я мучить казнию стыда.

> "O muza plamennoj satiry" (before 1825)

Elements of the folk and colloquial languages are even more varied and colorful in Puškin's prose dialogue, where, again, they occur not just in the speech of the lower classes but in that of upper-class characters as well (see, for example, the language of dialogue in *Poltava*, "Arap Petra Velikogo," *Kapitanskaja dočka*, etc.). Moreover, the speech of the lower classes is not at all undifferentiated for Puškin; his characters are well individualized.

Certain consistencies may be observed in Puškin's methods of selecting colloquial and folk terms. He avoided everything which was not generally known and generally employed. He had none of the exoticism of regional expressions, and he avoided terms from argots (with the exception of card-playing terms in *Pikovaja dama*, military terms in *Domik v Kolomne* and elsewhere, and conventional robber terms in *Kapitanskaja dočka*—in all of which the use of argot is justified by the conditions portrayed). He rarely utilized terms from professional dialects of the city (note, for example, the absence of merchants' language in "Ženix"). He generally avoided the conversational language of the bureaucracy—which played such a great role in Gogol' and Dostoevskij. In short, Puškin avoided all of those sharp social and professional dialectisms which were so characteristic of the Gogol' Natural School. Instead, his language vacillated between city colloquial and peasant expression, and, apart from those folk terms which had penetrated the everyday language of the intelligentsia, he drew most copiously on peasant and military speech styles (as in "Utoplennik," "Gusar," "Refutacija Beran-žera," etc.).

It is much more to the point, however, to trace the assimilation of folk elements in the author's own linguistic system—that is, in his literary language. As early as the mid-twenties, one can observe a rapprochement between the semantics of the folk language and folk poetry (see, for instance, "Telega žizni," 1825). Puškin's work on folk tales clearly reveals his methods of reproducing the epic simplicity of the folk style and his manner of synthesizing literary and oral creative traditions. When using the style of the folk tale, Puškin did not avoid the lyric formulas of the literary language. On the one hand, he added lyric tension and a generalizing content to the forms of folk poetry; on the other hand, he found the resources for a renewal and democratization of literary poetic styles in folk images and devices. Here are some examples of the reflection of lyrical or traditionally bookish phraseology in "Skazka o mertvoj carevne ..." (1834):

> Братья в горести душевной
> Все поникли головой.
>
> .   .   .   .   .
>
> Сотворив обряд печальный
> Вот они во гроб хрустальный
> Труп царевны молодой
> Положили ...
>
> .   .   .   .   .
>
> Вдруг погасла жертвой злобе
> На земле твоя краса;
> Дух твой примут небеса.

Note also the mixing of bookish images and expressions with those of folk poetry in the same tale:

> Но царевна молодая,
> Тихомолком расцветая,
> Между тем росла, росла,
> Поднялась — и расцвела ...
>
> .   .   .   .   .
>
> Ты встаешь во тьме глубокой,
> Круголицый, светлоокой,
> И обычай твой любя,
> Звезды смотрят на тебя.

This kind of mixture is particularly complex and varied in "Skazka o zolotom petuške," in which there are more exfoliations of literary and bookish elements:

> Застонала тяжким стоном
> Глубь долин и сердце гор
> Потряслося ...
> Царь, хоть был встревожен сильно,
> Усмехнулся ей умильно.

The process of reproducing the folk-epic style was not confined to stylized simplicity, naive folk expressions, and the broad use of colloquial language; it consisted also in re-creating the *Weltanschauung*—the spirit—of national poetry. V. D. Komovskij noted, in a letter to Jazykov, that, whereas one was always conscious that he was *reading* a tale of Žukovskij, Puškin's tales produced the impression that one was *hearing* them.

In his "Pesni zapadnyx slavjan," Puškin has a complex fusion of the folk poetic, the oral, and the bookish. There are elements of the style of the popular song, the tale, and, above all, the bylina.

> Слышит, воет ночная птица,
> Она чует беду неминучу;
> Скоро ей искать новой кровли
> Для своих птенцов горемычных.
> Не сова воет в Ключе-граде,
> Не луна Ключ-град озаряет,
> В церкви божией гремят барабаны,
> Вся свечами озарена церковь.
>
> "Videnie korolja"
>
> Тут и смерть ему приключилась.
>
> "Janko Marnavič"

(This same ending formula occurs in a number of the bylinas and songs of Kirša Danilov's collection.) Note the song-lyric formulas (also present in "Skazka o rybake i rybke"):

> Против солнышка луна не пригреет,
> Против милой жена не утешит.
>
> "Janyš Korolevič"

And note also the fairytale phraseology in the same poem:

> Круглый год проходит, и Феодор
> Воротился на свою сторонку.
> Вся деревня бежит к нему навстречу,
> Все его приветно поздравляют.

Alongside these popular poetic turns of phrase one finds bookish expressions and images from the literary language:

> Ужасом в нем замерло сердце ...
>
> "Videnie korolja"

> Рано утром, чуть заря зардела ...
>
> "Janyš Korolevič"

> Неподвижно глядел на него Марко,
> Очарован ужасным его взором.
>
> "Marko Jakubovič"

At the same time, Church Slavonic formulas (characterizing the Christian culture of the Slavs, in contrast to the culture of Turks and Tatars), freely invade this bylina cycle:

> Громко мученик Господу взмолился;
> "Прав Ты, Боже, меня наказуя!
> Плоть мою предай на растерзанье,
> Лишь помилуй мне душу, Иисусе!
>
> "Videnie korolja"

Sometimes the style fuses with the language of the Old Russian saint's-life narrative:

> Поднял он голову Елены;
> Стал ее целовать умиленно,
> И мертвые уста отворились,
> Голова Елены провещала.
>
> "Feodor i Elena"

And sometimes the bylina language tends toward the forms of the Old Russian heroic tale:

> Кровью были покрыты наши сабли
> С острия по самой рукояти.
>
> "Bitva u Zenicy-Velikoj"

The artless "popularness" of Puškin's folklore style is particularly palpable when one compares his verses to those of A. X. Vostokov. Vostokov, in "Žalobnaja pesn' blagorodnoj Asan-Aginicy" (1827), has:

> Успокоилась тогда Агиница,
> Обнимает брата с горькой жалобой:
> "Ах, братец, какое посрамленье мне!
> Выгоняют меня от пятерых детей!"

But Puškin, in "Čto beleetsja na gore Zelenoj" (1835), has:

> Воротилася Асан-Агница,
> И повисла она брату на шею —
> "Братец, милый, что за посрамленье!
> Меня гонят от пятерых деток."

It goes without saying, of course, that Puškin's "Pesni zapadnyx slavjan" contains no literary expressions which violate the spirit of folk poetry, while Vostokov's verses do.

From the end of the twenties, colloquial expressions freely enter the style of Puškin's authorial narrative. It is as if he were trying to unite extremes and bring together opposing varieties of literary styles. Note such a mixture of the popular with the bookish literary or the literary colloquial:

> Не ведаю, в каком бы он предмете
> Был знатоком, хоть строг он на словах,
> Но *черт его несет* судить о свете ...
>
> "Sapožnik" (1836)

Note also such mixtures as the following in Puškin's prose: *хлопнул* двери ему *под-нос;* заставал их без дела *глазеющих* в окно на прохожих; любил *хлебнуть* лишнее; со смеху чуть не *валялся; красно-рожий* старичок ... *гнуся,* начал читать.

The process of forming a new, democratic, national, literary language was connected with a figurative and ideological enrichment of the living Russian language. In accomplishing this enrichment, Puškin limitlessly expanded the boundaries of the literary language. He selected—from the old language, from Church Slavonic, from the eighteenth-century classical styles, and from early nineteenth-century romantic styles—everything bearing the clear imprint of the historical national character which could easily be brought together in generally understandable forms of expression, and which would give the Russian language pungency, freshness, and expressiveness.

14. PUŠKIN'S SIGNIFICANCE IN THE HISTORY OF THE RUSSIAN LITERARY LANGUAGE

The different elements of the Russian language found their equilibrium, for the first time, in Puškin. His unique synthesis forever erased the boundaries between the classical three styles of the eighteenth century. In destroying this schematism, Puškin created and sanctioned a diversity of national styles—or rather a diversity of stylistic contexts joined together by theme and content. As a consequence, the way was opened for limitless individual variation of styles within the bounds of a general literary norm. Gogol' had profound words for Puškin's role as a national poet. "In him," he claimed, "as in a dictionary, was contained the entire wealth, power, and flexibility of our language. He expanded its boundaries and showed us its entire breadth more than anyone else and further than anyone else." Turgenev wrote of Puškin: "There is no doubt that he created our poetic, our literary, language; and all we and our descendants need do is follow the path laid out by his genius." And Ostrovskij connected Puškin's name with the freeing of Russian thought from the yoke of convention, and with the appearance of the Russian literary language as an equal member of the family of West European languages.

However, the literary language did not at once follow the path laid out by Puškin. From the twenties through the forties, Russian literature, as if staggered by Puškin's great stylistic discoveries, tried to encompass those styles and dialects which were not utilized or exhausted by Puškin. These were various everyday city styles: the language of the bureaucracy, the language of the intelligentsia of non-noble origin, and the professional dialects. These forms of expression invaded the old linguistic norm and threatened it with serious disruption.

7   The Language of Lermontov

I. THE LANGUAGE OF LERMONTOV AND ITS RELATIONSHIP TO PUŠKIN'S LANGUAGE

Puškin's language contains the sources for all later trends in Russian poetry of the nineteenth century. His influence, direct or indirect, is palpable in all literary styles of the thirties and forties. Even resistance to Puškin and an avoidance of his poetic system (as in V. G. Benediktov's style) did not exclude dependence. The breadth of Puškin's creativity allowed both the romantics and the realists to utilize his artistic methods. Contemporaries could only continue and broaden Puškin's poetic reform.

The poetic styles of V. A. Žukovskij, I. I. Kozlov, A. I. Podolinskij, of E. A. Baratynskij, P. A. Vjazemskij, D. V. Davydov, of K. F. Ryleev, A. I. Poležaev, A. Odoevskij, of F. Tjutčev, S. P. Ševyrev, A. S. Xomjakov, N. M. Jazykov, of N. Kukol'nik, and, later, of A. V. Timofeev, V. G. Benediktov, and others—all were influenced by Puškin's language, although they followed other ways and byways at the same time. To be sure, these poets worked out new expressions and techniques in their artistic systems; yet all felt the need to do so in harmony with Puškin's example, to adapt their style to his.

The early Lermontov (up to 1836) had just such a conception of his literary and linguistic role. Although the influence of classicism was still present in the early Puškin, Puškin conquered classicism, and Lermontov did not have to return to its genres and styles. On the other hand, Puškin did not completely acknowledge the linguistic culture of romanticism; on the contrary, he occasionally resisted it and opposed his own style to it. Thus Lermontov, trying to utilize

the valuable portion of those poetic traditions which were not used
by Puškin, attempted to introduce tension and passion into the
Russian language. In the figurative language of B. Èjxenbaum, he
tried "to inflame the blood of Russian poetry, bring it out of its
state of Puškinian equilibrium."

The connection between Lermontov's language and that of
Puškin is obvious. Contemporaries noticed it, and later scholars
have pointed out many similarities. Lermontov's language was full
of Puškinian images, metaphors, and turns of phrase, particularly
in his early poetry. It suffices to give a single example. The following
lines are from *Evgenij Onegin* (VI, 31):

> На грудь кладет тихонько руку
> И падает. Туманный взор
> Изображает смерть, не муку.
> Так медленно по скату гор,
> На солнце искрами блистая,
> Спадает глыба снеговая.

Compare these lines from Lermontov's "Kavkazskij plennik"
(1828):

> Но роковой ударил час ...
> Раздался выстрел — И как раз
> Мой пленник падает. Не муку,
> Но смерть изображает взор,
> Кладет на сердце тихо руку ...
> ... Так медленно по скату гор,
> На солнце искрами блистая,
> Спадает глыба снеговая.

Later, in *Izmail-Bej* (1832), Lermontov had a more independent
version of the same Puškinian image:

> Лезгинец, слыша голос брани,
> Готовит стрелы и кинжал;
> Скопилась месть их роковая
> В тиши над дремлющим врагом.
> Так летом глыба снеговая,
> Цветами радуги блистая,
> Висит, прохладу обещая,
> Над беззаботным табуном.

In syntax as well, Lermontov continued to develop and deepen
the Puškin tradition. In his earliest poems, there is a tendency

toward freeing syntax of romantic diffuseness and indefiniteness—a tendency toward conciseness and clarity of poetic expression. Lermontov's stylistic emendations are interesting in this connection. In "Siluèt" (1830) he first had the following lines:

> Есть у меня твой силуэт:
> На память я его чертил,
> И мнится, этот черный цвет —
> Родня с моей душою был.

In the final text, these images were compressed into two transparent lines:

> Есть у меня твой силуэт.
> Мне мил его печальный свет.

At the same time, Lermontov, under the influence of Puškin's reform, brought the style of some of his genres ever closer to living speech, to the language of popular poetry, and to the styles of national antiquity. And his method of overcoming romanticism, his ways of synthesizing romantic and realistic forms of expression, remind one of the evolution of Puškin's language.

In the last period of his creative activity (beginning in 1836), Lermontov achieved an unusual simplicity and vitality, and the natural freedom of the conversational language. This is particularly evident in the following lines from "Valerik" (1840):

> На шинели
> Спиною к дереву лежал
> Их капитан. Он умирал;
> В груди его едва чернели
> Две ранки; кровь его чуть-чуть
> Сочилась. Но высоко грудь
> И трудно подымалась; взоры
> Бродили страшно, он шептал ...

Puškin's style was thus both a directive force and the main cohesive center for Lermontov. Only by adopting Puškin's mode of expression was Lermontov able to produce a synthesis of the varied but, at the same time, most valuable achievements of the romantic culture of the artistic word, and to create on its basis an original style of emotional confession. He achieved this in both lyric and drama, in both verse and prose.

2. THE PROBLEM OF A SYNTHESIS OF THE ROMANTIC CULTURE OF THE ARTISTIC WORD IN LERMONTOV'S EARLY LANGUAGE

Already in Lermontov's early language there is evident a striving toward a new, original unification of the most varied styles of artistic literature. Investigations have noted echoes and reflections of the language of Lomonosov, Kapnist, I. I. Dmitriev, Batjuškov, Žukovskij, Kozlov, Bestužev-Marlinskij, A. A. Del'vig, Baratynskij, Podolinskij, Odoevskij, Poležaev, and other poets in Lermontov's style. Contemporaries also noted this fact, and Kjuxel'beker wrote of Lermontov, in his *Dnevnik*, that "even in his very imitations there is something of his own, even if it be only the fact that he knows how to weld the most varied verses into a symmetrical whole—and that's no trifling matter."

There are, for example, many similarities and correspondences between the language of Lermontov and that of Žukovskij, particularly in Lermontov's early poetry. Compare the following lines from Lermontov's "Čerkesy":

> Лишь ветра тихим дуновением
> Сорван, листок летит, блестит,
> Смущая тишину паденьем.

with these from Žukovskij's "Slavjanka":

> Лишь сорван ветерка минутным дуновеньем.
> На сумраке листок трепещущий блестит,
> Смущая тишину паденьем.

The young Lermontov's many borrowings from Kozlov are no less obvious. One example should suffice. These lines are from Lermontov's "Kavkazskij plennik":

> Потом чрез вал она крутой
> Домой пошла тропою мшистой
> И скрылась вдруг в дали тенистой,
> Как некий призрак гробовой.

These are from Kozlov's "Knjaginja Natal'ja Borisovna Dolgorukaja":

> И меж кустов тропинкой мшистой
> Она пошла к горе крутой,
> И скрылась вдруг в дали тенистой,
> Как некий призрак гробовой.

It is characteristic, however, that as he built his works out of other peoples' images and turns of phrase Lermontov rejected archaic words or replaced them with living, conversational ones. For example, when he composed his "Čerkesy," Lermontov included a fragment from Dmitriev's "Osvoboždenie Moskvy," but he made stylistic changes. Where Dmitriev had Вдруг стогны ратными сперлись, Lermontov had Ворота крепости сперлись. Where Dmitriev had И се—зрю зарево кругом, Lermontov changed it to И видно зарево кругом.

Lermontov's artistic task was to create an original emotional union from a combination of the most varied expressions taken from both Russian and West European poetry (usually romantic). He wished to infuse a new style with profound semantic content and expressiveness, giving it unusual rhetorical force and sharpness and, at the same time, a national character. In this respect, his language was somewhat like that of Bestužev-Marlinskij, who confessed to the same tendencies. Bestužev-Marlinskij's influence on Lermontov is evident in Lermontov's tendency toward declamatory pathos, emotional rhetoric, and refined images and comparisons. In Lermontov's early dramas (in *Ispancy* or *Menschen und Leidenschaften*, for example) it is easy to find bombastic rhetorical images in the style of Bestužev-Marlinskij: Ревность в грудь ее, как червь, закралась; не слезы—камни уроните из глаз вы; О, не срывай покрывала с души, где весь ад, все бешенство страстей.

In striving toward a union of the most varied material, Lermontov borrowed striking, recherché comparisons from everywhere. B. Èjxenbaum noted that his youthful verses were overflowing with comparisons and that, in contrast to Puškin, he thus revealed a need for rhetoric. But at the same time (though not without the influence of Bestužev-Marlinskij on the one hand, and of Vjazemskij and Baratynskij on the other) Lermontov revealed unusual rhetorical power and inventiveness in his formation of sharp and convincing aphorisms, creating expressive and apt formulas which are often the central point of the poem. The following three examples are illustrative:

> Он тень твоя, но я люблю,
> Как тень блаженства, тень твою.

> Когда я свои презираю мученья,
> Что мне до страданий чужих?

А он, мятежный, просит бури,
Как будто в бурях есть покой.

By mixing and crossing established romantic formulas, Lermontov created new phraseological unities and series. For example, the image of a guest at an earthly banquet or the feast of life (borrowed from French lyrics) occurs more than once in Žukovskij. It also occurs in Puškin and Odoevskij, among others. Poležaev, on the other hand, had a different image for the same idea—the image of a superfluous participant in earthly existence. Lermontov combined the two images into a hybrid formula:

Ненужный член в пиру людском,
Младая ветвь на пне сухом;
В ней соку нет, хоть зелена, —
Дочь смерти — смерть ей суждена!

"Stansy" (1831)

He thus not only produced an original selection of the stylistic resources developed by Russian and West European poetry and an original synthesis of romantic devices, but he also created new forms of literary expression and continued Puškin's work of creating a national Russian literary language. On the one hand, he prepared the way for Nekrasov's civic pathos; on the other, he cleared away the overgrowths of romanticism and deepened the semantic system of Russian by adapting it to a new style of psychological realism.

In the early period of his work, Lermontov acquired a whole arsenal of artistic devices—images, metaphors, phraseological units, poetic aphorisms, and comparisons. He created an unusual variety of rhymes, metres, syntactic devices, alliterations, and strophic variations. He enriched and outdistanced the poetic culture of Puškin's time by having recourse to both popular and West European models. Such poems as "Ataman" (1831), "Volja" (1831), and "Pesnja" (1830) reveal the young poet's remarkably original work by their rhythmic and metrical novelty and complexity. At the same time, by precipitously passing from one genre to another and testing many different genres, he broke down the barriers between traditional "types" of poetry, and seems, in so doing, to have continued Puškin's reforming activity in a new direction.

3. THE PROBLEM OF THE FORMATION OF A NEW, "ORATORICAL" STYLE IN LERMONTOV'S LANGUAGE

Lermontov strove to make the Russian literary language capable of expressing the complex psychic conflicts and meditations of a strongly reflective personality. He wanted it to transmit the internal confession, political protest, and civic aspirations and ideals of such a personality, as well as the complex motives of its dissatisfaction with, and revolt against, contemporary society. He wished to infuse the artistic word with a more modern, everyday content, and to increase its ideological saturation and its emotional variety.

To achieve this goal, Lermontov, from the beginning of the thirties, worked at creating a convincing and effective oratorical style free of literary archaisms. From his early romantic experiments, he felt his way toward a broad oratorical style—a style with striking emotional pathos, profound and polished aphorisms, colorful and expressive epithets, declamatory intonations, questions and exclamations, sharp expressive effects, and a uniquely emotional syntax. A good example of Lermontov's declamatory style is his poem on the death of Puškin, "Smert' poèta" (1837), which B. Èjxenbaum characterized as the "passionate speech of an orator." Other examples may be found in his "Umirajuščij gladiator" (1836):

> А он — пронзенный в грудь — безмолвно он лежит,
> Во прахе и крови скользят его колена ...
>
> Что знатным и толпе сраженный гладиатор?
> Он презрен и забыт ... освистанный актер ...
>
> Напрасно: — жалкий раб, — он пал, как зверь лесной,
> Безчувственной толпы минутною забавой.

Lermontov's lyric style acquired an unusual emotional force and an oratorical tension which converted his lyrics into an emotional confession. Thence derive many of the unique qualities of his language. The leading role of passion entails fragmentariness, incoherence, and the repetition of images. The semantics of a word pale before its emotional tone, as in the following passage from "Demon" (1841):

> Я *бичь* рабов моих земных,
> Я *царь* познанья и свободы,
> Я *враг небес, я зло природы* ...

In Lermontov's oratorical style, epithets are endowed with the chief expressive role and receive the semantic stress:

> Отравлены его последние мгновенья
> Коварным шопотом насмешливых невежд,
> И умер он — с напрасной жаждой мщенья,
> С досадой тайною обманутых надежд.

"Smert' poèta" (1837)

At the same time, Lermontov's language acquired a whole set of other expressive constructions, which endowed speech with lyric agitation and pathetic tension. For example, the motif of deprivation, doom, and misfortune was connected with a tendency to frequently use chains of parallel items with the preposition без (без дружбы, без надежд, без сил; Без дум, без чувств, среди долин; Едва дыша, без слез, без дум, без слов). B. Èjxenbaum was of the opinion that Lermontov here relied on the poetic experience of Žukovskij and Kozlov.

In the oratorical style, the heightened emotional effect leads to destruction of the logical connection between images. The concrete designation of words comes into conflict with their expressive nuances:

> Я знал одной лишь думы власть, —
> Одну, но пламенную страсть:
> Она как *червь* во мне жила,
> *Изгрызла* душу и сожгла.

"Mcyri" (1840)

Occasionally, Lermontov's expressive images are transferred into a context far removed from the direct meaning of the surrounding words, as in the following application of the image "epigraphs of unknown creatures" to the signs on an old house:

> Как надписи надгробные, оне
> Рисуются узором по стене —
> Следы давно погибших чувств и мнений,
> *Эпиграфы неведомых творений.*

"Saška" (1836)

B. Èjxenbaum gave a very apt characterization of the declamatory element in Lermontov and the tendency of emotion to increase, to the detriment of simplicity and clarity. Commenting, for example, on the introductory formula of Lermontov's "Demon," he said

"Печальный демон, дух *ивгнанья*—evokes bewilderment if one fixes one's attention on it. Out of Puškin's дух отрицанья, дух сомненья—an expression which is completely understandable and normal for the Russian language—there arises, by analogy, something strange and incomprehensible: what is a дух *изгнанья?* Is it a дух *изгнанный* or a дух *изгоняющий?*"

This practice of selecting words for their expressive effect, which sometimes led to inexactitude, denotative contradiction, or logically unwarranted collocations, drew a negative response from Lermontov's older contemporaries, who were brought up on Puškin's style. Concerning these lines of Lermontov:

О как мне хочется смутить веселость их
И дерзко бросить им в глаза *железный* стих,
Облитый горечью и злостью!

one of them wrote: "An *iron* verse, *flooded* with anything you like, is an unfortunate expression. Imagine rage in the form of a liquid—that's bile! And now that bile, flowing along the iron strip of verse—really, that's not good! But the iron verse, without that fluid, is really very good."

Nevertheless, investigation of the evolution of Lermontov's language and style reveals that he strove to acquire an ever increasing conciseness and precision. His lyric style, full of antitheses, emotional repetition, and interrogative and exclamatory intonation, saturated with aphorisms, and vivid in anger, acquires its rhythmic and syntactic variety because of displacement of literary and conversational speech forms. The prose of everyday affective speech penetrates deeper and deeper into the structure of the literary language, acquiring new figurative and abstract meanings. Lermontov's language reveals a freedom greater even than Puškin's from the old, traditional styles connected with the church-book tradition.

4. THE SOCIAL AND DIALECTAL COMPONENT IN LERMONTOV'S LANGUAGE

Lermontov's language underwent a complex evolution. There is an enormous distance between his early attempts and his mature poetry (such as "Saška," "Skazka dlja detej," "Borodino," "Dary Tereka," etc.). But even in his early poetry there is a notable absence of the Church Slavonic element. Lermontov went even further than Puškin in excluding the obsolete. Occasional Church Slavonicisms such as

Смотрите, *враны* на дубах
Вострепенулись, улетели.

"Kavkazskij plennik" (1828)

and short-form adjectives and participles such as поникши ели, дружески обеты, в старинны годы gradually decreased in number and died out. In general, in Lermontov's style, the forms of the living language displaced Church Slavonic archaisms even in high-style genres.

The West European element played a much greater role in Lermontov's linguistic structure. The semantic forms of West European (largely French) poetry were the constructive center of Lermontov's style up to 1836. But, while retaining their significance, they gradually acquired a clear national coloration and merged with the native Russian element. Those French forms which were in conflict with the system of Russian gradually disappeared. The French element which had been established in the eighteenth century, however, was very much present in lexicon, syntax, and phraseology (Я взял свои меры; сделайте мне дружбу; он добр для меня; в первой моей молодости; вещи делают впечатление на сердце; подойдя к одному из отверстий, Юрию показалось). Also present were many borrowed words, such as индижестия, куртизанить, кокетиться, поменажируй.

Nevertheless, in his use of West European elements, Lermontov did not go far beyond the norms established by Puškin's reform. He avoided everything which was contrary to the "spirit" of the Russian language; but, like Puškin, he tried to enrich the semantic system of Russian with images, concepts, and phraseological units which had been developed by West European poetry. The French scholars de Vogüé and Duchesne noted that Lermontov's language had reflections of the images and phraseology of Chateaubriand, Hugo, Barbier, de Vigny, de Musset, and others. For example, the well-known comparison with an alligator in the depths of a well, which one encounters in *Vadim* and *Knjaginja Ligovskaja*, goes back to Chateaubriand's *Atala*.

At the same time that he was enriching the Russian literary

language with images from West European literature, however, Lermontov freed his style from classical and mythological images. In his early poems, one can still find a few phrases such as И Вакха милые дары or Диана осребрила, but they soon disappear almost entirely. In this fashion, Lermontov made a complete break with the literary language of the eighteenth century.

Living conversational Russian freely entered Lermontov's style beginning with the thirties. Even in his early language, lexical and morphological elements from colloquial speech appeared. He even used such forms as were normally excluded from the literary language of the thirties and forties. Examples are the use of the genitive plural in **-ов** for feminine and neuter nouns (стадов, толпа мадамов), the use of the nominative plural in **-ы** for neuter nouns (сердцы, кольцы, знамены, леты), the use of the genitive singular in **-мя** for neuter nouns like имя (не знал другого имя; не имел ни время, ни охоты), and the frequent use of adverbial participles in **-чи** (пируючи, сбегаючи, скрываючи).

For the most part, Lermontov introduced into the literary language those elements of the colloquial language and the peasant language which were all-Russian in their currency, and in this respect he continued Puškin's democratic reform. From the lexicon of professional jargons, he only used card-playing terms (compare Puškin's use of them in *Pikovaja dama*), military terms, hunting terms, and occasional colorful dialectisms.

5. LERMONTOV'S LANGUAGE AND POPULAR POETRY

Lermontov early realized (under the influence of Puškin's poetry, of course) that popular poetry was a vital source for Russian literature. In 1830, he made the following observation in his schoolboy notebook: "If I decide to look into folk poetry, I most likely won't look for it anywhere except in Russian songs. It's too bad that my nanny was a German and not a Russian—I heard no folk tales. There is undoubtedly more poetry in them than in all of French literature." However, in his very earliest poems connected with the themes of popular poetry there is no evidence of the influence of the popular language. Only in *Vadim* (1832), which extensively uses the resources of the colloquial language, does one sense the style of popular legends and robber songs. Here the speech of the characters—particularly that of the simple folk—bears the clear imprint of everyday realism.

Thus, even in his early work, there is present an interest in popular speech and popular poetry, which Lermontov could have known both from the folk themselves and from various song collections. At this time, he was more interested in robber legends and songs.

Lermontov's penetration into the spirit of popular poetry is most clearly manifested in the language and style of *Pesnja pro ... kupca Kalašnikova* (1837), in which we have reflections of old popular songs. The very family name, Kalašnikov, brings to mind the image of fighters of the same name in popular songs concerning Mastrjuk—and there are various phraseological parallelisms, as well. But Lermontov's "Kalašnikov" is not simply a mélange of fragments taken from popular songs. It is an independent re-creation, by a poet of genius, of the style of popular poetry, its motifs and images, and its popular poetic devices (epic descriptions, synonymic play, tautology, negative analogy, retardation, and the like).

In the last years of his life in the Caucasus, Lermontov again came close to the sources of popular poetry, and it was then that he wrote "Kazač'ja kolybel'naja pesnja" (1840) and "Dary Tereka" (1839). Yet there is no doubt that, both in the breadth of his utilization of folk material and in the variety and simplicity of his artistic re-creation of its style, Lermontov is far outdistanced by Puškin.

6. THE GROWTH OF REALISTIC TENDENCIES IN LERMONTOV'S LANGUAGE

Lermontov's developing interest in popular poetry, the gradual increase of the everyday conversational element in his language, and his growing tendency to depict what was contemporary and to explore the psychology of people of his own time—all are organically connected, in Lermontov's work, with the formation of a new style of psychological realism, and, at the same time, with a transformation of romantic poetics.

It is interesting to follow the transformation of a romantic style into a realistic one in Lermontov's work. In 1830–1831, in the poem "Pole Borodina," he compelled a simple soldier to deliver romantic tirades in the French fashion—sometimes with an admixture of odic archaism. There is little living Russian in the bookish rhetoric, and the folk element is utterly absent.

> Душа от мщения тряслася,
> И пуля смерти понеслася
> Из моего ружья.
>
> .   .   .   .   .
>
> Однако же в преданьях славы
> Все громче — Рымника, Полтавы
>   Гремит Бородино.
> Скорей обманет глас пророчий,
> Скорей небес погаснут очи,
> Чем в памяти сынов полночи
>   Изгладится оно.

In 1837, Lermontov wrote his celebrated "Borodino." Here, we have a national, realistic style which is striking in its artistic truth and simplicity. Some lines from "Pole Borodina" were transferred into it and, in their new surroundings, bear the clear imprint of popular poetic style. "Borodino" lacks the decorative clichés of the romantic style. Popular proverbial expressions and the soldier's colloquial language, while they are not obtrusive, give the narrative of the old soldier a clear nuance of the narrative style of popular epic (у наших ушки на макушке; французы тут как тут; постой-ка, брат мусью). Bookish and folk expressions and images are fused into a finished artistic whole.

> Вам не видать таких сражений ...
> *Носились знамена как тени*
>   В дыму огонь блестел,
> *Звучал булат,* картечь визжала,
>   Рука бойцов колоть устала,
> И ядрам пролетать мешала
>   Гора *кровавых тел.*

Many interesting contrasts may be found between "Pole Borodina" and the later "Borodino"; we will limit ourselves to one short one. In "Pole Borodina," Lermontov wrote И вождь сказал перед полками; in "Borodino," this became

> Полковник наш рожден был хватом ...
> И молвил он, сверкнув очами ...

Scholarship has noted that the old soldier of the poem is not centered on himself; he is constantly speaking of "our colonel" (see above), "our redoubt," "our breasts." In this fashion, Lermontov described the battle and not the individuals, the general and not the particular. This realistic mode of description was later taken up by Tolstoj, in his depiction of the psychology of war and the dynamics of combatant masses, in *Sevastopol'skie rasskazy* and *Vojna i mir*.

Lermontov not only searched for living, colloquial, popular, poetic coloration; he also sought out everyday, realistic situations and details to replace decorative, romantic pictures portrayed in the spirit of romantic folkishness. In this connection, it is interesting to compare the first version of the end of "Sosedka" (1840) with the style and images of the final redaction. The first version was as follows:

> У отца ты украдь мне ключи,
> Часовых разойтись поучи,
> А для тех, что у двери стоят,
> Я *сберег наточенный булат.*

The final version was:

> У отца ты ключи мне украдешь,
> Сторожей за пирушку усадишь;
> А уж с тем, что поставлен к дверям,
> Постараюсь я справится сам.
> Избери только ночь потемнее,
> Да отцу дай вина похмельнее,
> Да повесь, чтобы ведать я мог,
> На окно полосатый платок.

At the same time, Lermontov's style acquired a tendency to draw realistic pictures in conversational language, replacing prolix, even though detailed, descriptions. For example, in the poem "Valerik" (1840), the original description of the beginning of a battle was diffuse:

> Вот жарче, жарче ... Крик! ... Глядим:
> Уж тащат одного, — за ним
> Других ... и много ... ружья носят
> И кличут громко лекарей.

The final text has the same expressive coloration of living speech but it is a clear, simple, compressed image:

> Вот тащут за ноги людей —
> И кличут громко лекарей.

In the second period of his literary activity, Lermontov's language became so balanced by simple, accurate realism that at times it would read as prose were it not for the fact that it was saturated with feeling:

> Во-первых, потому, что много
> И долго, долго вас любил.

At that time also, Lermontov was attracted by the national Russian style of *Evgenij Onegin* as well as by the fabular language of Krylov. An example may be taken from his poem *Kaznačejša* (1836):

> ... Ее в охапку
> Схватив, с добычей дорогой,
> Забыв расчеты, саблю, шапку,
> Улан отправился домой.

Compare the following lines from Krylov's "Dem'janova uxa":

> Схватя в охапку
> Кашук и шапку,
> Скорей без памяти домой ...

The style of *Kaznačejša* contains many sharp aphorisms and expressions which quickly project clear, realistic images. Some of these even became popular phrases and enjoyed a wide circulation: времен новейших "Митрофан"; идеал девиц, одно из славных русских лиц; весь спрятан в галстук, фрак до пят, дискант, усы и мутный взгляд.

Lermontov thus gradually overcame the romantic style, and he declared his departure from romanticism in the following lines:

> Любил и я в былые годы
> В невинности души моей
> И бури шумные природы,
> И бури тайные страстей.
> Но красоты их безобразной
> Я скоро таинство постиг,
> И мне наскучил их несвязный
> И оглушающий язык.

But the realistic elements in Lermontov's prose style are even more expressive, complex, and significant.

7. THE LANGUAGE OF LERMONTOV'S PROSE

At the end of the twenties and the beginning of the thirties a crisis arose in the culture of the artistic word, and the question of the language and style of prose became unusually acute. Puškin, who at first called upon Vjazemskij and Bestužev-Marlinskij to work on the language of publicistic and artistic prose, himself turned to prose genres at the end of the twenties. The growth and significance of journalism were inseparably connected with the formation of new prose styles, which then became the center for a new system of the literary language. Puškin, Bestužev-Marlinskij, V. I. Dal', M. Zagoskin, A. Vel'tman, A. Pogorel'skij, I. Lažečnikov, N. Pavlov, N. Polevoj, V. F. Odoevskij, O. Senkovskij, and Gogol' were working intensively to develop a prose language system. It is obvious that Lermontov could not avoid participation in the national task.

Gogol' had a particularly high opinion of Lermontov's prose: "... no one in Russia has yet written such a correct and mellifluous prose. There is evident a greater penetration into the actuality of life here—a future great painter of Russian life was in the making." Čexov was of an even higher opinion: "I don't know of a better language than that of Lermontov. I would do the following. I would take his tale and analyze it as they do in the schools—every sentence and every part of the sentence ... And thus I would learn how to write."

However, Lermontov did not at once develop the austere, clear, and compressed style of realistic prose. His first attempts at prose belong to the tradition of romantic prose, which, in imagery, phraseology, and even, partly, in syntax, was close to the language of poetry. For example, the emotional, rhetorical style of the author's language and the speeches of the "elevated" (as opposed to lowly) characters in the novella *Vadim* (1832) are close to the language of romantic poetry. Compare Вадим имел несчастную душу, над которой иногда единая мысль могла приобрести неограниченную власть with the language of Lermontov's poem "Litvinka" (1830):

> В печальном только сердце может страсть
> Иметь неограниченную власть.

As far as the language of the character is concerned, one may compare Jurij's statement to Ol'ga—Мир без тебя, что такое? ... Храм без божества—with

> Что без нее земля и рай?
> Пустые звонкие слова,
> Блестящий храм без божества.
>
> "Ispoved'" (1830)

There are also many examples of vague, florid phraseology in the narrative style, such as: в книге судьбы его было написано, что волшебная цепь скует до гроба его существование с участью этой женщины. One also finds numerous instances of refined, romantic comparisons and melodramatic descriptions of feeling in the spirit and style of Bestužev-Marlinskij:

> Вадим дико захохотал и, стараясь умолкнуть, укусил нижнюю губу свою так крепко, что кровь потекла; он похож был в это мгновенье на вампира, глядящего на издыхающую жертву.

Even in *Vadim*, however, the rhetorical narrative style is mixed with realistic description of everyday scenes, and the speech of the lowly personnages is realistically differentiated. The following is a good example of realistic description:

> Борис Петрович с горя побил двух охотников, выпил пол-графина водки и лег спать в избе; на дворе все было живо и беспокойно; собаки, разделенные по сворам, лакали в длинных корытах ...

The same sort of stylistic bifurcation that we see in *Vadim* is present in Lermontov's early dramas. The pathetic, melodramatic style of his tragic heroes is closely connected with the artistic system of his romantic poetic language. B. Èjxenbaum correctly noted that Lermontov's tendency toward linguistic emotionalism brought the poet to verse drama, where rhetoric does not seem as melodramatic as it does in prose. But, at the same time, everyday scenes in Lermontov's early dramas are striking in their coarseness and in their realistic, even naturalistic, nakedness.

The precise, lively, compact, picturesque, and, at times, abstract language of *Geroj našego vremeni* (1839–1841) is Lermontov's highest achievement in prose. The epithet penetrates the essence of the object and becomes its characteristic definition. In this connection, Lermontov's corrections are interesting. A typical case is afforded by the phrase "The door opened, and a little hand (маленькая ручка) seized my hand." Initially, Lermontov had had "a hot hand" (жаркая рука), and the hint that a woman might be involved was absent.

In "Fatalist," there is a short and expressive aphorism: Ведь хуже смерти ничего не случится,—а смерти не минуешь. The rough draft had, in its stead, a long, romantic, philosophical discourse with a hint of declamation:

Весело испытывать судьбу, когда знаешь, что она ничего не может дать хуже смерти, и что эта смерть неизбежна, и что существование каждого из нас, исполненное страдания или радостей, темно и незаметно в этом безбрежном котле, называемом природой, где кипят [умирают], исчезают и возрождаются столько разнородных жизней.

Lermontov worked on analogies just as persistently and carefully. In the original description of Grušnickij's officer's uniform there was the following comparison: эполеты неимоверной величины *подобались двум котлетам.* The comparison was an exact one, but inappropriate to the personality of an enamoured ensign. It was changed to: эполеты ... были *загнуты кверху в виде крылышек амура.*

Lermontov brought the lyrical and narrative elements of prose into equilibrium. His language, consequently, does not have that predominance of verbs and verbal constructions which is characteristic of Puškin's language. The role of attributes is greater. In Lermontov's prose style a rapid, lively, verb-based narration commonly alternates with lyrical meditations which contain (in careful and limited use) the semantic peculiarities of his poetic language. Lermontov thus achieves a balance between all the basic grammatical categories, as the two following examples demonstrate:

я взял со стола, как теперь помню, червонного туза и бросил кверху; дыхание у всех остановилось; все глаза, выражая страх и какое-то неопределенное любопытство, бегали от пистолета к роковому тузу ...

. . . . . .

я возвращался домой пустыми переулками станицы; месяц, полный и красный, как зарево пожара, начал показываться из-за зубчатого горизонта домов; звезды спокойно сияли на темно-голубом своде, и мне стало смешно, когда я вспомнил, что были некогда люди премудрые, думавшие, что светила небесные принимают участие в наших ничтожных спорах ...

Lermontov's prose is completely lacking in the archaic overtones characteristic of Puškin's language. The prose of his last period is free of Church Slavonicisms and chancery language. *Geroj našego vremeni*, for example, does not have conjunctions like дабы, не токмо, но и, etc., which Puškin used in his prose writings.

At the same time, in *Geroj našego vremeni*, the narrative structure makes copious use of conversational language and everyday colloquial speech. Their clearest manifestation is connected with the figure of Maksim Maksimyč. His narration of the events in "Bèla" may serve as a case in point:

Печорин сделал несколько шагов к двери; он дрожал — и сказать ли вам? Я думаю, он в состоянии был исполнить в самом деле то, о чем говорил шутя. Таков уж был человек, Бог его знает! Только едва он коснулся двери, как она вскочила, зарыдала и бросилась ему на шею. — Поверите ли? Я, стоя за дверью, также заплакал, то-есть, знаете, не то чтоб заплакал, а так — глупость!

But the style of "Žurnal Pečorina," "Taman'," "Knjažna Mèri," and "Fatalist" is also saturated with the living national language. There are neither Church Slavonicisms nor any Gallicisms which would be contrary to the spirit of the Russian language. "Bookishness" disappears in the conversational style of a literary tale. A citation from "Knjažna Mèri" will illustrate these features:

Поздно вечером, т. е. часов в одиннадцать, я пошел гулять по липовой аллее бульвара. Город спал, только в некоторых окнах мелькали огни. С трех сторон чернели гребни утесов, отрасли Машука на вершине которого лежало зловещее облачко; месяц подымался на востоке; вдали серебряной бахромой сверкали снеговые горы ... Я сел на скамью и задумался.

In this passage, there is not a single excess or obsolete word. The syntactic structure is transparent. The sentences are compressed and laconic. Nominal, verbal, and attributive parts of speech are in harmonious proportion. It is the prose of a poet who knew how to deal with feelings and images; it is also the prose of a realistic observer and an acute psychologist.

8. LERMONTOV'S SIGNIFICANCE IN THE HISTORY OF THE RUSSIAN LITERARY LANGUAGE

Lermontov's language was of enormous importance for the history of literary Russian. He prepared the way not only for Nekrasov but also for Turgenev, Tolstoj, and Dostoevskij. The stylistic traditions of the eighteenth century were totally and irrevocably overcome and rejected. Lermontov brought into general use the best achievements of the romantic culture of the artistic word. He cleansed the romantic style of imagistic extremes and the insipid ornamentations of romantic phraseology. He brought about that national synthesis of the narrative and the "metaphysical," abstract, bookish language for which Puškin strove. He made the semantic system of the literary language more profound by creating new forms of compressed and colorful expression of ideas and complex emotions.

In Lermontov's language, artistic force and expression are combined with an extreme conceptual profundity. This ideological pithiness appeared so clearly, even in his poetic language, that Belinskij announced: "For Lermontov verse was only a means for expressing his ideas, profound but, at the same time, simple in their merciless truth." Lermontov created the analytical method of expressing emotions which was later elaborated, in various directions, by Turgenev, Tolstoj, and Dostoevskij. The aphoristic pointedness and laconism of Lermontov's language reached the highest level—outdistancing the aphoristic style of Vjazemskij and Baratynskij:

> И дерзко бросить им в глаза железный стих,
> Облитый горечью и злостью.

This manner reminds one of the turns of phrase of Baratynskij, who, in his early poetry, beautifully expressed what the French call *pointe*. In Lermontov, Puškin's aphoristic style acquired psychological depth, romantic colorfulness, and the analytical precision of abstract exposition.

Lermontov's language had an influence not only on the styles of artistic literature but also (together with Gogol''s language) on the styles of journalistic and publicistic prose which, beginning with the forties, assumed a central position in the system of the Russian literary language.

8

Mid-Nineteenth-Century
Literary Styles

I. DIFFERENCES IN THE FORMS OF WRITTEN EXPRESSION AND THE
NORMS OF LINGUISTIC TASTE BETWEEN HIGHER SOCIAL LEVELS
AND THE RAZNOČINEC-DEMOCRATIC INTELLIGENTSIA IN THE
THIRTIES AND FORTIES

In the thirties and forties, the "fashionable" styles developed by
Karamzin and his followers lost their leading role. Some of them
underwent complex changes by adapting to the linguistic habits,
both written and spoken, of different social strata. In 1828, Orest
Somov noted that the poetic language had become standardized,
but that the language of prose still lacked firm norms. He drew an
analogy between the relatively stable situation in poetry and the
cult of French in higher social circles: the nobility, knowing Russian
and French equally well, nonetheless often preferred to speak and
write in French simply because French was a language with well-
developed and readily available norms.

But the stylistic canons established by the older literary tradition
were crumbling. Poetry was relinquishing its leading role to prose
genres. The relationship of socially based dialects to literature was
changing. The literary language was gradually finding a new
foundation in the culture of the raznočinec* intelligentsia and in

---

* [A *raznočinec* was an educated (often highly cultured) man who did not belong to
the nobility. He could be of merchant, burgher, or clerical origin. He could also come
from the ranks of *déclassé* noblemen. His social views tended to be liberal, democratic,
and even revolutionary. More rarely, he was a conservative. The members of this "class"
had become a rather important social, political, and literary force by the forties and
fifties of the nineteenth century. L.L.T.]

other democratic strata. Their manner of speaking, their democratic forms of expression (sometimes accompanied by a superficial tendency toward florid bookishness) frightened the older nobility. I. I. Dmitriev, an associate of Karamzin, called the new forms of literary expression "marketplace." He noted that, while on the one hand Europeanisms and borrowings were leaving the literary language and passing into the language of the masses, on the other hand the language of literature was being vulgarized and democratized: Я право иногда боюсь, чтобы мужики не заговорили по-французски, а мы *по-ихному*. He felt that the language of *Biblioteka dlja čtenija* contained "banal, incorrect expressions, overheard at bivouacs, in marketplaces, and in flour-dealers' shops." In an appendix to his memoirs, *Vzgljad na moju žizn'*, Dmitriev provided a list of new and old expressions, directing his attack mainly against the *Biblioteka dlja čtenija* and *Moskovskij telegraf*. "Let us," he said, "by way of example, write down some of the newly introduced words, along with a translation of them into the language of Lomonosov, Šiškov, and Karamzin ... :

In the new way	*In the old way*
суметь	уметь, сладить
словно	как бы, подобно
поэтичнее	стихотворнее, живописнее
огромные надежды, огромный гений	это прилагательное прикладывалось только к чему-нибудь материальному: *огромный дом, огромное здание.*
пехотинец, конник	пеший, сухопутный, солдат, ратник конный, всадник. Нынешние авторы, любя подслушивать, оба сии названия переняли у рекрутов.

In connection with these evaluations, it is interesting to observe what the nobleman Irten'ev, in L. Tolstoj's *Junost'*, had to say about the speech of raznočinec students: "They used the word глупец instead of дурак, словно instead of точно, великолепно instead of прекрасно. They used движучи, etc. All this seemed to me bookish and revoltingly disordered." He later added: "Our comprehension was completely different. There was a gulf of nuances which, for me, constituted the entire charm and meaning of life and which was completely foreign to them—and the other way around."

There were many such plaints, but they were to no avail. Even such a proponent of the linguistic culture of the nobility as F. I. Buslaev had to admit, in 1844, that "The so-called Karamzin style, which many people now use, has, for the most part, adopted properties which are only negative. These are: gracefulness of the period, smoothness of the phrase (which sometimes becomes color-lessness and flabbiness), measured prose (cloying in its extremes), and Slavonicisms which, since they occur in worn-out expressions, endow the language with pomposity and theatricalness. And so on."

All of these observations merely testify to the fact that the norms of literary expression had changed and that a new social stratum with more clearly democratic attitudes was gradually becoming the arbiter of linguistic taste. The period from the thirties through the fifties was a turning point in the Russian literary language. But the new styles were very different from each other, contradictory, and mixed. The tradition of the literary language of the salon collided and mixed with the new raznočinec styles. Most often it was subordinated to them; but sometimes it conquered them in certain respects. Most proponents of the new styles were united in their negative opinion of the church-book culture and the turn-of-the-century rhetorical literary styles founded on it. And, for all the differences among them, an effort was made to make the new styles a genuine expression of the national language culture. They were presented as the voice of an awakened national and social self-consciousness. To be sure, in the stylistic ferment of the twenties and thirties, contemporaries could not yet guess which linguistic tendencies were to dominate prose and replace the old literary tradition. But, beginning with the second half of the thirties, Belinskij and Gogol' were powerfully moving Russian literature and the literary language along a new path.

For a time, these new, "progressive" styles were opposed by what Turgenev called "the pseudo-majestic school," which had brought the rhetoric of the "high" romantic style of the preceding epoch to its extreme limit in the language of Zagoskin, Bestužev-Marlinskij, Kukol'nik, P. Kamenskij, Timofeev, Benediktov, and others. But this current also died out toward the end of the thirties and the beginning of the forties.

2. THE BASIC TENDENCIES IN THE DEMOCRATIC REFORM OF THE
RUSSIAN LITERARY LANGUAGE

At the basis of the styles now being formed, there lay, despite their social differences and internal contradictions, four general tendencies. These were inherited from the previous linguistic culture, in part, but they were somewhat transformed.

There was a tendency toward a greater limitation of the high, Slavonic tradition and toward a destruction of the devices of Slavono-Russian rhetoric. Some social groups even desired a complete break with the old church-book tradition.

There was a stylistic insistence on living speech, on popular dialects, and on the written and oral dialects, jargons, and styles of the city. The dialectal center, however, might differ from one style to another, depending on the social basis of the style, and ranging from one dialect to another—from the speech of upper social layers to the bourgeois colloquial language, which was close to the language of the peasantry.

There was a closer interaction between the literary language and the professional dialects of the city. This meant the introduction into literature of many professional and expressive variations of that everyday speech which was characteristic not only of the bureaucracy but also of various categories of the bourgeoisie, peasantry, and city craftsmen. At the same time, antithetically, there were increased efforts to elaborate an all-national linguistic system.

Finally, there was a tendency to establish permanent national norms of expression on a "popular" foundation. There was a search for such national forms of the literary language as would, by virtue of their "national" content, be an expression of the "spirit" of the Russian nation. This concentration on national forms of expression did not, however, exclude West European, particularly French and German, connections.

3. THE STRUGGLE AGAINST REMNANTS OF THE CHURCH SLAVONIC
TRADITION. THE FORMS THE STRUGGLE TOOK AND THEIR SOCIAL
AND IDEOLOGICAL BASES

The reaction against the church-book tradition found a clear, although sociologically varied, expression in various groups of the intelligentsia during the thirties.

O. I. Senkovskij put the question of the relationship of Russian to Church Slavonic in a very extreme form, pointing out that, in West European cultures, the feudal language of the church had played its historical role but then had ceased to have any influence. He insisted that "The Slavonic language must remain in the tradition of our Orthodox Church and be at the exclusive service of the needs of the Faith ... it has nothing to do with Russian literature." It was therefore deemed necessary "to rupture the friendship between the Russian and the Slavonic word, establish the independence of the Russian language, and put a boundary between the two languages so that, in the future, they no longer mix but go each its own way." He contended that Russian grammars were concocted of a mixture of the two languages and that, consequently, there was no grammar of Russian. The stylistic break with Church Slavonic, according to Senkovskij, should result in a change in the phraseology and syntax of the literary language. "For the sake of readability," short sentences should replace constructions with lengthy participles, "endless pronouns," adverbs, and adjectives. In general, all "turns of phrase not characteristic of the logic of Russian" were to be rejected. In his opinion, the lexicon and phraseology of Church Slavonic were contradictory to the norms of an "elegant conversational language." They should be replaced by words of the conversational language of "good society" —defined as the conversational language of the city intelligentsia, which Senkovskij considered to be the structural base for an all-national language.

The stylistic declarations of the thirties, which provided varying views of the future structure of the literary language and varying evaluations of its past, are interesting. A typical case is that of N. Nadeždin, who expressed his opinion in 1836: "The reestablishment of the dignity of the Russian language is very important, not so much out of petty consideration of national self-esteem as for the fact that, by defining its relationship to other languages, one frees it of the danger of foreign, inappropriate influence. The influence of Church Slavonic was just that. It smothered national Russian speech at the very beginning and, for a very long time, hindered its development into a living, national literature." Nadeždin noted the one-sidedness of Lomonosov's reform and rejected Slavophile theory and practice. "Lomonosov's language was still artificial, bookish, too isolated, and too elevated above the living, popular speech." He pointed out that there was no single conversational language common to the soldier, the peasant, the landowner, the scholar, and others, and he called for a reunion of popular speech with the literary language, cautioning, however, that such a reunion avoid vulgar folkishness. "All of these various elements," he felt, "must be melted down and reforged into one pure, educated, refined, conversational language which books would not be ashamed to contain ..."

Given his position, it is understandable that Nadeždin also rejected Karamzin's reform as biased and socially limited. Karamzin, according to Nadeždin, "began to coddle and curry the Russian language, in order to make out of it those little dolls with which French literature of the time filled ladies' boudoirs." Nadeždin disapproved of the pretension displayed by the upper strata of society that their language was the basis for the literary language, and he called for the cooperation of various social groups: "No estate, no select circle of society can have exclusive importance as the model for literature. Literature is the voice of the people; it cannot be the privilege of a single class, of a single caste ... The basis of national unity is language, and it must be understandable and available to all."

Writers like V. I. Dal', who strove to make the spoken popular language (sometimes, even, with regional coloring) the basis of the literary language, also rejected the church-book culture. Dal' believed that it would be the task of the "middle estate" to create a genuinely national system of the Russian language. But he did not see, as yet, any middle estate: "... the mean which we seek does not yet exist. We have only extremes. The language of the highest estate is half-Russian; the language of the lowest estate is a folk language." Therefore, Dal' envisioned the creation of a common language through a synthesis of the language of the upper classes and that of the folk. "Russian expressions and syntax have remained only among the folk. The language of educated society and our written language have been ground down into a vulgar, colorless speech which can be translated, word for word, into any European language." Thus we have, in changed form, an anti-Western conception with a folk and peasant coloration. Dal' rejected Church Slavonicisms as unnecessary ballast: "... the efforts of the Slavonicists—out-of-place, strained interpretations—remain voices crying in the wilderness." Writing about the content of his *Tolkovyj slovar' živogo velikorusskogo jazyka*, Dal' stated: "Our church language has been excluded; what has been accepted are those of its expressions which have entered the living language as well as common terms for items having to do with faith and the church." (This pronouncement, however, did not stop him from recording such words as дланъ, глад, младой, and even спона, стогна, угобжать, дщи, сице, etc.).

In Dal''s conception, therefore, the literary language and, in general, the written language of the upper levels of society were placed under the control of folk dialects. In his opinion, the literary language of the noble tradition had retained almost nothing of a national character.

4. CHANGES IN ATTITUDE TOWARD CHURCH SLAVONICISMS

The resistance to the church-book tradition on the part of the progressive intelligentsia of the thirties and forties was different from that of writers of the Karamzin school. Differences between literary styles were conditioned by differing conceptions of Church Slavonicisms and differing usage of them in various social strata. Forms of the church language which were already considered archaic by the noble intelligentsia still survived in raznočinec spheres. Words which some considered Russified and belonging to literature seemed to others to be "vulgar Slavonicisms." A Slavono-Russian lexicon of 1831 considered such words as спутник, туземец, шествие, юность Slavonic. On the other hand, N. A. Polevoj considered even such words as рукоплескание, скрежет, святилище Russified.

All these contradictions in the literary styles of the thirties and forties were particularly evident in the work of V. I. Dal'. In his opposition to the old, bookish literary language, Dal' also opposed semi-educated imitation of it, claiming that, "In common literary usage, we meet many bad words which have been put in circulation in place of more euphonious and expressive words." It would seem as if Dal''s judgment were similar to Puškin's concept of the language of bad society. But it is very likely that many of Dal''s own neologisms of the type самовщина, мертвизна, ловкосилие would have met with Puškin's adverse judgment; for many of them bear the same imprint of bourgeois bookishness which revolted Puškin's linguistic taste. Although he rebelled against polysyllabic Slavonicisms such as усовершенствование, руководствуемый, семейственный, and the like, Dal' himself made wide use of word formations of a Church Slavonic type. On the other hand, when Dal' submitted examples of his ideal, folk, dialectally localized language to Žukovskij for judgment, Žukovskij opined that one could speak thus only with Cossacks and then only of things well known to them.

It is interesting that Turgenev, in the forties, ironically called the styles of the "pseudo-majestic school" "seminary" styles, thereby underlining their archaic, bookish, church manner. He wrote, concerning a novella by Kukol'nik:

The author ... in order, in some fashion, to delineate his characters, tinted them with some sort of seminary coloration. We have called the coloration of the new novella "seminary" and we will immediately demonstrate why. For example, here is how Mak-Stefens speaks: "Умереть с голоду! За то, что в *тайниках природы* я открыл ее новую силу ... За то, что *попечительная* натура *моими устами* этой же столице, целому миру — *изволит поведать одну из благодетельных тайн своих* ... " Lilla, Maks-Stefens' daughter, together (купно) with her mother, Betsi, bears that same coloration.

5. THE INSTABILITY OF LITERARY AND WRITTEN STYLES IN THE LANGUAGE OF VARIOUS DEMOCRATIC GROUPS OF RUSSIAN SOCIETY IN THE THIRTIES AND FORTIES

The originality of the democratic conception of the boundaries and content of the Church Slavonic bookish current is explained by the fact that, in democratic circles of society, different norms of literary and written expression had been formed. In comparison to the aristocratic salon styles, there was a different attitude toward the concept of "literariness." It consisted, above all, in the selection of, and preference for, some one word form out of two or more variants. Moreover, the preferred form would be one which was earlier considered less literary and less normal. For example, according to various testimonies, снова would be selected in place of вновь, лишь in place of только, нисколько in place of нимало, and so on. There were also changes in the meanings and uses of words; for instance, разбор came to be used in the sense of рецензия, and сложиться came to be used in the meaning of устроиться (in speaking of circumstances). Methods for creating neologisms also indicate changes in grammatical and semantic norms in comparison to the previous system of the literary language. For example, the archaic, church-book suffix **-овение** became productive, and thus words like исчезновение, возникновение (on the model of Church Slavonicisms like отдохновение) appeared in the forties. The verbal pair вдохновить–вдохновлять was created even though it disturbed the pattern of a morphological word-forming series (cf. вдохнуть–вдохновение, возникнуть–возникновение, etc.).

Thus, stylistic traditions were vacillating at a moment of crisis in the system of the literary language. The meanings of words became unstable. They were broadened and changed, as if the new social groups which were announcing their rights to the literary language had no command of their full range of uses. Colloquialisms mixed with the written language.

One can derive some knowledge of the vacillations in the written and spoken language of the thirties and forties from a sort of handbook of common stylistic errors (*Spravočnoe mesto russkogo jazyka*) which was published in 1839 and reissued in 1843. A few examples will illustrate the kinds of problems which were being faced.

It was noted, for one thing, that generalization of the meaning of some words obscured the original meaning: *Бал.* Балом называется собрание, в котором танцуют; называть этим словом большой обед, ... неправильно. Так же должно говорить: *на бале*, а не *на балу*. On the basis of such obscuring of the original meaning, pleonasms arose. The careless inexactitude of colloquial usage broke into literature: *Будни.* Не должно говорить *будние дни. Будни*, без прибавления слова *дни*, уже означает непраздничные, рабочие дни.

The manual provided a whole series of examples testifying to the identification of words which were synonyms or near synonyms, but which differed stylistically. The nuances preserved by the old literary tradition were being obliterated in the new styles of the literary language. For example: *Доктор* ... Обыкновенно употребляют слово *доктор* вместо слова *врач. Место рождения.* Слово *месторождение* употребляется только, когда говорят о минералах. *Всходить.* Часто употребляют слово *входить* там, где должно говорить *всходить* ... Confusion of homonyms also occurred: *Газ, газ. Газ*—название прозрачной ткани; *газ*—воздухообразное вещество; поэтому должно писать: *газовое освещение,* а не *газовое.*

Vacillations in old syntactic and phraseological norms, caused by the influence of the spoken language, were also noted: *Лекарство.* Не должно говорить: *лекарство против чахотки,* ... говори *лекарство от чахотки* ...

A principle for *selecting* colloquial forms was put forward. Morphologically unjustified, "vulgar" variants were rejected: *Их.* Не должно говорить *ихный брат, ихная очередь. Очень.* Не должно говорить: *оченно холодно.* Также не правильно выражение: *очень прекрасно.*

6. NEW FORMS OF LITERARY PHRASEOLOGY

The differences between the new literary styles and the former ones are particularly apparent in phraseology. To be sure, the basic phraseological tendencies of the thirties and forties had not yet become established. But the general principles of semantic deviation from older norms and contradiction in the very structure of the new phraseology are nonetheless interesting. There were two diametrically opposed tendencies: a soberly realistic and practical reflection of life, and a romantic, philosophical overembellishment and rhetorical idealization of it. Thus, in the rhetorically strained metaphors of the period, there was either an inorganic mixture of bookish and everyday words or an absence of any semantic correspondence between the images—which were drawn partly from the romantic poetry of the twenties and thirties and partly from life's practical side.

Good examples of such a style may be found in N. A. Polevoj's

Očerki russkoj literatury (1839): Угрюмый опыт останавливает мечту и щиплет крылья моего воображения; Раздушенный выродок французской литературы давал пирушку дремлющей русской душе и крепко спавшему русскому уму; Тысячи рифмачей писали запоем пошлости. In Polevoj's letters to his brother we find examples such as the following: Ведь жизнь-то значит счастье и наслажденье, а я откупорил стклянку с этим небесным газом—он вылетел и теперь, как ни запирай эту драгоценную сткляночку,—она пуста. Я как будто забыл о делах, этих мерзких червях, которые точат нас заживо.

Thus, this phraseological rhetoric à la Bestužev-Marlinskij either soared in empty and contradictory metaphors and abstract, periphrastic descriptions of feelings, or it descended into the material world—often into the mundane detail of professional or technical activity. The sources of this style, of course, are to be sought in the romantic literature of the twenties and thirties. Bestužev-Marlinskij's language has a bacchanalia of such romantic periphrases and descriptive metaphors. Instead of saying застрелить, he says запечатать рот свинцовой печатью; instead of попасть в полынью и утонуть, he says ночевать с карасями под ледяным одеялом. And he often has personifications which are very pretentious: Кавказ носит ледяной шлем на гранитном своем черепе; по углам развеваются кружева Арахны.

A. I. Gercen characterized this romantic language as a *jargon de la puberté;* and Turgenev tried to reproduce the phraseology of the thirties in the language of Mixalovič in *Dvorjanskoe gnezdo:* волны жизни упали на мою грудь; я был тут орудием судьбы,—впрочем, что это я вру,—судьбы тут нету; старая привычка неточно выражаться ... It is interesting to compare phrase-making of the Bestužev-Marlinskij or Polevoj type with the comically pompous phraseology of a letter of petition sent to Puškin in 1835 by a certain raznočinec: С телом, истомленным адскою болезнью ... которая, как червь, по капле в день сосет кровь из его сердца; я хотел убить жар сердца и души подобно мужам древности, etc. But such extremely tense rhetorical pathos, with its comic disparity, came to be considered a fault toward the beginning of the forties, as evidenced by Belinskij's conflict with Bestužev-Marlinskij's epigones.

The metaphors and images of the new style often had a concrete basis. The abstract was passed through the prism of the well known, the everyday. Thus one gets the impression of playful irony, of comic disparity. Examples of such everyday, even professional, metaphorizing may be found in parodies of the language of *Biblioteka dlja čtenija:* С головами раскаленными, как говорится ныне, всем тем, чем питался пиитический их дух; перепалка трескучего пламени чувств; Нет средств удержать удивления, которое заставляет перекипать сердце через край (уподобление в этом случае сердца котлу или горшку, в котором перекипает через край жидкость, только что унижает предмет и больше ничего). Sometimes the metaphorizing could even take on a scientific character, as in Любовь *разложила меня в стихии* всех возможных чувствований, и, если бы она меня поцеловала, я бы в один миг *испарился.*

This phraseology—which was not characteristic of all groups of Russian society of the thirties and forties (witness the language of such writers as M. P. Pogodin, V. I. Dal', Ja. Butkov, and others) —is also interesting for its orientation toward objects and concepts in the spheres of production, technology, and natural science. (In the artistic literature of the *nobility* of the time, V. F. Odoevskij, who readily used concepts from natural science, or, more accurately, from idealistic "natural philosophy," occupied a quite isolated position.) The search for new, more complex, "scientific," semantic forms and the introduction of these into the literary language led into the broad areas of natural science and social science.

But before radical changes in the general semantic and lexical system of the literary language are discussed, it is necessary to describe the basic stylistic contradictions in literary development, and to sketch out, from all angles, the boundaries of the literary language—in the new meaning of that term.

7. THE STRUGGLE AGAINST PHRASE-MAKING IN THE NAME OF A REALISTIC DEPICTION OF LIFE

At the same time that romantic phraseology was being adapted to new social needs, a struggle against it was in progress, in the name of simple, precise realism. I. A. Gončarov, in *Obyknovennaja istorija,* sharply depicted the collision of the two phraseological tendencies in the persons of the Aduevs—the nephew and his uncle, a businessman of the new type. Conversations such as the following take place between them:

"Меня влекло какое-то неодолимое стремление, жажда благородной деятель-
ности; во мне кипело желание уяснить и осуществить …"

Петр Иваныч приподнялся немного с дивана, вынул изо рта сигару и наво-
стрил уши.

"Осуществить те надежды, которые толпились …"

"Не пишешь ли ты стихов?," вдруг спросил Петр Иваныч.

"И прозой, дядюшка, прикажете принести?"

"Нет, нет! … после когда-нибудь; я так только спросил.

"А что?"

"Да ты так говоришь …"

"Разве нехорошо?"

"Нет, может быть, очень хорошо, да дико."

Beginning in the mid-thirties, Gogol' (especially in the first volume of *Mertvye duši*) tirelessly worked at destroying the clichés of the florid romantic style, which was so divorced from practicality. The call to action had already come from Puškin. In the second half of the thirties, Belinskij began an energetic attack against "wild phrases and a strained, high, passionate style," making Bestužev-Marlinskij, and, later, the whole rhetorical school, his prime targets. He became the propagandist of a realistic style. The clearest and most individualized expression of this struggle with romantic phrase-making, however, is to be found, beginning with the fifties, in Tolstoj's creative writing.

Tolstoj's literary banner bore the motto "simplicity and truth." He fought for a realistic style, for a merciless unmasking of pure wordplay, and for an exact, colorful, and unpolished reproduction of reality.

Of course, the very devices and principles of Tolstoj's realism were ideologically conditioned by the norms of a world-view which defined for itself the artistic mode of cognition and the ways in which literature could embody reality. Thus, in the semantics of the literary language, the functional connections between objects, phenomena, events, concepts, and characters are depicted as they are conceived by a given social milieu. The actual, objective essence of objects and concepts is often not depicted immediately and directly, but, rather, through the prism of the cultural tradi-tions of the given society—through the prism of its ideology, its mythology, and the various conditions imposed by its "civilization." These conditions, by creating a unique rhetorical covering over reality, can completely distort and even obscure the real structure of the world and the true meaning of words.

In Tolstoj's view, it was necessary to start, not with words, but with facts, with life. It was necessary to start with the living phenomenon, seeing it from the point of view of its internal essence, and then to proceed to its designation, testing the accepted meaning of words against the facts. Thus, Tolstoj's entire story "Nabeg" is constructed on the variations of images and events connected with the definition of the word "bravery." According to Tolstoj, the adequate and objective designation of an object, the meaning of a word, is conditioned by the correspondence and connection of the word with the entire context of the genuine, "national," Russian life and ideology. Words may be only a covering, and not an uncovering, of the true content of cognition. They may be pure actors' phrases, a pose, presenting some imaginary feature of character or emotion imposed by false concepts. The unmasking of such phrases constitutes a unique peculiarity of the style of Tolstoj, which is a further development of the realism of Puškin and Gogol'. Tolstoj polemically opposes a direct designation of the object to the romantic phrases which only obscure the true essence of the object. In the novella *Kazaki*, he depicts mountains through the perception of the hero—a device which rejects the conventional, romantic, literary phraseology of Bestužev-Marlinskij and his epigones.

In the same fashion, Tolstoj, in the fifties, fought against the rhetorical language of the "fashionable" novel, with its affected, romantic phraseology and solemn declarations of emotion. In the novella *Semejnoe sčast'e*, a characteristic dialogue takes place, of which the following is an excerpt:

"А мне кажется, что и мужчина не должен и не может говорить, что он любит" сказал он.

"Отчего?" спросила я.

"Оттого, что всегда это будет ложь. Что такое за открытие, что человек любит? Как будто, как только он это скажет, что-то защелкнется, хлоп — любит. Как будто, как только он произносит это слово, что-то должно произойти необыкновенное, знамения какие-нибудь, из всех пушек сразу выпалят. Мне кажется, — продолжал он, — что люди которые торжественно произносят эти слова: 'я вас люблю,' или себя обманывают, или, что еще хуже, обманывают других."

The unmasking of a discrepancy between "phraseology" and actuality is used as a convincing polemic device in a *sui generis* style of realistic depiction. Two styles of reproducing reality are juxtaposed: the one is false, romantically elevated, emphatic, and does not correspond to actual life; the other reflects the "genuine" course of events and calls objects by their "true" names. The method is used to good effect numerous times in *Vojna i mir*, as can be seen from the following extracts of a description of how Nikolaj Rostov described a battle (the description, at the same time, parodies the romantic battle tradition of Bestužev-Marlinskij's followers):

Не мог он им рассказать так просто, что поехали все рысью, он упал с лошади, свихнул руку и изо всех сил побежал в лес от француза ... Рассказать правду очень трудно; и молодые люди редко на это способны. Они ждали рассказ о том, как горел он весь в огне, сам себя не помня; как буря, налетал на каре; как врубался в него, рубил направо и налево; как сабля отведала мяса, и как он падал в изнеможении, и тому подобное. И он рассказал им все это.

Tolstoj directs the same method against the rhetorical style of "historians." He often first gives a "simple" (or, more accurately, a "simplified"), naively direct, convention-free, description of an event or definition of an object—and only then points out the conventional designation of it. Or, on the other hand, he will at once reveal, by means of the device of an absurdly ironic comparison, the senselessness of the term and the falsehood of the accepted concept. For example, he writes (in *Vojna i mir*): "The military term 'cut off' has no sense whatever. One can 'cut off' a piece of bread, but not an army. 'To cut off an army'—bar its road—is impossible, for there are always plenty of places to go around and there is the night, during which nothing can be seen." It is from this aspect that one must view the typically Tolstojan "infantile" descriptions of such ceremonies as the church service (in *Voskresenie*), or his opinions of the traditional view of the course of world history.

This ideological struggle with conventional, literary word-masks and abstract terms which either obscure concepts or lack them (from the point of view of the author) colors Tolstoj's publicistic prose of the fifties and sixties.

8. THE LITERARY LANGUAGE OF THE THIRTIES THROUGH THE
FIFTIES AND PEASANT DIALECTS

The specifics of what constituted "literariness" during this period
came not only from changes in stylistic tastes and a critical attitude
toward tradition, but also from a new evaluation of the literary
significance of various class and professional languages. Most of
the democratic intelligentsia of the period rejected localized variants
of the peasant language as material for a general literary language.
In *Moskovskij telegraf*, N. A. Polevoj insistently stressed the idea
that what was of literary value in the language of the folk was only
that which had a chance of becoming national in usage. Even
V. I. Dal', for all his sympathies for the language of the folk,
sanctioned only that linguistic material which had passed through
broad strata of the city population or which was directly comprehensible within the bourgeois conception of language. A "sensitive
ear," according to him, should protect the "citizen" from a "spoiling
of the literary language" with local, regional expressions. But that
same "Russian ear and Russian sense," in his opinion, would find,
in the language of the folk, a "multitude of splendid, irreplaceable
expressions, which ought to be accepted into the literary language."
At the same time, Dal' objected to distorted expressions taken
from the language of the lower classes of the city.

In this process, therefore, of purging folk elements and qualifying
their literary value, everything which was strongly localized or
distorted was rejected, on the grounds that it could not pretend
to national currency. Another criterion which was of basic importance was that of the "picturesqueness" of the word, its expressive
force. The literary fate of an expression was determined by the
possibility of directly perceiving the image, by the "internal form"
of the folk word, and by the possibility of its "etymologization" on
the basis of everyday experience.

In general, the city intelligentsia (especially that of the capital)
and the bureaucratic circles often regarded the peasant language,
and particularly its regional forms, with scorn. Senkovskij, for
example, completely barred the "coarse, peasant language" from
literature and derided the "bast-shoe school," one of whose representatives was Dal'. For Senkovskij, the language of peasants was

a wild and petrified form of aboriginal, uneducated expression, and he insisted that the old Russian aristocracy could not have been coarse in its speech. In a review of Vel'tman's novel *Lunatik*, Senkovskij quoted the following conversation:

"Э, э, что ты тут хозяйничаешь?"
"Воду, брат, грею."
"Добре, засыпь, брат, и на мою долю крупки."
"Изволь, давай."
"Кабы запустить сальца, знаешь, дак он бы тово."
"И ведомо. Смотрико-сь, нет ли на поставце?"

and commented, in part: "This is called *belles lettres!* It is very regretful to us that Mr. Vel'tman, who has no lack either of education or of talent, has recourse to such greasy ingeniousness."

Such an attitude toward the language of the peasantry was in sharp social contrast to the tendency of other writers to rely on the regional exoticism of village speech (compare the language of Gogol', D. V. Grigorovič, Turgenev, and others). There could not be a complete ban on peasant, or even regional, words; there could only be restrictive measures. This was all the more true in that the very theme of the village, embodied in Russian literature of the forties à la George Sand, led to peasant dialects. But peasant speech here took on a different role than it had had in the previous tradition. It was not assimilated into the "author's" language, and there neutralized. It served, rather, as a means to provide local color, to show the author's sympathy toward the village, and to assist in a sentimental description of the life of the peasant. By "citing" peasant expressions, the author either brought his point of view into concord with linguistic "self-definition" of the village or created the illusion of naturalistic portrayal. Thus, there was normally no generalization of peasant language (compare Dal''s style). It remained a characterizing token of certain literary genres.

There were attempts at inclusion of exotic or, at least, ethnographic peasant expressions in the author's language. Grigorovič, for example, used peasant expressions in his novel *Derevnja* (1846), but his use of dialectisms was not entirely skillful and selective. Turgenev's account of the reception of the novel serves as an excellent commentary both on its language and on the whole question of the role of peasant speech in the literary language of the time. He pointed out that the novel was a pioneering effort at a Russian "village history." He then commented that I. I. Panaev, having found some laughable expressions in it, held the entire novel up to scorn and delighted in reading passages from it at the homes of friends. But then Belinskij found the novel to be significant and, on the basis of it, predicted the turn that Russian literature was soon to take. There remained nothing for Panaev to do but continue reading passages from it—praising them.

These examples show that, despite differing attitudes toward peasant dialects on the part of different social groups, such dialects played a comparatively insignificant role in the "normal" literary language of the time. Between them and the literary language stood the language of the city, in all its professional, functional, and class varieties.

9. THE SATURATION OF THE LITERARY LANGUAGE WITH ELEMENTS OF THE CITY COLLOQUIAL LANGUAGE AND PROFESSIONALISMS

In the forties and fifties, the social dialects of the city became an important source for enlarging the literary language with elements from living speech. The composition of these dialects depended on their proximity to peasant speech and on their degree of sub-ordination to literary styles. Literature, in its basic current (the naturalistic school), was now oriented toward everyday life, toward linguistic divisions based on estate, class, and profession. The task of a literary style became that of depicting the way of life of some milieu by using its language. Two examples will suffice to demonstrate the new forms of the literary language and the new social evaluations and redefinitions of expressions.

In the thirties, the expression бить по карману (meaning to "get someone in his pocketbook") entered the literary language. Senkovskij revealed the social content of the expression in an ironic description of the conduct of Bulgarin and other literary entre-preneurs of the time. When someone attempted a literary venture, he claimed, the entrepreneurs would immediately attempt to bring him under their control. If that failed, they would take the necessary steps (unfavorable reviews, journalistic attacks) to bring the venture (or book) to financial disaster.

Another example of change in the meaning of an expression is the fate of the adjective паркетный (parquet). In the first decades of the century it had received a transferred meaning and could be used as an epithet to describe the foppish individual who walked about the parquet floors of the salons of the nobility. It had a pejorative connotation and only appeared in a few set phrases, of which the most frequent was паркетный шаркун. But this slightly ironic pejorative meaning later became more complex and more pejorative in the speech of broad democratic circles. It is sufficient to note the use of the word in Dostoevskij's *Bednye ljudi* and "Dvojnik." The reason for the strongly pejorative meaning was the social differentiation connected with parquet floors in the first half of the nineteenth century. A parquet floor could be found at a social level not lower than that of a very wealthy landowner (and then only if he did not adhere to "old-world" principles), and people unused to them would sometimes rub their soles with chalk in order to avoid disaster on the ballroom floor.

Paralleling the changes in meaning, there occurred a process by which the literary language was enriched with words, expressions, and turns of phrase from various city strata. The literary language began to accept many "borrowings" from class and professional dialects. There was, for example, a widespread use of terms from finance and industry. Compare the following excerpt from a letter of N. A. Polevoj: Счастлив, кто возьмет у будущего вексель, хоть на одну строчку в истории. The style of the author's narration, which is usually considered the literary norm, came closer to the spoken language of the city, and even of the village. In a story by Nekrasov, one can have an expression such as: Поджал под себя ноги, и *пошла писать*. And, in a story by Grigorovič, we have: (русский человек) за словом в карман не полезет.

Nekrasov, in his sketch "Peterburgskie ugly," made a manor serf use the word ерунда, and then immediately noted: "A lackey's word, equal to дрянь." Dostoevskij stubbornly asserted his literary right to use the term стушеваться, which he had taken from the professional language of draftsmen and endowed with a transferred meaning. Such instances are very typical of the general style of the epoch.

However, it is also characteristic that, at the same time, a systematic collection and broad literary canonization was made of the professional lexicon which served the everyday needs of the landowner. During the thirties and forties there appeared *sui generis* literary encyclopedias which provided quite a broad sampling of the linguistic material of the landowning nobility. Also symptomatic was the appearance, in 1843, of a terminological dictionary of rural economy, containing twenty-five thousand words. Reviews praised the work for its value to the young landowner, to the bureaucrat on village assignment, and so on. But its value was not confined to technical affairs; for, in that its codification of terms secured them the right to literary usage, it had its influence on the literary language too. A number of words in the dictionary (which had not been recorded in earlier dictionaries of the Russian Academy) became established in literature precisely at this time.

Thus the boundaries of the literary language, which had been established at the turn of the century and had been somewhat extended in the direction of the languages of the landowners and peasantry in the twenties, were now broadly opened to include the everyday language of various city social and professional groups.

10. THE GROWING SIGNIFICANCE OF BUREAUCRATIC DIALECTS

Among the social dialects of the city, the language of the bureaucracy was the most significant by virtue of its composition, its range of usage, the number of its speakers, and its general position within the over-all structure of the colloquial language of the city. In the thirties and forties, both the oral and the written language of the bureaucracy were copiously introduced into literature, especially into its narrative and publicistic styles. In the sphere of artistic prose, elements from the bureaucratic language became the basic linguistic material for constructing the narrative tale; and they freely entered dialogue.

The language of the chancery not only directly affected the literary language but it also became the object of artistic stylization and parody. For example, in Dostoevskij's "Dvojnik," the narrative is comically larded with the peculiarities of bureaucratic language: *положил* ждать; *для сего* нужно было, *во первых*, чтоб кончились как можно скорей *часы присутствия*. In his story "Gospodin Proxarčin," there are examples such as: *неоднократно замечено* про разных лиц; *могуче форменная фраза*. In Grigorovič's tale

"Loterejnyj bal," we have examples such as: страстный любитель музыки, театра и вообще изящнего, *как-то; вопреки долга,* чести, приличия. Note also the wide use in literature of such terms as замарать репутацию, состряпать дело, дело десятое, крючок, etc.

In his *Zapisnye knižki,* Gogol' made much use of terms dealing with the bureaucratic mechanisms and with bureaucratic practice.

II. THE CRISIS IN THE LINGUISTIC CULTURE OF THE OLD NOBILITY IN THE THIRTIES AND FORTIES

The old aristocratic literary and linguistic culture was undergoing a crisis. Expression and style, in the thought and artistic activity of the aristocratic literary circles, were "clothed in the mirages of history and art." These circles tried to resurrect, in the mind of the reader, images of various styles and cultures. In the ruling literary styles of the first quarter of the nineteenth century, the artistic word was understood in two contexts and united them. One was the context of everyday life, and the other was the context of *belles lettres,* with its images, symbols, themes, and its stylistic culture. Therefore, words and phrases with certain denotations were given certain connotations within the composition of a work. These directed the reader's consciousness toward certain allusions to everyday life, while, at the same time, as echoes of other, preceding artistic works, they symbolically reflected complex and varied subjects and themes of Russian or world literature.

In such an intellectual culture the world was apprehended through the intermediary of the book and the style. Karamzin admitted that spring would not have appeared so beautiful to him were it not for the fact that Thomson and Kleist had described its beauties for him.

> Ламберта, Томсона читая,
> С рисунком подлинным сличая
> Я мир сей лучшим нахожу;
> Тень рощи для меня свежее,
> Журчанье ручейка нежнее;
> На все с веселием гляжу,
> Что Клейст, Делиль живописали;
> Стихи их в памяти храня,
> Гуляю, где они гуляли,
> И след их радует меня.

"Derevnja"

In the realistic styles of the forties and fifties, however, this whole sphere of conceptual forms almost disappeared. For the new realistic school, the most important element in the word was its direct signification, its everyday base. Such a tendency led to a breakdown in the concept of "artistic language." The understanding of actuality became more profound; the representation of the internal world of the individual became more complex. It is characteristic that Tolstoj, reading Puškin, noted in 1853: "I was reading *The Captain's Daughter* and, alas, I must admit that Puškin's prose is now old—not in style, but in mode of exposition. Nowadays, going (correctly) in a new direction, an *interest in details of emotion* is replacing the interest in events themselves. Puškin's tales are somehow barren."

12. THE DEVELOPMENT OF A PHILOSOPHICAL, JOURNALISTIC, AND PUBLICISTIC LANGUAGE. BELINSKIJ'S SIGNIFICANCE IN THE HISTORY OF THE RUSSIAN JOURNALISTIC AND PUBLICISTIC LANGUAGE

In the thirties and forties, the lexical and phraseological systems of the literary language underwent change—but so did the semantic structure. New ideological links were being sought. Various styles underwent a redistribution of functions and influences. The poetic language, which was the bulwark of literary styles and the laboratory for developing new means of literary expression, lost its significance. The very concept of "literature" was restructured. "Belletristics" (the term беллетристика was apparently firmly established in the literary language by Belinskij), that is, a half-publicistic and half-artistic prose genre, became the center of literature. It was directed at a cultural, political, ideological, and moral reeducation of society. Newspaper, journalistic, and publicistic styles gradually came to occupy the center of the stage.

The problem of a "metaphysical" (abstract, publicistic, popular-scientific) language was intensified in this period. In the beginning of the nineteenth century, all of Russian upper-class society had sought means for creating such a language on the basis of the semantic system of the French language. To be sure, in the twenties, the "Lovers of Wisdom" sought a philosophical terminology for expressing the German idealistic philosophy of Schelling. Compare the philosophical terms in the language of Prince Odoevskij: проявленние, субъективный, объективный, аналитический, синтети- ческий. But at that time the philosophical style of the "Lovers of Wisdom" did not achieve general literary recognition. A much greater influence was exerted by the lively intellectual labor engendered by Hegel in Russian intellectual circles between the thirties and the fifties. Gercen, in his *Byloe i dumy*, very clearly and accurately characterized the language of this Russo-German philosophical thought:

No one at that time would have disavowed phraseology such as this: Конкрес- цирование абстрактных идей в сфере пластики представляет ту фазу самоищущего духа, в которой он, определяясь для себя, потенцируется из естественной имманентности в гармоническую сферу образного сознания в красоте. It is noteworthy that here the Russian words sound even more foreign than the Latin ones ... Our young philosophers did not just ruin their phraseol- ogy. Their understanding, their relationship to life and actuality, became schoolboyish and bookish ...

The results of this work on a philosophical lexicon, however, entered the general literary system by way of the language of journalism. Calques from the German language for the expression of abstract social and philosophical concepts became established in literary usage: образование–*Bildung*, мировоззрение–*Weltanschauung*, целостность–*Ganzheit*, предполагать–*voraussetzen*, исключительный–*aus- schliesslich*, and many other compound words, the first element of which is само-, such as самоопределение–*Selbstbestimmung*.

V. G. Belinskij played an enormous role in the diffusion of such abstract terms through Russian society. Turgenev, in his memoirs, was later to recall that, for several years during the middle period of his activity, Belinskij evidenced a special passion for the jargon of Hegelianism—for its *Schlagwörter*. Compare the following citation from Belinskij:

Распадение и разорванность есть момент духа человеческого, но отнюдь не каждого человека. Так точно и просветление: оно есть удел для немногих ... Чтобы понять значение слов *распадение, разорванность, просветление*, надо или пройти через эти *моменты духа*, или *иметь в созерцании их возможность*.

Along with the philosophical terminology from Germany came terminology connected with socio-political and socio-economic disciplines. Some of these terms also came from Germany, but most came from France. Bulgarin's denunciation of Belinskij has a characteristic writing of the suffix **-изм** as **-исм** (социалисм, комунисм, и пантеисм в России). Note also the following excerpts from Belinskij's famous letter to Gogol': Россия видит свое спасение не в *мистицизме*, не в *аскетизме*, не в *пиэтизме*, а в успехах цивилизации, просвещения, *гуманности;* поборник *обскурантизма* и мракобесия, etc.

Thus, an intense effort was made to create an "abstract" publicistic language, and the result was a unique socio-political lexicon of the intelligentsia. Society was much more attracted to "civic" themes than it had been formerly. What had once been philosophical dogma now became "convictions," and the very term, убеждение, became characteristic of the intellectuals' lexicon at the end of the forties.

Belinskij's cardinal role in the introduction of philosophical terminology is confirmed by the many complaints and parodies of him by his contemporaries. One illustration will suffice. It comes from N. Kulikov's comedy *Škola natural'naja* (1846):

> Вот *индивидуум* ... или простой *субъект,*
> Сам заключась в себе, не двигатель массивный,
> Рельефно, может быть, сам выступит вперед,
> Но *пафос,* творчество с ним вместе пропадает ...
> Объекта же *принцип* в сочувствиях *гуманных* ...

Belinskij understood that it was not possible to avoid foreign borrowings in the process of forming a Russian scholarly, critical, and publicistic language. On the other hand, he was well aware that such terms should be used with care, and in limited quantity. He felt impelled to make a defense of his own usage, and based his defense on two principles: that many of the terms he used had been in use before and had not provoked any attacks, and that such abstract terms were the common property of every educated German.

It is clear that Belinskij's work in reforming the abstract lexicon of Russian had great influence on the succeeding history of the literary language. Belinskij refashioned the Russian literary language, in its prose genres, in a manner parallel to that of Lermontov and Gogol', and often in the same directions. It would therefore be incorrect to limit his role in the history of Russian publicistic styles to lexical and phraseological innovations. What he fought for was an exact, simple, understandable, "educated," artistic style for the exposition of every theme, even a scholarly one. He objected to inexact word usage in the poetry of Benediktov. And, in a review of some philosophical books, he noted that he had found a period in one of them that covered almost four pages, and he commented: "A truly philosophical style, but by no means a Russian one! The study of philosophy must be preceded by a study of grammar, since the exposition of philosophy must be preceded by the ability to express oneself in one's own language clearly, understandably, and sensibly."

Thus, gradually, the styles of an abstract, journalistic, and popular-scientific language were being created. They utilized both philosophical terminology (of the idealistic school) and the socio-political terminology based on it. They also utilized the terminology of natural science and technology. The humanistic, esthetic education of the turn of the century was now being complicated by an education based on science, technology, and political economics. As an encyclopedic dictionary of 1847 pointed out, in its preface, education had now come to all classes of society (as proven by the fact that journalistic literature now encompassed all branches of human knowledge), and it was therefore necessary for ordinary people to know something of subjects which had formerly been known only to scholars.

The ground was being laid for a national Russian publicistic and scholarly prose. Russian gradually became capable of an independent expression of abstract terms—without the aid of foreign borrowings. The process is illustrated by one of the characters in Turgenev's novel *Dym:* "Concepts found favor and were adopted; foreign forms gradually evaporated; the language found substitutes in its own bosom. And now your faithful servant, an absolutely average stylist, sets about translating any page of Hegel without using a single non-Slavic word."

But only in the second half of the nineteenth century did the new publicistic and scholarly styles became more or less established. From the thirties through the fifties, there was only a fermentation and mixture of various socio-linguistic styles.

13. VACILLATION IN THE GRAMMATICAL SYSTEM FROM THE
THIRTIES THROUGH THE FIFTIES

The same contradiction and instability, characteristic of a transitional epoch, were also present in the grammar of the literary language. From the thirties to the mid-fifties, there was a tendency to standardize the grammar, thereby completing the grammatical normalization begun by the Karamzin school (which took on a one-sidedly dogmatic character in the grammatical works of N. I. Greč). If one is not afraid of paradoxes, one can put forth the following thesis: as the literary language of the forties and fifties came closer to various styles of the spoken language, the grammar of the normal literary language (particularly of the language of journalism) tended to become more bookish. This contradiction is a trait typical of a transitional stage. At the same time, there was a greater tendency to regularize the grammatical tradition by removing the grammatical doublets permitted by the previous epoch. Normalization also continued to reject the relics of regional colloquialisms. Forms which had been condemned by the Karamzin tradition, but which had continued to exist in literary usage, were now weeded out of the grammar, as follows:

(1) Toward the beginning of the fifties, colloquial declensional forms of neuter nouns in the class of время disappeared. Compare, for example, the following forms of the genitive: не знал другого имя (Lermontov); поверь, что у него ни время ни охоты на это нет (Krylov); Это было б лишь время трата (Puškin).

(2) Neuter nominative plurals in -ы, which still occurred in the thirties and forties, were gradually weeded out. Note the following examples: и были вечера светилы, как яркие паникадилы (Žukovskij); письмы, колесы (Puškin); яйцы (Vjazemskij). Gogol' and Lermontov frequently used such forms.

(3) Instrumental singulars of the type неделью from feminine nouns in -я were forbidden (they could still be found, e.g., in Puškin's correspondence).

(4) The number of adverbial participles in -учи, -ючи was gradually reduced in the literary language, even though they continued to appear sporadically in the second half of the century (in

a small number of verbs). Tolstoj noted that they were preserved for a long time in raznočinec colloquial speech.

(5) The range of usage of the iterative aspect was reduced and many of its forms died out.

But, at the same time that the system of the literary language was being freed of relics of the low style, there was a noticeable shift of grammatical norms in the direction of the conversational language of the city:

(1) The sphere of use of the nominative plural in **-a** for masculine nouns continued to increase.

(2) There was a tendency to mix up the prefixes of certain verbs: for example, the prefixes **в-, вз-** (въехать instead of взъехать, etc.). Note the following (from Lažečnikov): проворно влезла на стену.

(3) New elements from the colloquial language were often in evidence. For example, a new modification of the semelfactive aspect, of the type толканул, дерганул, penetrated the literary language. At first, it meant "scarcely do something." From this meaning there developed a sense of instantaneousness with a nuance of sharpness or force. It first was used in "folk" dialogue, and then became established in the literary language. Note the following example from Turgenev: Голос ее как ножом резанул его по сердцу.

There was also a characteristic renewal and strengthening of a whole series of specifically bookish forms:

(1) Adverbial participles in **-я** were reduced in number, limited by strictly defined grammatical bounds, and replaced by formations in **-в** (and even **-вши**). Greč ruled that prefixed verbs must form their adverbial participles from the past and not from the perfective future (thus посадив and not посадя; вынесши and not вынеся), although he allowed exceptions in verse and in reflexive verbs (e.g., убоясь, возвратясь).

(2) With a reduction of adverbial participle forms in **-я**, a reevaluation of the forms in **-в, -вши** took place. Even though the forms in **-в** were the preferred literary forms, forms in **-вши** gradually acquired literary citizenship, losing their specifically colloquial coloring. Such forms were used by S. Aksakov, Gončarov, Turgenev, Grigorovič, Dostoevskij, and others. As the number of

adverbial participles in **-я** became limited, a number of them became pure adverbs (нехотя, молча, сидя, лежа, не глядя, etc.). Vostokov, in his grammar, considered знав, знавши equivalent; and he required that the second element be inserted before the reflexive particle (e.g., знавшись). On the other hand G. Pavskij, in 1842, stated that the forms in **-ши** were unpleasant to the ear and should be avoided. In the second half of the century, such grammatical strictures were abandoned.

(3) In the area of participial forms, the official, chancery style had an influence. It led to the formation of participles in **-щий** from perfective verbs to form a future participle. Compare the following examples from Gogol': человек не *предъявящий* никаких свидетельств; *приедущий* из столицы.

Other bookish grammatical tendencies became fully evident only in the second half of the century and they should therefore be discussed during our study of grammatical stabilization toward the end of the century.

In phrasal and sentence syntax, one can note the dying out, at this time, of certain archaic constructions which had been inherited from Church Slavonic.

(1) There was a gradual reduction in the use of быть with the dative of the short-form past passive participle in constructions such as the following: присудил его *быть посажену* на кол (Puškin); Он нашел средство *быть выпечатану* и даже *прочтену* (A. I. Turgenev).

(2) The use of a genitive case with the preposition от to express the actor with a passive participle gradually died out. Note the following: приглашенный от правительства (Žukovskij); покинут от друзей (Lermontov).

(3) The use of a double accusative, that is, an accusative object and an accusative modifier (usually a participle) linked with it in the predication, was curtailed. Note the following: которого привел *связанного* к себе на двор (Puškin); видела его *сидящего* (Batjuškov). The modifier gradually began to appear in the instrumental case.

(4) One of the characteristic phenomena of the period was the broad development of the predicate instrumental.

Thus, between the thirties and the fifties, the shifting of the boundaries between the literary language and living speech, the process of reevaluating what constituted "literariness," and the process of achieving a rapprochement between the literary language and the everyday conversational language with its various dialects —all were reflected in basic grammatical changes.

14. CHANGES IN THE PHONETIC NORMS OF THE LITERARY LAN-
GUAGE

In the sphere of phonetics, the first problem to arise was that of the phonetic shape of borrowed words. At the turn of the century, the pronunciation of such words obeyed either the norms of the colloquial language or else those of the language from which the loan word was taken. Educated society, therefore, often had two pronunciations for such words. Some loan words had been able to establish themselves in the colloquial form: ярманка, анбар, азарт, лилея, шлафор (or шлафорк). In others, parallel forms were allowed, such as английский, аглицкий, английнский; пашпорт, пачпорт, паспорт; etc. On the other hand, the majority preserved their foreign pronunciation.

The democratic strata of society had no firm tradition for the pronunciation of borrowings. Quite the contrary. There was considerable vacillation between a bookish pronunciation based on spelling (sometimes with accent shifts) and a colloquial "distortion" of the phonetic form. A unity in norms of pronunciation had to be established. The problem had already been faced at the turn of the century, when the salon styles were "purged" of "low" colloquial elements. Now the rule was advanced that the borrowed word must be pronounced as it was spelled in Russian. The orthoepic work of 1843 (*Spravočnoe mesto russkogo jazyka*) which was mentioned earlier in this chapter gives interesting examples of vacillations in pronunciation. According to it, one was to write and pronounce амбар, шампанское, камфора, лампа, and not анбар, шанпанское, канфора, ланпа. Transpositions and dissimilations of liquids and nasals were forbidden. One was to write пелеринка, рапира, пантомима, and not перелинка, лапира, пантомина. The pronunciation [ry] instead of [ri] after a consonant was forbidden: бриллиант, and not брылиант. Morphological distortions of borrowed words were noted: припорция, пришпект, instead of пропорция, проспект.

It is important to note that the foreword to the book specifically states that the book is not concerned with errors made by the common folk; it is concerned with errors found in the conversational language of good society, in literature, and in journals and newspapers. In this connection, the pronunciation of certain Russian and Church Slavonic words assumes a particular historical interest: one was supposed to write отсрочка, понравиться, поздравить, нынче, жизнь, ужас, and not отстрочка, пондравиться, проздравить, нонче, жисть, ужесть.

Some of the pronunciation rules for native and foreign words show the increased influence of the spelling-oriented Petersburg pronunciation on the phonetic system of the literary language. Three categories of pronunciation are particularly interesting for their reflection of Petersburg speech patterns:

(1) A palatalized pronunciation of **р** before labials and velars (in instances of the so-called "secondary full vocalization") was declared to be regional: one was supposed to write and pronounce верх, первый, сперва, and not верьх, перьвый, сперьва.

(2) The pronunciation [čn] was declared the normal one, in contrast to [šn]: гречневый, коричневый, свечник, and not грешневый, коришневый, свешник. By the forties of the nineteenth century, the Muscovite colloquial pronunciation [šn] was much reduced.

(3) A palatalized pronunciation of **ц** before **и** was noted in foreign words: the pronunciation медицина was recommended over медицына. However, there were differences of opinion on this matter, depending on how close the grammarian stood to the speech patterns of Petersburg.

In the second half of the nineteenth century, Petersburg pronunciation increased its pretensions to being a general literary norm.

In summarizing the discussion in this chapter, the basic processes in the history of the Russian literary language in the period from the thirties to the middle of the fifties were the following: (1) limitation and stylistic transformation of Church Slavonicisms; (2) a change in the relationship between the literary and conversational languages, with the influence of the spoken language increasing; (3) professionalization and dialectization of the literary language, largely on the basis of the social, stylistic, and dialectal variants of the language of the city; (4) disintegration and transformation of the former aristocratic artistic styles; (5) the formation of publicistic, journalistic, and popular-science genres and a growth in their significance; and (6) a growth in the literary significance of raznočinec-democratic styles.

9 The Language of Gogol'

I. THE POSITION OF GOGOL''S LANGUAGE IN THE LITERARY
CONFLICTS OF THE THIRTIES, FORTIES, AND FIFTIES

Gogol' was the literary personality who stood at the center of the linguistic conflicts of the thirties, forties, and fifties. Most of the literary styles of the period had some relation to him. He also exercised a decisive influence on the style of literary publicistics. Tendencies toward professionalization and democratization of the literary language found support in his works. The realistic treatment of everyday dialogue in literature had its origin in his linguistic system. Gogol''s images and his methods of depicting reality entered into the "general" system of literary expression. To be sure, not all aspects of his work were of equal value in the eyes of his contemporaries. The Ukrainian element had a sympathetic reception only among his Ukrainian compatriots. The archaic, romantically rhetorical, and Church Slavonic elements—and the ideology connected with them—did not achieve a further development in the dominant literary styles. What was to be reflected in the literary language as "Gogolian" was largely his complex expressive forms of comic ridicule and irony, as well as his marvelous gift for handling dialogue.

Gogol''s linguistic system was extremely comprehensive; it both included the styles of the preceding period and reflected the complex influence of city and rural speech. Furthermore, his language, being that of a man from another country, was not entirely bound by the old aristocratic speech culture; it was full of dialectal "inaccuracies." All this put Gogol''s language halfway between the old literary styles and the new.

Gogol''s epoch was a revolutionary one in the history of the literary language. New national, democratic transformations of the literary language were coming into being. In his search for an independent literary position, Gogol' was naturally to go through many vacillations and deviations. His language contained both revolutionary and archaizing tendencies, which were further complicated by his bilingualism. Nonetheless, his linguistic and stylistic evolution was part of the general literary life of the period. He did not immediately establish an independent attitude toward all the literary and linguistic problems of the time. His position changed in the course of the thirties, and only toward the very end of that decade did he develop a consistent, broad, and harmonious conception of literature and language. *Mertvye duši* (1842) was a literary manifesto which revealed Gogol''s idea of the essence of a national language policy.

2. THE DIALECTAL AND STYLISTIC COMPOSITION OF GOGOL''S LANGUAGE UP TO THE SECOND HALF OF THE THIRTIES

Apart from traditional, "neutral," literary resources, the language of Gogol''s works, up to the mid-thirties, contained four elements: Ukrainian; the Russian conversational and everyday colloquial language styles; the Russian language of official business (largely in its chancery styles, with an occasional admixture of the bureaucratic conversational language); and the romantic styles of Russian artistic and publicistic language. Their mutual relationship and interaction had already undergone a complex evolution by the middle of the decade.

Gogol''s attempt to enter immediately into the mainstream of Russian poetry with his verse epos *Ganc Kjuxel'garten* ended in failure. Its immaturity in style, language, and poetic technique was obvious. The complex situation in the literary stylistics of the twenties was unfamiliar ground to him. The element of "provincialism" was all too evident in the language of the young poet. He therefore took a different stylistic path, one dictated for him by the national and social milieu from which he came, by the interest of the Russian nobility in Walter Scott, and by the romantic interest in the "folk," which led to a fashion for "Little Russianism."

For his exercises in the "high" style of the literary language, Gogol' selected not only the lyrical and narrative genres of romanticism, but also the genres of critical-publicistic and historical articles. This was the path of romantic rhetoric, which supplied the styles of the literary language of the twenties and thirties with new forms of abstract symbolism and phraseology. (Compare the prose language of D. Venevitinov, Prince V. F. Odoevskij, I. Kireevskij, N. Polevoj, N. Nadeždin, and the early works of Belinskij.)

The idea of "folk" in the Russian literary language of the beginning of the nineteenth century was closely connected with the process of working out an artistic depiction of national types. The need for nationalization and democratization of literary expression led beyond the linguistic norms of the noble salon. There was a whole series of storytellers from the provincial nobility, the merchant class, and the bureaucracy (cf. Puškin's *Povesti Belkina* and the novellas and tales of M. Pogodin, O. Somov, V. Dal', V. Ušakov, and others). On the linguistic level, this meant the introduction of fresh elements from the spoken language into the language of literary narrative. In his stories, Gogol' used both the Russian and Ukrainian national languages. From the point of view of the chauvinistic outlook of the time, however, Ukrainian was merely a provincial variant of Russian. It was viewed as a language for local domestic uses. And it was only in this function that it could enter Russian nineteenth-century literature, where it was used to portray national Ukrainian types (usually in a comic light).

However, the romantic conception of "folk" at the beginning of the century connected the conversational colloquial language with the oral literature of the folk *and* with Old Russian church literature. It is understandable that such a romantic interest in the "folk" would lead, by virtue of its exoticism, to the social success of the Ukrainian language and Ukrainian folk literature. In an article on Ukrainian songs, Gogol' pointed out that only recently, in "times of a striving for independent existence and for one's own folk poetry," had Ukrainian songs attracted attention as songs and not just as melodies. His evaluation of the literary significance of folk poetry was characteristic of the time: "It all bears the stamp of a pure, primordial infancy and, therefore, of great poetry." The Ukrainian element was thus viewed from two aspects: as a means for describing Ukrainian provincial types, and, in folk poetry, as a source of lyricism in the conventional style of Ukrainian literary melodies.

Belinskij, in a book review written in 1841, provides a good example of the attitude of contemporary Russian society toward the Ukrainian language. Belinskij was of the opinion that the Ukrainian language had existed at the time when the Ukraine was independent. Beginning with the time of Peter the Great, however, the Ukrainian upper classes, out of historical necessity, had become Russified. The language of the folk themselves had deteriorated. Consequently, by Belinskij's time, the Ukrainian language had become merely a dialectal variant of Russian. The Ukrainian language of former days was preserved only in monuments of folk poetry. On this basis, Belinskij considered the literary resources of the Ukrainian "dialect" severely limited and thought it symptomatic that Gogol' had decided to write in Russian even though he loved the Ukraine.

Gogol''s own attitude toward Ukrainian was the conventional literary one and is evident in *Večera na xutore bliz Dikanki* (1831), even in the linguistic evaluations of the heroes themselves. Pure Ukrainian is considered a "peasants' dialect" and Russian is considered "educated." In the beginning of "Noč' pered Roždestvom," the blacksmith, Vakula, expresses himself in the conventional, literary, Russo-Ukrainian conversational language, in the Russian colloquial language, and in the language of novels: Чудная, ненаглядная Оксана, позволь поцеловать тебя. He also uses the language of folk poetry in its literary form: Стоит, как царица, и блестит черными очами. And he knows the language of bourgeois "men of the world": Дай Боже тебе всего, *добра всякого в довольствии, хлеба в пропорции!* When the action is transferred to Petersburg, the whole linguistic atmosphere changes. Signs of an artificial juxtaposition of Ukrainian and Russian appear: "Что ж земляк," сказал приосанясь запорожец и желая показать, что он может говорить и по-русски: *"што, балшой город!"* Кузнец и себе не хотел осрамиться и показаться новичком, *притом же, как имели случай видеть выше сего, он знал и сам грамотный язык.* "Гоберния знатная!" отвечал он равнодушно ... This conventional literary function of Ukrainian is emphasized even more when the Cossacks speak to Potemkin and the Tsaritsa. They fall into pure Ukrainianisms (which are printed in italics), and Vakula is amazed that a Cossack who had demonstrated such a good knowledge of the "educated language" should suddenly shift into "the coarsest peasant dialect, as it is commonly called."

Gogol' was, therefore, far from making a sociological differentiation within the Ukrainian language itself. He made his social divisions evident by his methods of mixing Ukrainian with Russian. But even here the scope is not broad. Gogol' wrote, in the conventional literary fashion of his time, about the "dancing and singing" Ukrainian people, about Cossacks, provincial bureaucrats, and old-world landowners. Only at the end of the thirties, when he was reworking the text of *Taras Bul'ba*, did he face the questions of class differentiations, of the sociological nature and historical significance of folk poetry, and, generally, of the "language" of the Cossacks.

The Ukrainian admixture in Gogol''s narrative style is inseparable from the character of the narrators, who represent a world of provincial, backwoods farmers, far from "fashionable" society. From the viewpoint of society, the speech of the Ukrainian farmer had to be considered the language of peasants. But Rudyj Pan'ko, the fictitious publisher of *Večera*, objected that the characters were by no means "farm peasants." They were the village aristocracy, like the country narrators of Walter Scott. But, even in this milieu, social divisions are evident. There is a stylistic antagonism between the language of the village rhetoricians (Foma Grigor'evič, for example, whose side Rudyj Pan'ko takes) and the comic young lord from Poltava, who is depicted as a city "aristocrat" and an advocate of the romantic literary style with its "clever" language.

The novelty of Gogol''s style consisted in the open democratism of his admixture of the Ukrainian "folk" language. Characteristically, Gogol' clearly democratized and Ukrainianized the language of Foma Grigor'evič. But it is also significant that the language of *Večera* became more and more "urbanized" and tended to lose its folkish, Ukrainian character in the second half of the collection. This urbanization of the Russo-Ukrainian style reached its culmination in *Mirgorod*. Here, Gogol''s narrative style made a definite break with the Ukrainian folk language. Grammatical and lexical Ukrainianisms are still present, but they no longer have a stylistic or characterizing function (except, of course, when they are used for local color). The Ukrainian folk language is freely used only in dialogue.

Gogol' now sharply differentiated between the Ukrainian language and the styles of Ukrainian folk poetry. A study of his work on *Taras Bul'ba* shows that the very idea of literary "Ukrainianism" underwent transformation when Gogol' adopted the point of view of Russian nationalists. The phraseology and symbolism of Ukrainian folk poetry and the colorful semantic and syntactic forms of Ukrainian songs were now considered to be living sources of the "Slavonic" national spirit and were handled in the manner of the Homeric poems. But the Ukrainian language had become, for Gogol', a provincial dialect of Russian. Folk Ukrainianisms became, in his language, provincialisms within the context of the Russian colloquial language. Their function and role, particularly in the sphere of verbal aspect and government, became unimportant, although Gogol' carried on a fierce struggle against them at the end of the thirties and beginning of the forties. The initial versions of *Ženixi* and *Revizor* contained sporadic Ukrainianisms, but all such "provincialisms" were rejected in the final versions.

The process of urbanization of Gogol''s language led to a toning down of the folk element. The colloquial element took on more "worldly," city forms. This was foretokened by traces of seminary language which were present in the speech of Foma Grigor'evič and later passed into the narrative style of "Vij," *Taras Bul'ba*, and the fragment "Učitel'." But the language of narration of "Noč' pered Roždestvom" already contained such expressions from the "official" colloquial language as бедный чорт припустился бежать, как мужик, которого только что *выпарил заседатель*, etc. The tale concerning Ivan Fedorovič Špon'ka saw an increase in the role of the city colloquial language. The connection between city colloquial and various official and unofficial sub-styles became, at the same time, stronger and more noticeable. On the one hand, one encounters occasional items from schoolboy argot (урока в зуб не знал) and military argot (стал в вытяжку), and, on the other hand, there is a flavor of the language of the chancery (Эти дела *более* шли хуже, *нежели* лучше; *долгом почитаю предуведомить*).

Vacillation in usage of colloquial forms is clearly evident in the language of *Mirgorod*, as well. In the narrative prose of

"Starosvetskie pomeščiki," colloquialisms are colorless and rare. On the other hand, "Vij" has many colloquial expressions (*фукнул* в обе руки; философ ... издал глухое *крехтание;* etc.). Colloquialisms in the language of the tale of the two Ivans are even more striking and complex. Here, we have the uninhibited, coarse, provincial, unceremonious, everyday conversational language, which turns, now toward the "folk" language, now toward the "official" language. The language is motivated by the figure of the narrator, Rudyj Pan'ko, but now it appears (from such phrases as уходился страх) as if he had moved to a provincial county seat. The fact that the fictitious narrator belongs to the same milieu as the actors erases the boundary between the narration and the actors' dialogue.

The transfer of action to Petersburg signalled a break with the provincial, "Ukrainianized," colloquial language. In the Petersburg tales, Gogol''s language absorbed more and more elements of the everyday speech of the city technical intelligentsia, of the bureau-cracy, and of army officers. But these elements were still poorly represented during the first half of the thirties. Instead, Gogol' used "neutral" elements from non-aristocratic circles. Note the following in the language of "Portret": мужики обыкновенно *тыкают* пальцами; о чем *калякает* народ; не хвастал, не *задирался; отпустить спроста* глупость; etc. Similar elements occur in "Nevskij prospekt": вот он *продрался-таки* вперед; Миллера это *как бомбою хватило;* живет *на фуфу;* etc.

Elements of the uninhibited colloquial language also penetrated Gogol''s descriptive and publicistic language. This mixture reveals a conscious artistic goal—to break down the old system of literary styles. (Compare Puškin's broad use of conversational constructions and conversational lexical elements beginning at the end of the twenties.) The following examples are from Gogol''s articles of this period: ум человека, *задвинутый крепкою толщею,* не мог иначе *прорваться;* вся Европа ... *валится* в Азию; всякий ... *топорщится* произвесть эффект.

Similarly, the romantic style of the young Gogol' was charac-terized by unmotivated lapses into the colloquial, as in алые, как кровь, волны *хлебещут* и толпятся вокруг старинных стен. At the same time, periphrases of the high romantic style were accompanied by an antithetical ironic use of descriptive expressions within the colloquial language of comic narration, as in разноголосый лай прорезал *облекавшую его тучу задумчивости.*

Thus, Gogol' followed Puškin in bringing the literary language closer to the conversational language of non-aristocratic circles. Colloquialisms were introduced into the author's narration. Although Gogol', up to the mid-thirties, still did not have very rich resources of "non-literary" terms in his language, and although he used relatively few exotic Russian provincial and "folk" expressions, he nonetheless strove to introduce elements of the city and country colloquial language into the system of literary expression. These colloquial elements he mixed with an official, chancery style which, together with the bureaucratic conversational language, he felt to be the language of governmental affairs.

The language of narration in the first half of *Večera* has only sporadic officialisms; the tale of Špon'ka has a somewhat greater admixture; but the tale of the two Ivans is the real beginning of this linguistic element in Gogol''s language, containing such phrases as: хотел что-то *присовокупить;* табак, *адресуемый* в нос; бумагу *пометили, записали, выставили нумер, вшили, расписались*; etc., etc. We also encounter the *argot* of officialdom: *забежать зайцем* вперед; *состряпало* такую бумагу; etc.

The official language of the chancery, sometimes clothed in irony, became a distinct element in the Petersburg tales. For example, we have, in "Nevskij prospekt": *написать отношение* из одного казенного места в другое; в их голове ералаш и целый *архив начатых и неоконченных дел.* In "Zapiski sumasšedšego" and "Nos," the bureaucratic-conversational and chancery elements are significantly increased, subordinating to themselves all other social nuances and variations of colloquial speech. In "Zapiski sumasšedšego," for example, we have such phrases as the following: Я не понимаю выгод служить в департаменте: *никаких совершенно рессурсов;* он увидел, может быть, *предпочтительно мне оказываемые знаки благорасположенности;* событие, *имеющее быть* завтра; etc. It is interesting that, while Gogol''s publicistic style of the first half of the thirties was quite free of Church Slavonic, it revealed at the same time a connection, sometimes direct, sometimes ironic, with the chancery language. Note phraseology such as the following: счесть *итог* всех книг, *пожалованных* в первоклассные.

The chancery language was so deeply imbedded in the structure of Gogol''s style that he did not understand the campaign of the "Smirdin school" against elements of the chancery language in the general literary language. He could not comprehend why Senkovskij made such a great matter out of two pronouns, сей and оный. It remained for Puškin, in a polemic with Gogol', to point out that they were merely symbolic of a campaign against the whole system of the old literary language, which was founded mainly on Church Slavonicisms and chanceryisms, particularly in its lexicon, morphology, and syntax. Puškin defended the literary language against Senkovskij. But, for Puškin, the center of "literariness" was a synthesis of living Church Slavonicisms, Europeanisms, and forms of the city and folk languages. Gogol', on the other hand, following (in the early thirties) the principle of contrast as a base for romantic creativity, tried to combine colloquial styles of the "middle estate" with the literary language of romanticism.

Gogol''s attention was immediately fixed on the romantic styles of the Russian literary language, which, in turn, were nourished by the poetic culture of the preceding period. These styles combined romantic neologisms, echoes of the sentimental tradition, and archaic church-book expressions. Moreover, romantic writers were proceeding with an intensive process of assimilating West European phraseology, artistic themes, images, syntactic devices, and compositional schemes. The system of romantic styles had a mixture of national elements—from various historical eras—and Europeanisms. Up to the mid-thirties, Gogol' took a very eclectic stand concerning the different varieties of the romantic language. He used freely the language of the Žukovskij school (note the widespread use of adjectives—often in the neuter singular—in noun function), the Germanized romantic style of the Lovers of Wisdom (note the language of some of his articles of the period), the nightmarish language of the French École furieuse (as in "Krovavyj bandurist" and "Portret"), and some of the peculiarities of Bestužev-Marlinskij's language.

Gogol' was carried away by the "melody," "language harmony," "sound hues," picturesque tension, and the abstract hyperbolism of romantic images, metaphors, and periphrases. His romantic language has the characteristic predominance of "individualizing" epithets, metaphoric attributes, and, in general, of the abstract types of qualitative evaluation which united the language of romanticism with the sentimental styles, but which are striking in their emotional tension, abundance of semantic antitheses, and metaphorical contradictions. (Note the following series of contradictory adverbs from "Starosvetskie pomeščiki": я знал его влюбленным нежно, страстно, бешено, дерзко, скромно ...) Gogol' went through a long and complicated process of freeing himself of romantic catch-phrases, but he did not become completely free of them until the period of *Mertvye duši* (note, in "Ženščina": дрожащие губы пересказывали мятежную бурю растерзанной души).

However, Gogol', in that "waterfall" (his favorite image at the beginning of the thirties) of romantic metaphors, discovered new forms of poetic semantics and developed a new theory and practice of constructing and using artistic images. At the start, the romantic styles were the furnace in which Gogol' fused the forms of the colloquial language with new European phraseology and Church Slavonicisms.

Gogol''s attitude toward the West European element in the romantic styles may be illustrated by a multitude of words, phrases, metaphors, and syntactic devices: оно [лицо] непременно должно было все *заговорить конвульсиями;* возжечь этой верой пламень и ревность до *энтузиазма;* жадные узнать новые *эволюции и вариации* войны. But Gogol' himself was no innovator in the translation and adoption of Europeanisms. He only developed and varied the metaphoric and phraseological forms adopted by Russian romanticism. He was aided in this by the archaic traditions of the high styles of eighteenth-century poetry, which were saturated with Church Slavonicisms.

At this time, Gogol' used the Church Slavonic language in three different ways. First, he used Slavonicisms for the comic structuring of periphrase and metaphor as applied to "low" objects in the comic-narrative style. Second, he used them to form the speech of personages belonging to the church culture (such as Foma Grigor'evič, and Afanasij Ivanovič in "Soročinskaja jarmarka"). Third, he transformed Church Slavonicisms into new semantic and phraseological forms in the romantic styles. Some examples are the following: [Zeus] гневно бросил ее *светодарною десницей;* душа потонет в эфирном *лоне души* женщины; кладут пламенный крест на *рамена* и спешат с энтузиазмом в Палестину.

Of course, the Church Slavonicisms could also be preserved in their pure form in the romantic styles (*совокупление их всех вместе;* also, in the speech of the monk in "Portret," *меня ... милосердый создатель сподобил такой неизглаголанной своей благости*). However, within the general context of the romantic styles, Church Slavonicisms underwent drastic changes.

It should also be pointed out that Gogol' made the same abrupt transitions from the elevated to the lowly when he used Church Slavonic that he did when he used other linguistic resources. For example, in his article "Boris Godunov" we have the following: *прения их воздымают бурю и запенившиеся уста горланят на торжищах.*

The growth of national tendencies in Gogol''s work led inevitably to his renunciation of many of the linguistic devices which were associated, at the beginning of the thirties, with the idea of European romantic styles of the literary language. His dissatisfaction with romantic genres and styles became clearly defined in 1834 and 1835. He was still sympathetic to the romantic revolution in "Arabeski"; but now he felt that the work of its followers, while rejecting unsatisfactory literary forms, was introducing an equal amount of other harmful material. He thus adopted the slogan of a synthesis of "the old and the new" to replace the romantic chaos.

His *Mertvye duši* was supposed to effect that "classical" synthesis of vital old and new linguistic elements and sketch out the framework of the future all-national literary language.

3. GOGOL''S CAMPAIGN AGAINST ANTI-NATIONAL STYLES OF THE RUSSIAN LITERARY LANGUAGE IN THE NAME OF NATIONAL REALISM

The language of *Mertvye duši* (like that of "Šinel'") is a structural unification of different stylistic layers. Each of these layers corresponds to a definite scheme of artistic reality and a definite mask adopted by the author. Further, in the composition of *Mertvye duši*, two methods of depicting life are strictly opposed. One is based on the reproduction of life "as it actually is," with the language, psychological types, and world-outlook characteristic of such an approach. Things are called by their "real" names. For the sake of "literalness," the author seems to sacrifice all literary canons. He introduces into the narrative style the language of various classes, particularly peasant language, professionalisms, and all sorts of argots. But against the background of this colorfully realistic, unpretentiously coarse language there appear forms from the conventional literary styles which Gogol' is rejecting. This second method of depiction in *Mertvye duši* is based on a parodistic display of the conventional literariness of the "anti-national" styles of the Russian language—for the purpose of unmasking their lack of correspondence to reality.

Gogol' considered the literary language of the upper classes to be infected with a passion for the foreign. He objected to foreign influence on the semantics of native Russian words and to the tendency of foreign words to supplant native ones. Consequently, he rejected the Europeanized, fashionable literary styles. He also opposed the conversational language of the upper classes, whose passion for French, German, and English he believed to be detrimental to the native language. In this respect, he stood opposed to the "Smirdin school" headed by Senkovskij. It was no accident that Senkovskij fought against Gogol''s language in the name of an "elegant, noble, refined language."

Gogol' ironically commented on the "salutary value" of French for the Russian language, but announced that, for all his respect for French, he would not introduce a "phrase of any foreign language whatever" into his Russian poem *Mertvye duši*.

His struggle against the "fashionable-European" language of the nobility also took the form of a comic depiction of the periphrases and "Gallicisms" which abounded in the speech of members of the lower ranks of bureaucrats and landowners who were imitating the language of the aristocratic salons. His depiction concerned, above all, the "language of ladies," which he characterized thus: "The ladies of the city N were distinguished, like many Petersburg ladies, for their extraordinary carefulness and decorum in the use of words and expressions. They never said я высморкалась, я вспотела, я плюнула, but said я облегчила себе нос, я обошлась посредством платка ..."

Such a satirical attack on the "delicate language" of ladies united Gogol' with those literary and social groups which, guided wholly or partly by the principles of "populism," opposed the Russo-French styles of the upper classes and their provincial imitations. In actuality, Gogol' was close, in this respect, to the attitude which Puškin took. But Gogol''s democratism was more direct and one-sided; it was more categorically opposed to the artificial stylistic norms of "fashionable" society, with their mannered rhetoric and their dependence on French. Gogol' was thus closer to Dal''s position. He went further than Puškin in his use of peasant language (including dialect) and of various styles of the city colloquial language.

The dialogues of the women in *Mertvye duši* abound in Gallicisms and French quotations (for example, *скандальозу* наделал ужасного; ну, просто *оррёр, оррёр;* даже подкладывать ваты, чтобы была совершенная *бельфам*). Characteristically, Gogol' also included in the language of his provincial ladies such archaic Gallicisms as were banned from the upper classes and considered as belonging to the language of merchants and petty bureaucrats (Как, неужели он и протопопше *строил куры*). He satirized emotional hyperbolism of the kind which had already been ridiculed by N. Novikov (*Словом, бесподобно! Можно сказать решительно, что ничего еще не было подобного на свете*). And he mocked French linguistic mannerisms (*Ах, жизнь моя; Ах прелести!*).

To these traditional forms of speech of "society women," however, which had already been ridiculed in the satirical literature, Gogol' added new emotional phraseological devices to depict, in a comic light, the "poetry of fancy": Это такое очарование, которого просто *нельза выразить словами. Вообразите себе:* полосочки узенькие, *какие только может представить воображение человеческое.* The sentimental sweetness and false, cloying politeness of society women found their expression in a flood of caressing diminutives: *веселенький* ситец; *полосочки узенькие, узенькие; эполетцы* из *фестончиков.* At the same time, Gogol' emphasized the closeness of ladies' language to the rhetorical forms and phraseology of the sentimental romantic styles: Она статуя и *бледна, как смерть; вооруженный с ног до головы в роде Ринальда Ринальдина.*

The style of the letter sent to Čičikov by an unknown lady comically depicts the basic devices of the sentimental salon style. There is a parody of the emotional lexicon in тайное сочувствие между душами. There is also a comic representation of the tense emotional tone of the salon style and its forms of expression: Письмо начиналось очень решительно, именно так: "Нет, я должна к тебе писать!"; *эта истина скреплена была несколькими точками, занявшими почти полстроки.* Gogol' also parodies the device of the rhetorical question: Что жизнь наша!—Долина, где поселились горести. Что свет!—Толпа людей, которая не чувствует. Compare Karamzin, in "Dva sravnenija":

> Что есть жизнь наша! сказка,
> А что любовь? ее завязка!

It is particularly interesting that the letter to Čičikov also contains a phrase from Puškin's *Cygany*, presented in a contrastingly comic manner: приглашали Чичикова в пустыню,—оставить навсегда город, где люди в *душных оградах не пользуются воздухом.*

With no less accuracy and sharpness, Gogol' represented the sentimental phraseology of the ladies' style in those "hints and questions" which were directed at Čičikov "from the fragrant lips of ladies": Где находятся те *счастливы места, в которых порхает мысль ваша?*

Gogol' put the style of the "modish" novel of the thirties—the rhetorical style of the school of Bestužev-Marlinskij—on a level with the Europeanized Franco-Russian language of society women. He ironically characterized the speech of the governor's wife as belonging to the salon speech depicted by fashionable writers of the time, and Čičikov's manner of speaking was ironically juxtaposed with that of fashionable heroes:

Герой наш ... уже готов был отпустить ей ответ, вероятно, ничем не хуже тех, какие отпускают в модных повестях Звонские, Ленские, Лидины, Гремины и всякие ловкие военные люди, как, невзначай поднявши глаза, остановился вдруг, будто оглушенный ударом ... Чичиков так смешался, что не мог произнести ни одного толкового слова и пробормотал, чорт знает что такое, чего бы уж никак не сказал ни Гремин, ни Звонский, ни Лидин.

Such an ironical attack against the fashionable sentimental style, particularly against its manner of describing beautiful women, even creeps into the language of Čičikov's meditations at a ball. The hypertrophy of epithets in the language of the salon styles and in the poetic language of Benediktov and his school is comically emphasized by Čičikov's thoughts about women's eyes:

Ну, попробуй, например, рассказать один блеск их: влажный, бархатный, сахарный — Бог их знает, какого нет еще! и жесткий, и мягкий, и даже совсем томный, или, как иные говорят, в неге, или без неги, но пуще нежели в неге, — так вот зацепит за сердце, да и поведет по всей душе как будто смычком.

In such fashion, Gogol' openly opposed his own style of narration and depiction to the norms which had become established in the salon styles of the first half of the nineteenth century, with their orientation toward the linguistic and artistic tastes of "fashionable ladies."

Along with his opposition to salon styles, Gogol' also began a literary campaign against the mixture of semi-French and semi-peasant styles in Russian romanticism. He expressed himself in ironic terms concerning the contemporary historical novels which were a mélange of peasant and regional speech and reflections of French semantics.

Gogol' now opposed realistic styles to romantic ones. In the first versions of *Mertvye duši*, his alienation from the romantic style was expressed by the broad use of romantic phraseology and images—negated or transformed. In the final version, romantic images and Europeanisms were replaced by a Church Slavonic phraseology reminiscent of the images of eighteenth-century odes. Such changes are evident in the language of lyric digressions; but the new principles of stylistic construction and new semantic forms are especially striking in the development of themes having to do with the passions. In the early versions, we have a romantic lexicon (cf. the epithets безумно, слепо, упоительный, восторженный, вечнозовущий) and a romantic phraseology (вперивши очи свои в иной мир, несется он мимо земли; полный благородных слез за свой небесный удел, не ищет он ничего в сем мире). All of this leads to Gogol''s style of the period of "Arabeski," "Portret," and "Nevskij prospekt." In the final version of *Mertvye duši*, however, Church Slavonic images, phraseology, syntax, and the entire semantic system are at a far remove from the Europeanized styles of romanticism. They are directly based on the ideology of the church sermon: бесчисленны, как морские пески, человеческие страсти; растет и десятерится с каждым часом и минутой безмерное его блаженство; Но есть страсти, которых избранье не от человека; Высшими начертаньями они ведутся.

The scholarly and philosophical language, between the twenties and the forties, was connected with the semantics of the West European romantic styles. It now seemed to Gogol', as it would later to Gercen, like an anti-national collection of foreign terms and obscure words. In directing Čičikov to a bookshelf in the library of the colonel, Koškarev, Gogol' comically derided the

Russo-German style of the philosophical jargon of the thirties and forties: Что ни разворачивал Чичиков книгу, на всякой странице— *проявление, развитие, абстракт, замкнутость, и сомкнутость,* и чорт знает чего там не было! In Gogol''s opinion, the outstanding features of the Russian scholarly language were its objectivity, realism, and laconism. The Russian scholarly language should be free of phrase-making, rhetoric, and sentimental romantic "coloring" and "sweet-ening." It should not have class limitations; it should be understood by everyone. Such a style, according to Gogol', was in sharp contrast to the language of "German philosophy." The wellsprings for a truly national scholarly language should be Church Slavonic, folk poetry, and the "national" (mainly peasant) language.

Thus, Gogol' believed that the basic resources for a truly national Russian language had been forgotten. These resources had been preserved in "the depths of peasant life" and in the spiritual culture of the church. "Elevated words" should be taken from the biblical language of the church, and "precise appellations" should be selected carefully from provincial dialects. Russian, in this fashion, would be capable of achieving heights unattainable by any other language and a simplicity accessible to the most uneducated. Upper-class society had forgotten its native resources, but, according to Gogol', there was no harm in this. Members of high society had now had the opportunity to chatter out all the nonsense and unclear concepts which were part and parcel of a foreign education, *without* sullying the pristine clarity of the native language. They could now return to it "prepared to think and live with their own intelligence and not a foreign one."

4. THE UNMASKING AND DISCLOSURE OF OFFICIAL RHETORIC AND STYLISTICS

As is evident from what has been said above, Gogol' became convinced that it was impossible either to understand or to depict Russian actuality with the resources of "Western" literary styles. These styles did not correspond to "the spirit of the Russian language or the psychological make-up of the Russian people." The next task was to unmask that falsehood in the relations of words to objects which had become established in Russian life and in the national literary and conversational styles. This task required a comic writer to penetrate more deeply into the reality depicted, by accepting its language and its styles of official, social, and everyday intercourse, and by using these in such a way as to demonstrate the gap between the word itself and its true meaning.

Thus the socio-linguistic content of Gogol''s narration became extremely complex. His tendency to utilize the linguistic resources of the milieu under description became greater, and his use of them became more detailed. To this end, the styles of the conventional language remained, for Gogol', his basic material. He knew that the official styles of the business language played a great role in the structure of these conventional styles and in the unification of their class, professional, urban, rural, and jargon dialects into a single, national, conversational language which was the wellspring for the literary language. He tried to purify that wellspring by filtering out hypocritical and false forms of expression.

The principles underlying the official semantics of the upper classes were unmasked in *Mertvye duši*. The falsehood of designations, their lack of correspondence to reality, was revealed: при всех таких похвальных качествах он мог бы остаться ... тем, что называют в обширном смысле: "хороший человек," т. е. весьма гаденький, обыкновенный, опрятный человек, без всяких резких выпуклостей. The conventionality of a concept was sometimes revealed by an ironic treatment of the meaning attached by society to some word or other: Более не находилось ничего на сей уединенной или, как у нас выражаются, красивой площади. Gogol' satirically demonstrated the magic power of words connected with money and rank, which change one's attitude toward objects even when no personal gain is involved:

Виною всему слово *миллионщик*, — не сам миллионщик, а именно одно слово; ибо в одном звуке этого слова, мимо всякого денежного мешка заключается что-то такое, которое действует и на людей–подлецов, и на людей ни се, ни то, и на людей хороших, словом — на всех действует. Миллионщик имеет ту выгоду, что может видеть подлость, совершенно бескорыстную, чистую подлость не основанную ни на каких расчетах.

But the main objects of Gogol''s attacks were forms of official, business, and chancery stylistics. The high point of such attacks occurs in that part of the second volume of *Mertvye duši* which is devoted to a depiction of Colonel Koškarev's village. It is a prime source of accusatory stylistics, and it provided the starting point of Saltykov-Ščedrin's devices for parodying the bureaucratic language. The anonymous report concerning Čičikov's request contains the casuistry of the chancery language, the aimless and senseless irony inherent in it, the peculiarity of its semantics, and its close connections with Church Slavonic and Church Slavonic rhetoric—all in a grotesquely exaggerated form. First, the very concept of the "soul" is examined from the civil and metaphysical points of view:

В изъяснении того, что требуются ревизские души, постигнутые всякими внезапностями, вставлены и умершие. Под сим, вероятно, они изволили разуметь близкие к смерти, а не умершие, ибо умершие не приобретаются. Что ж и приобретать, если ничего нет? Об этом говорит и самая логика ...

Then the expression "dead souls" is examined from the point of view of the literature of the church, and the conclusion is reached that the word "dead" is out of place, since souls are immortal.

Thus, in Gogol''s depiction, Russian reality of the time was as if enmeshed in thin nets of bureaucratic chancery lexicon, phraseology, and stylistics. These elements appear in a particularly clear, and hence absurd, light when there is an ironic revelation of the non-correspondence between conventional semantics and the true nature of things.

Church Slavonicisms which had become part of the solemn official style were adopted into Gogol''s narrative style and were endowed with the clear stamp of the author's irony: В разговорах с *сими властителями,* он очень искусно умел польстить каждому.

The falsehood and conventionality of the bourgeois and noble business rhetoric are unmasked with particular force and clarity in the speeches of Čičikov. His language is extremely variegated. His speech and even his person are a synthetic embodiment of a mercantile society undergoing the capitalistic process and infected with a passion for acquisition. Gogol' even has Čičikov's speech undergo stylistic and expressive variation depending on the social and financial position of the person to whom he is talking.

By such means, Gogol' rejected the canons of the noble and bourgeois official and everyday speech as being hypocritical and false.

5. GOGOL''S CONCEPTION OF THE PRINCIPLE OF MIXTURE OF
LITERARY STYLES WITH VARIOUS DIALECTS OF THE SPOKEN
LANGUAGE AS A BASE FOR A NATIONAL RUSSIAN LANGUAGE
SYSTEM

As his realistic tendencies developed, Gogol' came to have a clearer
idea of the audience he was addressing: his readers were "the
middle class in its entirety." It therefore followed that he must
establish a national source of literary expression and, by means of it,
break down the old linguistic system of the literary language.
Puškin had already discovered the artistic method—a synthesis of
the author's narrative style with a selection of speech forms characteristic of the heroes depicted and their everyday milieu. In this
fashion, the door had been opened to all sorts of urban and rural
dialectal and jargon variations.

The language of *Mertvye duši* contains a whimsical mixture of
literary forms with various styles of the spoken language. The most
common element, and the clearest, is the everyday speech of the
depicted milieu. The fact that he is garnishing the narrative style
of *Mertvye duši* with expressions and syntactic constructions taken
from the milieu being described is often commented upon by the
author himself: ... была у них ссора за какую-то бабенку, свежую
и крепкую, как ядреная репа, по выражению таможенных чинов-
ников. The stock phrases of the colloquial language are introduced
into the narrative style with the aid of the introductory phrases
как говорится or что называют: Но Собакевич *вошел*, как говорится,
в самую силу речи; Если же между ними и происходило *какое-
нибудь-то*, что называют "*другое-третье*," то оно происходило втайне.

But, even independently of the author's stylistic comments, the
sheer quantity of colloquial expressions in the narrative style of
Mertvye duši testifies to the author's increasing sense of compatibility
with the speech of the milieu he is dealing with: А уж там в стороне
четыре пары *откалывали мазурку;* Скрипки и трубы *нарезывали*
где-то за горами.

Elements of the "service style" of the bureaucratic dialect played
a great role in the everyday colloquial language and were therefore
much used in Gogol''s narrative passages: Ему хотелось, не отклады-
вая, все кончить в тот же день: *совершить, занести, внести* и потом

вспрыснуть всю проделку шипучим под серебряной головой; Фарфор, бронзы и разные батисты и материи получали ... всякого рода *лизуны.*

The device of ornamenting the narrative with the colorful expressions of the characters and their milieu was also responsible for the fact that *Mertvye duši* is speckled with the phraseology and syntax of the chancery language and the bureaucratic dialect: чтобы *немедленно было учинено* строжайшее разыскание; чиновники невольно задумались *на этом пункте;* при выпуске *получил полное удостоение* во всех науках.

By the same token, expressions from the familiar speech of various social strata and the expressive sayings of the city colloquial language entered Gogol''s narrative style in a broad stream: Своя *рожа* несравненно ближе, чем всякая другая; Наконец, он *пронюхал* его домашнюю семейственную жизнь; совал капусту, *пичкал* молоко, ветчину, горох, словом: *катай, валяй;* живой и бойкий русский ум, что не *лезет за словом в карман...* а *влепливает* его сразу как пашпорт на вечную *носку.*

Proverbs and sayings, which had wide currency in the colloquial language, were also extensively used in the narrative language of *Mertvye duši* (Пойдут потом поплясывать, как нельзя лучше, под чужую дудку—словом, начнут гладью, а кончат гадью), as were dialectisms (Дом господский стоял одиночкой *на юру;* Собакевич *пришипился* так, как будто не он), and colloquial syntactic constructions (Видели ... гнедого жеребца на вид и не казистого, но за которого Ноздрев божился, что заплатил десять тысяч; темнота была такая—хоть глаз выколи).

The variety of mixture of literary and colloquial elements was conditioned by vacillations in the narrative style itself—by metamorphoses of the "image of the author" and changes in his mode of expression. The interrelationship of the various masks of the author is expressed in sharp changes of tone. Occasionally, the author even adopts the pose of the familiar, simple storyteller:

Дамы города N были ... *Нет, никаким образом не могу: чувствуется, точно, робость.* В дамах города N больше всего замечательно было то ... *Даже странно — совсем не подымается перо, точно свинец какой-нибудь сидит в нем. Так и быть:* о характере их, видно, нужно предоставить сказать тому, у кого поживее краски и побольше их на палитре; а нам придется — разве два слова о наружности и о том, что поповерхностней.

6. THE BREADTH OF INCLUSION OF CLASS, PROFESSIONAL, AND REGIONAL DIALECTS IN GOGOL''S LANGUAGE

Gogol' endeavored to utilize the professional dialects of the peasantry, the landowners, and the city circles. He considered the peasant language, in its various forms, to be the quintessential "element" of the national language.

He carried to the ultimate the principle of mixing various literary styles with various dialects of the spoken language. Actually, even the speech of his characters is built on such a principle—even though there are limitations, such as that of the social station of the speaker. In the mine of the national language, Gogol' found unused strata of "native" Russian "treasures." According to him, the mixed linguistic stock of the "middle estate" should be transformed, semantically cleansed, and "sanctified" through the medium of these basic elements.

The basis of the national style, for him, was the folklore and everyday life of the peasant. The language of the peasant interested him not only in its all-Russian aspects, but also in its dialectal peculiarities. The admixture of peasant words (both rural and professional) is very evident in *Mertvye duši*, where we have many examples such as the following: столько же *поставов* холста должна была наткать ткачиха; у мужиков давно уже *колосилась* рожь, *высыпался* овес, *кустилось просо*, а у него едва начинал только *итти хлеб в трубку*, *пятка колоса* еще не завязывалась. Gogol''s broad knowledge of peasant botany was reflected in his landscapes from the end of the thirties onward. No writer of the previous period except Dal' had such a variety of "botanical" colors.

Gogol' freely used the dialectal as well as the general peasant lexicon, and even noted down items which did not appear, later on, in Dal''s dictionary. Some of these he used in his fictional prose, as in the following item from the second volume of *Mertvye duši:* приказал выдать даже по *чапорухе* водки за усердные труды. Investigation of the language of the various versions of *Mertvye duši* shows that dialectisms and professionalisms penetrated ever more deeply and broadly into the narrative style. Gogol''s *Zapisnye knižki* shows that he also had an intense interest in peasant crafts and technical specialties, and in the terminologies connected with them.

The jargons of the everyday life of landowners were close to the peasant language. Gogol' made wide use of national Russian culinary terminology (for example, Korobočka's food, Sobakevič's dinner, the postmaster's snacks, and the "Homeric gluttony" of Petux). The jargon of hunting was also part of the landowners' linguistic experience, and it entered the Russian literary language early. One need only mention the broad use of hunting terms in S. Aksakov, Turgenev, and L. Tolstoj. They are also abundantly present in Gogol''s narrative language. In *Mertvye duši*, the description of Nozdrev's kennels is colored with many terms from the jargon of hunting—as is Nozdrev's speech itself.

Expressions from the language of gamblers also gave Gogol' material for reproducing the language of the landowning milieu. One dialogue between Nozdrev and his son-in-law, Mižuev, is almost entirely composed of gambling terms and phrases (although Nozdrev's language is closer to that of cardsharps). There are elements of the gambling jargon in *Revizor;* and, in *Igroki*, Gogol' masterfully reproduced not only the language but also the ideology of cardsharps. In *Mertvye duši*, Gogol' also utilized those familiar, everyday variations of the gambling language which P. A. Vjazemskij had dreamed of collecting (since he thought that the language, folklore, and anecdotes of gamblers were a good reflection of national character). In his description of the game of whist at the governor's, Gogol' gave a masterful reproduction of the free and easy linguistic creativity in the sphere of gambling: Выходя с фигуры он ударял по столу крепко рукою, приговаривая, если была дама: "Пошла, старая попадья!" если же король: "Пошел, тамбовский мужик!" Lastly, Gogol' did not neglect military jargon. One will note elements of army language in the speech of Nozdrev and in the language of *Igroki*.

The language of administration, the subtleties of official stylistics and rhetoric, and the "official" masks of bureaucrats—all underwent intense study by Gogol', as one can see from the appropriate sections of his *Zapisnye knižki*.

There can be no doubt that, as far as the spoken language was concerned, Gogol' was drawn most of all to the forms of the national colloquial language and the different varieties of the colloquial language of the city. Most of the phrases in *Zapisnye knižki* belong to that general, everyday linguistic stock which was used by the broad masses of the peasantry but which was not unknown to other social strata as well. By way of example, note the following lexical items in the narrative style of *Mertvye duši:* Чичиков будучи человек весьма щекотливый и даже в некоторых случаях *привередливый;* родственница, бывшая при его рождении, низенькая, коротенькая женщина, которых обыкновенно называют *пиголицами.*

Gogol''s language was the first in the history of Russian literature to make use of the entire range of "vulgarisms" and argotisms of city and village life. Note the following from *Mertvye duši:* Пирушка, как водится, кончилась дракой. Сольвычегодские уходили на смерть устьсысольских, хотя от них понесли крепкую *ссадку на бока, под микитки и в подсочельник.* The argotism подтибрить is noted down in *Zapisnye knižki* and utilized artistically; compare the following example from "Vij": Богослов уже успел *подтибрить* с воза целого карася.

Gogol' also had a particular interest (evidenced in *Mertvye duši* and *Zapisnye knižki*) in the professional terminology of buying and selling, and in the folklore, life, and dialects of merchants. The "gallant" language of merchants and burghers also found clear expression, both in Gogol''s literary sketches and in his artistic prose. He noted examples of vulgar etymologization of borrowed words, which often give an impression of punning. Note the following examples from *Mertvye duši:* Что ты вечно выше своей сферы, точно пролетарий какой; тут с этим соединено и буджет и реакция, а иначе выйдет павпуризм. The language of merchants in the second volume of *Mertvye duši* is constructed on the norms which are evident in Gogol''s notebooks. Vulgar bookishness, "gallantry," and an attraction for Europeanisms are the basic traits of the language of these merchants.

It is now necessary to take a closer look at those linguistic resources which Gogol' considered to be the core of the future national language.

7. GOGOL''S CONCEPTION OF THE STRUCTURAL BASES AND STYLISTIC NORMS OF AN ALL-NATIONAL RUSSIAN LANGUAGE. IDEALIZATION OF CHURCH SLAVONIC AND THE "FOLK" LANGUAGE IN GOGOL''S PUBLICISTIC WORKS

Gogol' declared that the language of the peasantry and Church Slavonic were the structural and ideological bases of a national

Russian language. They were to supply the artistic means for renovating the literary system which had served society but which had been rejected by Gogol', in some of its styles, as lacking in internal development and incapable of expressing elevated and profound ideas. The search for philosophical, moral, social, and political support for the author's stance in the ideology, mythology, and dogmatics of the church led Gogol', in the last period of his life, to the feeling that it was necessary to revise the relationship between the literary language and the professional cult language of the church. Archaic Slavonicisms and the symbols and formulas of church rites were now introduced by Gogol' into the literary language—largely into its publicistic styles.

The entire structure, including the semantic structure, of Gogol''s publicistic language changed in the mid-forties. The language of church books and the dialectic language of the church became the ideological center of his publicistic stylistics and rhetoric. The romantic expressive devices of his publicistics of the thirties were now neutralized, destroyed, or reformed. Images from the church books now penetrated the author's semantic system, where they tended to subordinate to themselves the phraseology and symbolism of everyday speech and literary exposition.

Very characteristic of Gogol''s devices of publicistic word usage and semantics in this period is the following etymological discourse:

We still senselessly repeat the word просвещение. We never paid any thought to where that word came from or what it means. The word exists in no other language but ours. Просветить does not mean to teach, or to instruct, or to educate, or even to enlighten. It means to illuminate a man through and through in all of his powers—not just in his mind alone. It means to take his entire nature through some sort of purifying fire. The word is taken from our church, which has been pronouncing it for almost a thousand years despite all the darkness and clouds of ignorance which surround her—and she knows why she pronounces it.

The lexicon and phraseology of Gogol''s language were now filled with elements of church mythology and symbolism: Карамзин ... ничего не зарыл в землю и *на данные ему пять талантов истинно принес другие пять;* Перед тобой *разверзается живописный источник;* как начертанные на воздухе *буквы, явившиеся на пиру Валтасара.*

In the period after the publication of the second volume of *Mertvye duši,* Church Slavonic was, for Gogol', primarily a poetic language. According to him, it contained an inexhaustable lyric power to which a poet "inflamed with the necessity of sharing his emotions" would turn. Gogol''s style, when he was describing lyric "enthusiasms," was filled with Church Slavonicisms, particularly when he was characterizing an ode or a hymn.

His patriotic attitude toward the Russian language led him to search for synonyms for Slavonicisms in the national colloquial language. In doing so, he ignored the stylistic nuances and distinctions which had been established in aristocratic circles. His religio-moralistic tendency found its most one-sided expression in his *Vybrannye mesta iz perepiski s druz'jami* (1847). Here we find clearly expressed the moralistic mysticism of his comparisons and the logical basis of "the most daring transitions from the sublime to the simple in one and the same speech": О главном только позаботься, прочее все приползет само собою. Христос недаром сказал: "Сия вся вам приложаться."

The tendency toward an everyday, matter-of-fact representation of phenomena, which was characteristic of Gogol''s artistic prose and which he carried over into publicistic prose because of its rhetorical expressiveness, often led to a sharp clash between bookish phrases and everyday qualifications of objects and actions: желание быть лучше и заслужить рукоплескание на небесах, *придает ему такие шпоры*, каких не может дать наисильнейшему честолюбцу его ненасытимейшее честолюбие; сердца их чокнуться с вашим сердцем, как рюмки во время пирушки.

Of course, neither the style of Gogol''s publicistics of the forties nor its later influence can compare with that of his earlier artistic works. But for a complete understanding of the contradictory development of his style and his historico-literary "methodology," it is necessary to consider the style of *Vybrannye mesta*.

Since certain forms of the solemn official style and elements of the chancery language were historically connected with Church Slavonic, Gogol' could hardly avoid a mixture of them, particularly since one of his main themes in the forties was the union of church and state. In his opinion, the church element should revitalize the false and moribund formulas of the bureaucratic language (which he had ridiculed in his earlier works). But the high genres of official rhetoric had always drawn upon the rhetorical resources of Church Slavonic, so Gogol' was merely following an old tradition. To be sure, the patriarchal and church elements predominated over the official chancery rhetoric in Gogol''s publicistics. But his attempt to bring about a reconciliation between the two spheres merely made him return to that church-chancery rhetoric against which he had struggled so successfully in his earlier work.

For this reason, Gogol''s publicistic language contains many chanceryisms and bureaucratic expressions: полная любовь не должна принадлежать никому на земле. Она должна быть *передаваема по начальству*. Note such chancery turns of phrase as the following: покуда не выступит перед вами ясно вся цепь, *необходимым звеном* которой *есть* вами замеченный *чиновник*. Metaphors and images from the sphere of administrative organization enter even into the area of abstract ideas and religious and ethical concepts, establishing law and order in the spiritual world: Ум не есть высшая в нас способность. *Его должность не больше как полицейская; верховная инстанция* всего есть церковь. At the same time, Gogol' made wide use of contemporary merchant life in his spiritual economics: Вы можете во время вашей поездки ... произвести взаимный благодетельный размен, как расторопный купец: забравши сведения в одном городе, продать их с барышом в другом, всех обогатить и в то же время разбогатеть самому больше всех.

But the living folk element was, for Gogol', more organically fused with Church Slavonic than any other. For him, the national language was a form of national self-determination. What interested him most in the Russian language was its "internal essence and expression"—the "justness and aptness of its words" on the one hand, and its "harmony" on the other. The treasury and the creator of "apt" speech were the "simple folk," mainly the peasant mass. The peasant element in the language, representing a stock of Russianisms and a host of dialectisms untouched by European civilization, was as fresh a force as Church Slavonic. And the literary language should, in Gogol''s view, absorb the world-outlook preserved in the speech of the folk. (Such an attitude brought Gogol' close to the position of Dal', although Dal' rejected the role of Church Slavonic in the Russian literary language.)

In conjunction with these views, Gogol' believed that a characteristic property of Russian was its capacity for "the most daring transitions from the sublime to the simple in one and the same speech." The problem of the artist was to bring the two elements into structural unity. According to Gogol', such an artistic ideal was accomplished by Žukovskij in his translation of the *Odyssey*. He connected this dualism of expression with a duality of basic literary resources—the force of lyricism opposed to the force of sarcasm. In his view, Russian lyricism had its origins in biblical soil, and it is characteristic that he considered the thirties and forties (a period of decline for lyric poetry) a predominantly lyrical period.

At the same time, the familiar, conversational, often folkish, component of the conversational language corresponded to Gogol''s conception of Russian national simplicity and truth—his conception of the "general and national" style. Therefore, the same well-tested method that he had used elsewhere, of using simple words to portray nature, retained its force in Gogol''s publicistics as well. That is one of the reasons for the sharp and precipitous transitions from the solemn to the vulgar in the language of *Vybrannye mesta*. In addition, both stylistic inertia and social habit had their effect in the use of familiar and vulgar words without comic motivation and without any intent at ironic debasement: потомство плюнет на эти драгоценные строки; только в глупой, светской башке могла образоваться такая глупая мысль; стыдно тебе ... не войти до сих пор в собственный ум свой ... , а захламостить его чужеземным навозом.

8. GOGOL''S INFLUENCE ON THE FURTHER DEVELOPMENT OF THE RUSSIAN LITERARY LANGUAGE

The return of Gogol' the publicist to the Church Slavonic linguistic and ideological culture in the last period of his life meant his estrangement from the progressive styles of the forties. Resistance to Church Slavonic was the slogan of the majority of the literary groupings of the time (for example, the Natural School—represented by I. Panaev, Nekrasov, V. A. Sollogub, in part, Turgenev, etc.— and the school of Sentimental Naturalism—headed by Dostoevskij). Contemporaries were ready to view Gogol''s retreat as a compromise with the sentimental-romantic linguistic culture of the nobility (Kukol'nik, Timofeev, etc.). Turgenev, in the forties, characterized the style of the school as "seminary," thus alluding to the church-book element in its language. But Gogol' differed profoundly from this school by virtue of his rejection of West European influences and his broad understanding of the composition and limits of the Church Slavonic element in the Russian literary language.

At the same time, the democratism of Gogol''s attraction to the peasant language, to local dialects, to various city styles, and to different bureaucratic styles sharply separated him from previous literary styles. In this respect he was close to Dal', but, unlike Dal', he drew heavily on the linguistic material of the older, bookish styles.

Gogol' was unable to achieve a synthesis of the "old" and the "new." Later literary styles were far removed from the antiquarian efforts of Gogol''s publicistics and from his conception of lyricism. Even the language of the Slavophiles remained apart from his publicistic style. But his "new" element proved victorious. The reliance on the living language, on various professional and social dialects, became the slogan of the realistic school (Nekrasov, the young Dostoevskij, Saltykov-Ščedrin, Turgenev, and others) and the basis of a new system of the literary language. Gogol''s methods of unmasking the falsehood and hypocrisy in various official styles were the impetus for the development of an accusatory publicistic language which reached its highest point in the work of Saltykov-Ščedrin. Gogol''s dramatic characterizations led to searches for new methods of depicting national types and became an object of imitation and emulation in the works of Pisemskij and Ostrovskij.

Expansion of the Bases
of the Literary Language

In the second half of the nineteenth century, and in connection with the growth of national self-consciousness, the process of democratization of the literary language became broader and more profound. The literary styles of the nobility were supplanted and transformed under the influence of the speech of the broad national masses. Saltykov-Ščedrin drew an effective contrast between "noble melodies" and the "stigmatized language" of accusatory publicistics of the second half of the century. And Dostoevskij, in a letter of 1871, declared that Turgenev's work was the literature of landowners and that this literature had said (brilliantly, in the case of Tolstoj) all that it had to say.

Linguistic and stylistic contradictions within artistic literature became more intense. The very concept of what was "artistic" began to change. In a letter of 1859, Saltykov-Ščedrin complained that the time for artists had not yet come. The existing artists smelled of "slander and the seminary," and were unable to conquer form. "Since Turgenev, you feel a certain rage toward these artists."

The sharp change of attitude toward the system of the literary language was connected with a break from the tradition of the artistic literature of the previous period and with the development of national publicistic and scholarly styles. From the second half of the eighteenth century through the thirties of the nineteenth, the

237

basic structural center of the literary language was occupied by artistic styles (at first verse, then prose). Beginning with the second half of the nineteenth century, however, the concept of "literary language" was separated from the concept of "artistic expression." The development of journalistic and publicistic genres, of the popular-science article and the tract, brought to the fore the problem of a publicistic and popular-science language. I. V. Kireevskij wrote: "In our time, artistic literature comprises only an insignificant portion of literature ... In our time, artistic literature has been replaced by journalistic literature." He further noted that journalism was not restricted to periodicals, but had spread to most literary forms. Everywhere, interest was concentrated on the demands of the moment. "The novel," said Kireevskij, "has been transformed into a statistics of manners; poetry—into occasional verses ..."

N. S. Leskov's comments about the relationship between the literary language and artistic expression are extremely interesting. He noted that the author had to be able to control the voice and language of his hero and not "fall from an alto to a bass." He further noted that: "To learn the speech of every representative of numerous social and personal situations is quite difficult." In reply to the accusation that his language was mannered because he tried to reproduce the speech of the peasants, the demi-intelligentsia, etc., he stated: "It is more difficult for the literary man to assimilate the uncultured language and its living speech than to assimilate the literary language. That is why we have few stylistic artists, that is, people who control the living, and not the literary, speech." Starting from different convictions, but in the same spirit, Tolstoj spoke of the relationship between the literary language and the artless spoken language. He had seen from experience that the reader missed no nuances in anything written in the simple Russian, rather than the literary, style. He thought that the artless language of the people was incomparably more artistic and expressive than the language of Turgenev's novels or that of *Vojna i mir*.

All these statements testify to the fact that, in the second half of the nineteenth century, the process of collision and mingling of various bookish and conversational elements within the system of the literary language was becoming more intensive.

2. THE ENTRANCE OF IMAGES FROM ARTISTIC LITERATURE INTO THE GENERAL LITERARY LANGUAGE

The growth of the influence of scholarly and publicistic prose, the development of "belletristics"—which Belinskij still opposed to pure artistry—created new types of interaction between the artistic language and various genres and styles of the bookish and conversational languages. Artistic literature now played a reduced role in the creation of general norms of literary expression, but it rapidly enriched the inventory of the literary language with individual word forms, phrases, and depictive devices.

The device of literary citation and the device of using suggestive formulations became favorite methods of achieving rhetorical effect. Citations, sayings, and *bon mots* from the artistic works of various authors entered into general literary usage. Some examples follow: from Gončarov—жалкие слова; Обломов; from Nekrasov—до хорошего местечка доползешь ужом; размышления у парадного подъезда; from Ostrovskij—жупел; жестокие нравы, сударь, в нашем городе; Чего моя нога хочет; from Saltykov-Ščedrin—благоглупости; головотяпы; Иудушка; мягкотелый интеллигент; эзоповский язык; from L. Tolstoj—с изюминкой (an expression which had its origin in the proverb не дорог квас, дорога изюминка к квасу, but which Tolstoj popularized); образуется; от ней все качества; from Dostoevskij—бедные люди; униженные и оскорбленные; карамазовщина; from Turgenev—дворянское гнездо; живые мощи; лишние люди (Turgenev is also normally credited with introducing the terms нигилизм, нигилист; but he merely renewed and popularized terms which had already had a complicated history before he wrote his novel *Otcy i deti*); from Pomjalovskij—кисейная барышня; from Čexov—недотепа; человек в футляре; from A. K. Tolstoj— против течения (originally from the Bible); from Tjutčev—мысль изреченная есть ложь; from Gor'kij—бывшие люди; рожденный ползать летать не может; человек—это звучит гордо; and, of course, the language of publicistics swarmed with Kuz'ma Prutkov's apothegms.

Apart from such individual phrases, the literary language took compositional devices, methods of characterization, rhetorical principles, and various forms of symbolic expression from artistic works.

3. THE DOMINANT STATUS OF THE PUBLICISTIC STYLES

As artistic styles changed their composition and function, the relative positions of genres in the literary language underwent drastic change. The linguistic styles of journals, newspapers, and popular science achieved a dominant position and even influenced the language of artistic literature. They were the main source for the lexical enrichment of the conversational language of the intelligentsia. That language had undergone a philosophical reform under the influence of Schelling and Hegel from the twenties through the forties and now, for the most part, was evolving within the ideological atmosphere of publicistics.

Differentiations in lexicon, word usage, and the like, took place, conditioned by social, ideological, and political groupings within the intelligentsia. Semantic and phraseological usages bore the imprint of the world-outlook and political convictions of the writer and reflected the evolution of social ideas. For example, in the forties the word прогресс became established; but, toward the end of the fifties, its use in "official documents" was forbidden by order of the Tsar. In the fifties and sixties the word среда, in the meaning of the French *milieu*, achieved a firm position in the language. Terms and expressions such as the following are characteristic of N. A. Dobroljubov's publicistics: инициатива; субъект человеческой породы; экземпляр; начала общественной жизни; принцип невмешательства (non-intervention); etc. The language of A. F. Pisemskij has words and phrases like закон *гуманности;* эмансипация; миропонимание; веяние минуты; русская община; and the like. Note also the following conversation in one of Pisemskij's works: "Нам нужны люди с характером, с темпераментом, люди твердых убеждений, а не разваренные макароны." "Господи, где вы этаких фраз нахватились! ... Вас, вероятно, всем этим нашпиговала наша литература." A somewhat similar speech is delivered by one of the characters in Turgenev's novel *Dym:* "... разве все эти фразы, от которых так много пьянеет молодых голов: *презренная буржуазия, souveraineté du peuple, право на работу*, разве оне тоже не общие места?" In the seventies and eighties such terms as шкурный вопрос, шкурный инстинкт, увенчание здания (concerning the constitution) achieved

currency. M. P. Pogodin coined the expression рыцари сви-
стопляски with reference to the *Sovremennik*, when it was under
the editorship of N. G. Černyševskij. The term либеральная раз-
мазня was coined in the publicistics of the eighties. Saltykov-
Ščedrin played a particularly important role in the development of
publicistic styles.

Through the medium of publicistics, various terms and slogans
became established in the speech of different social strata (compare,
for example, the particular revolutionary meaning which дело,
великое дело acquired in the language of the revolutionarily inclined
intelligentsia of the sixties). The struggle between differing political
ideologies was thus directly and sharply reflected in semantics.

4. THE ENRICHMENT OF THE LITERARY LEXICON

The process of enriching the literary language with abstract,
scholarly, and intellectual lexical items still continued intensively.
Many former professionalisms now entered the literary language,
occasionally acquiring new, abstract shades of meaning. New words
(mostly abstract) were created; old words acquired new meanings.
Many terms from the folk and colloquial languages now achieved
literary canonization.

The tempo and basic tendencies of this lexical growth may be
traced through the additions which Baudouin de Courtenay made
in Dal''s dictionary. Even if one excludes highly specialized (non-
literary) terms and confines oneself to only the first three letters
of the alphabet, one still finds a great number of barbarisms:
абзац, аборт, абсурд, агитировать, аграрный, аккомодация, аллите-
рация, альбумен, альтернатива, альтруизм, антисемит, аншлаг, апломб,
артикуляция, бактерия, бетон, буржуй, вокализм, and many others.
Moreover, many words which were entered in Dal''s dictionary
had changed their meaning; many words arose after the sixties;
and many more came into the literary language from outside of it,
such as бессодержательность, бесформенный, брехунец (lawyer), впе-
чатлительность, вскидчивый (quarrelsome), вспрыски, белоперчат-
ное фарисейство сытой морали (the earning of money through
occupations not characteristic of the given social class or occupation),

всесокрушающий, судебно-медицинское вскрытие, and so forth.

Other investigators also noticed lacunae in Dal''s dictionary: бесправие, бесшабашный, наглядность (*Anschaulichkeit*), причинность (*Kausalität*), неизменяемость, общинник, отожествление, праязык, самоуничтожение, уподобление, etc. Occasionally, such words came from the colloquial language or from professional languages and argots: бронзовый (in the meaning of "exaggerated" or "false," from the language of finance), военщина, иеримиада, культ, отмочить штуку (to do or say something extravagant), санитарный, суммация. Ja. K. Grot noted the absence from Dal''s dictionary of such words as the following, which were current in the literary language of the sixties: деловитый, забастовка, мировоззрение, миросозерцание, общедоступный, пиджак (peajacket), чек (check).

What was characteristic of these nineteenth-century neologisms was a lack of differentiation between bookish terms (sometimes created following Church Slavonic norms) and colloquial terms (sometimes having a provincial, regional character). Bookish words mixed with colloquialisms, and stylistic norms were unstable. Many words which had previously been considered colloquial now became literary: быт, суть, рознь, строй, отчетливый, дословный, корениться, обрядовый, противовес, самодур, проходимец. On the other hand, archaic, church-book types of word formation were renovated: научный, даровитый, настроение, творчество, представитель, сопоставление, голосование, etc. Bookish neologisms such as the following came into being: водораздел, замкнутость, крепостничество, мероприятие, непререкаемый, представительство, обольщение, собственник.

For the historian there is particular interest in the words and expressions which reflect the growth of industry, commerce, and capitalist relations: чьи-нибудь акции поднялись, упали; потерпеть крах; надежды, планы лопнули; крупный вклад во что-нибудь; выйти в тираж; свести счеты с кем-нибудь. Compare the following in N. S. Leskov's novel *Na požax:* я задумал было и жениться, конечно не по расчету и не по прикладным соображениям, однако этому, как кажется, не суждено осуществиться, и я эту *статью* уже *выписал в расход.*

5. THE SPREAD OF FOREIGN WORDS AND BORROWED TERMS IN
THE LITERARY LANGUAGE OF THE SECOND HALF OF THE NINE-
TEENTH CENTURY. THE COMPOSITION AND FUNCTION OF BOR-
ROWINGS

The same ideological conflicts which affected the semantic system
of the literary language served also to bring Russian thought into
contact with various West European theories, discoveries, and
achievements. Consequently, the literary language continued to
absorb borrowed words, phrases, and syntactic constructions. At the
end of the sixties, Ja. K. Grot noted the currency of such constructions as the following: рассчитывать на кого, на что; делать кого
несчастным; иметь жестокость; предпослать что чему; пройти мол-
чанием; разделять чьи-либо мысли; прежде нежели сказать; иметь
что возразить; иметь что-нибудь против. According to him, in the
sixties and seventies still more such constructions were added:
считаться с чем (*tenir compte de quelque chose*); человек такого закала
(*un homme de cette trempe*); немыслимый (*undenkbar*); etc.

The tendency toward "scientific" forms of expression led to a
saturation of the literary language with West European borrowings.
For the most part, they belonged to the spheres of natural, social,
and economic sciences, civics, manufacturing, the political, economic, and juridical foundations of civic life, personality traits, and
norms of social conduct. The judgments of contemporaries in connection with such borrowings, whether they passionately favored or
passionately opposed them, are of historical interest as testimony to
the literary canonization of borrowings. For example, Ja. K. Grot
noted a "whole legion" of verbs of the form формулировать, изоли-
ровать, to which he particularly objected because they constituted
a "double deformation"—that is, a French word had been first
reformed with a German suffix, -*ieren*. He observed that, to reduce
such "deformity," many people began using infinitives of the type
формуловать, on the model of older verbs like атаковать. Grot was
a confirmed Westerner; but he nonetheless advised caution in the
selection of foreign words, particularly abstract terms which might
be easily misused, as in the following example from the speech of
a young, provincial landowner: Без рыску нет шансов на авáнтаж.

Purists railed against the flood of borrowings and against the

misuses of borrowed words that resulted from a lack of understanding of their meaning in the language of origin. Compare the
following passage from Turgenev's novel *Nov'*:

В разгоряченной атмосфере голушкинской столовой, завертелись, толкая и
тесня друг дружку, всяческие слова: *прогресс, правительство, литература,
податной вопрос, церковный вопрос, денежный вопрос, судебный вопрос, классицизм,
реализм, комунизм, интернационал, клерикал, капитал, администрация, органи-
зация, ассоциация* и даже *кристализация*.

It is interesting that Europeanisms of an official, business, political,
and technical coloring even entered the language of poetry. Note
Nekrasov's use of such words as the following: агент, афера, бир-
жевик, брошюра, гонорар, дебоширствовать, дивиденд, квитанция,
колоссальный, коммунизм, радикал, ретроград, субсидия, тариф,
фельетон, etc.

The particular selection of borrowed words depended on the
ideological and social divisions in Russian society. B. Èjxenbaum
noted that Tolstoj's penchant for mathematical and physical
terminology was a result of his opposition to raznočinec "realists,"
with their Darwinism and their "tendency to make history a branch
of natural science." The conservative, noble camp made ironic
attacks against the materialistic, natural-science terminology of the
Nihilists. The phraseology of Bazarov in Turgenev's *Otcy i deti*
typifies this point of view: "Look at the class of mammals (к какому
разряду млекопитающих) to which this person belongs." In the
sixties, Tolstoj opposed a physical and mathematical terminology to
this natural-science terminology; thus the philosophical-publicistic
portions of *Vojna i mir* utilize terms from physics, mathematics,
mechanics, and astronomy.

The second half of the nineteenth century witnessed the "uni-
versalization" of a host of terms in the literary language which
originally belonged to the language of natural science. As these
terms became current, they developed new meanings which reflected
the world-outlook of one or another social milieu. V. V. Rozanov,
in his book *Uedinenie*, wrote the following:

In my day—during my lifetime—certain new words were created. In 1880, I
called myself a психопат, laughing and enjoying a new, apt word. Up to that
time (I think), I heard the word from no one. Then (the time of Schopenhauer)
many people began to call themselves and others by it; then it appeared in the
journals. Now it's a term of abuse, but originally it meant an "illness of the spirit,"

à la Byron, and was used for poets and philosophers. Werther was a психопат. Then, later, came the word декадент, and again I was among the first. That was before we ... heard of Brjusov. And A. Belyj was not yet born.

6. THE VARIETIES OF WESTERNIZING TRADITIONS IN RUSSIAN LINGUISTIC CULTURE

Even though the Russian literary language, by the middle of the nineteenth century, had enriched itself with many terms for abstract concepts and had developed numerous methods of forming words to express complex ideas, certain intellectual circles still continued the tendency toward a closer rapprochement between Russian and West European languages. In general, the tendency was characteristic of those strata of society which were closely connected with the preceding linguistic culture and which continued to live in the intellectual atmosphere of the West European literary languages. Gercen, whose language contained many Gallicisms, is an example.

Proponents of a greater rapprochement would argue that a Russian term either lacked the generality of a corresponding term from a West European language or was so general that it could not express all the nuances expressible in a West European language, which would have a whole constellation of terms for the same general concept. Often, these general terms belonged to the sphere of polite social relations. It was felt, for instance, to be a sign of intellectual poverty that Russian had only two terms, вежливость and учтивость, for the concept of politeness itself, whereas French enjoyed the richness of *civilité, politesse, urbanité, galanterie, courtoisie,* and *honnêteté.* In this connection, it is interesting to note a conversation which takes place in Turgenev's novel *Nov'.* Sipjagina accuses Kallomejcev of using too many French words, a habit she considers old-fashioned. He replies that not everyone has such control over Russian as she has, that he has great respect for the official language of the Russian state, and that, further, he has great respect for Karamzin. But then he goes on:

"Но русский, так сказать, ежедневный язык ... разве он существует? Ну, например, как бы вы перевели мое восклицание: 'De tout à l'heure: C'est un mot!' — *Это — слово!?* Помилуйте!" "Я бы сказала: '*Это удачное слово.*' " Калломейцев засмеялся. " '*Удачное слово!*' Валентина Михайловна! Да разве

вы не чувствуете, что тут ... семинарией сейчас запахло ... Всякая соль
исчезла ...''

The democratic creation of words by the newspapers and journals
did not satisfy those (largely noble) social circles which had their
origins in the preceding esthetic culture. In some literary styles,
the influence of West European linguistic constructions was still
very great. Note the following Gallicisms in Turgenev's language:
Он брал аккорды рассеянной рукой, d'une main distraite; Маша
в присутствии матери вооружилась jusqu'aux dents, как говорят
французы; etc. And note the following Anglicism: Мнения, казав-
шиеся дерзкой новизной, — стали всеми принятым, общим местом—
"a truism," как выражаются англичане.

During the fifties and sixties, L. Tolstoj's connections with French
literature were also very close. Although he was later to try to
break these ties, his narrative language of this period was still very
close to the French artistic styles of the upper classes. To be sure,
this feature of his language was, in part, connected with the fact
that he was describing the everyday speech of aristocratic circles.

In *Vojna i mir*, for example, the author's language contains many
of the traits of the Russo-French styles of the literary language of
the first third of the century. The lexicon, phraseology, and syntax
of *Vojna i mir* clearly reflect the language of the old nobility, avoiding
the journalistic neologisms and publicistic phraseology of the sixties,
as well as the archaic Church Slavonicisms of the previous period.
Because *Vojna i mir* swarms with Gallicisms, it has an old-fashioned
air about it, since even such "Europeans" as Turgenev had, by
that time, already cleared their narrative style of the turn-of-the-
century Europeanisms of the old nobility. The Gallicisms in *Vojna
i mir*, however, were consistent with the style of the epoch being
portrayed. As a matter of fact, such literary archaisms were still
present in the "polite" language of the fifties and sixties. Compare
the following examples of lexical, phraseological, and semantic
Gallicisms from *Vojna i mir*: Ростов *делал* эти *соображения;* Он
ненавидел ее и навсегда *был разорван с нею;* Тузы, *дававшие мнение*
в клубе; Вся фигура Сперанского *имела особенный тип; разорвать*
этот *досадный ему круг смущения; вино ее прелести ударило ему в голову;
врач необыкновенного искусства;* Граф Растопчин *держал нить разговора;* после той *среды могущества,* в которой он так недавно нахо-
дился; Люди этой партии *имели в своих суждениях и качество и*

недостаток искренности; сделал вид задумчивой *нежности.* Similar phraseology was present in the narrative style of Tolstoj's early works. Note the following example from *Junost'*: Я был *в расположении духа пофилософствовать; я ... сделал* себе уже ясное *понятие* об ... Thus, a social and stylistic contact took place between the author's language and that of characters from the upper social circles. It was in this fashion that the "style of the period" was reproduced.

One must remember, therefore, that the Gallicisms of *Vojna i mir* serve the function of historical stylization. They characterize the style and cultural attitudes of the milieu being depicted—particularly that of the Petersburg aristocracy, which Tolstoj reproduced in a satirical light. The author's translations of aristocratic conversations often have Gallicisms (occasionally intentional ones): Генуа и Лукка *стали не больше как* (*ne sont plus que*) поместьями фамилии Бонапарта; *я из хороших источников знаю* (*je sais de bonne source*); etc. There can be no doubt that Tolstoj consciously exaggerated the French coloring in aristocratic speech by laying bare the method of translating French phrases. Occasionally he even commented on such calques. The method is used most openly in *Anna Karenina* to create the impression of French conversation: "Алексей *сделал нам ложный прыжок*,"—сказала она [Бетси] по-французски; "я не могу быть *католичнее* папы,"—сказала она.—"Стремов и Лиза Меркалова—Это *сливки сливок общества*," etc., etc.

One must therefore differentiate between the typical peculiarities of Tolstoj's language and its occasional stylistic variations. Moreover, a sharp distinction must be drawn between his own narrative style and the Russo-French language of the aristocratic circles he depicted in *Vojna i mir* and *Anna Karenina.* His route toward that national style which he achieved toward the end of the century, and which he thought should be accessible even to the uneducated, was nonetheless very complex and difficult. He acquired such a broad grasp of the living language that he gradually freed himself from the old, aristocratic, literary tradition. This process accelerated beginning with the seventies; but his language of the fifties and sixties contained many Gallicisms and syntactic remnants of the literary language of the beginning of the century.

He has, for example, a dangling use of the adverbial participle, independent of the subject of the main clause: нынче, *увидав* ее мельком, *она ему показалась* еще лучше. Note, in the text of *Vojna i mir*, the following correction made in the edition of 1873: Когда Пьер вошел в калитку, его обдало паром replaced пройдя в калитку, Пьера обдало паром.

To this same area of turn-of-the century Russo-French syntax belongs the crossing of participial and relative constructions: люди этой партии, большею частью *не военные и к которой* принадлежал Аракчеев, думали и говорили; Подольский полк, *стоявший* перед лесом *и большая часть которого* находилась в лесу.

Also characteristic of *Vojna i mir* is the interdependence, or hybridization, of relative and nonrestrictive clauses: Пойдет ли он по старой, прежней дороге, или по той новой, *на которой он твердо верил что найдет* возрождение к иной жизни; "*К которым вы предполагаете, что я принадлежу?*"—спокойно ... проговорил князь Андрей.

French influence is also evident in a more independent use of participles. From the point of view of the norms of Russian literary syntax, these are anacolutha: Необычайно странно было Балашову после близости к высшей власти и могуществу, после разговора три часа тому назад с государем *и вообще привыкшему* по своей службе к почестям, видеть тут ... враждебное ... к себе силы. Such a use of dangling syntagmas is characteristic of Tolstoj's syntax in general and must also be viewed as the product of French influence: Наташе, видимо, поправились эти, *вне обычных условий жизни*, отношения с новыми людьми.

In Tolstoj's method of constructing his syntactic groupings, there is evident a unique use of prepositions which is, again, due to French influence: Барклай ... делается еще осторожнее *для* решительных действий; В обоих случаях русские были *в превосходных силах.*

French influence is probably also responsible for Tolstoj's passion for constructions with с (*avec*) and в (*dans, en*), which often form dangling, semi-independent syntagmas. As a matter of fact, almost every designation of a person, object, or action is accompanied by explanatory additions introduced by these prepositions: Он лежал высоко на спине *с своими, костлявыми*, покрытыми лиловыми узловатыми жилками *руками*, на одеяле, *с уставленным прямо левым глазом*, и *с скосившимся правым глазом, с неподвижными бровями и губами;* каждый полк *в своей безмолвности и неподвижности* казался безжизненным телом. Note also the insertion of one construction with с into another of the same form: M-lle Georges *с* оголен-ными, *с ямочками,* толстыми *руками.*

Such examples clearly illustrate the close connection between Tolstoj's language, in his early period, and the Russo-French styles of the literary language of the first half of the nineteenth century.

Certain Russian literary styles, especially in the sphere of artistic narrative, continued to imitate West European languages (especially those with an analytical structure—French and English) even in the second half of the century. The aristocratic circles of Russian society sought, in French and English, an antidote for the confused, artificially bookish constructions, the terminological complexities, and the "professional" phraseology of the new publicistic style—a style which, in many respects, still based itself on the chancery language.

7. THE INTERACTION BETWEEN THE PUBLICISTIC STYLES AND THE STYLES OF THE OFFICIAL AND CHANCERY LANGUAGE

Publicistic, scholarly, and, to some extent, even artistic styles of the literary language interacted with the official, chancery language. At any rate, expressions from the chancery language were introduced into these styles and, conversely, the chancery language reflected to some extent the novelties of the language of the press. This connection between the publicistic genres and the language of officialdom was most clearly reflected in the work of Saltykov-Ščedrin—often in a parodistic, satirical interpretation.

The newspaper language aided in the dissemination of chancery terms, as in the language of G. Uspenskij: возвышая голос *до еликовозможной степени.* It also established certain "free usages" in the "general" language, such as the use of благодаря with negative as well as positive concepts. The official language, in turn, adopted some of the phraseology of the newspapers; for example, in the seventies, it accepted the popular locution идти в разрез с кем-нибудь, чем-нибудь.

Contemporary purists objected to the appearance, in the literary language, of Church Slavonic and archaic elements which had been preserved in the language of the chanceries. Examples of such items are буде, вящще, нарочитый, таковый, обоего пола, instead of если, более, нарочный, такой, обоих полов, respectively. Objection was also raised to certain types of syntactic construction, such as отношение с чем, согласно чему, instead of the "correct" отношение к чему, согласно с чем. Occasionally, Germanicisms made their way into the newspaper language by way of the language of Petersburg bureaucracy; so, for example, a complaint was raised that во внутрь России was a calque of *ins Innere des Reiches*, and that it led, by analogy, to the construction из внутри. From the language of officialdom, also, came new collocutions of verb plus noun, such as заслушать какой-нибудь отчет; доклад был заслушан.

The expansion in the use and formation of one grammatical category, the deverbative noun, owes its origins to the demands of the chancery language. The language of bureaucracy (and publicistic styles as well) had need of a compact, analytical, syntactically monotonous style, particularly for the expression of abstract concepts. With reference to the verb, this meant the creation of many verbal nouns in **-н-** and **-т-**. Note the following examples (from the language of G. Uspenskij): *приподнятие* и *мановение* указательным пальцем; процесс *отворяния* крови. Sometimes these are connected with a parodistic allusion to chancery business, as in о *сдернутии* меня с кресла за ногу. Such forms enjoyed wide usage even in the poetry of writers with a civic orientation; they mainly involved official, bookish, or specialized words, and they often had a Church Slavonic or archaic coloration. Compare the following examples from the language of Nekrasov: водворение, назначение, кучение, утоление, кружение, поругание, борение, стенание, стяжание.

In official, scholarly, and publicistic styles it was occasionally necessary to obliterate or blur the individualized, often familiar and concrete, depiction of action which was frequently a property of the simple form of the verb. For this purpose, a periphrastic construction was used, consisting of a more or less abstract verb, which designated the action in general (or which had lost all or nearly all concrete meaning of any sort), and a deverbative noun, which designated the specific content of the action. For example, нанести удар (instead of ударить), совершить ошибку, произвести кражу, вступить в соглашение, вести разговор, etc. Sometimes these constructions came from the Church Slavonic tradition (одержать победу), and sometimes they were calques of West European phraseology (принять меры, делать впечатление, дать аудиенцию, иметь успех).

Such constructions had undergone intensive development from the middle of the eighteenth century onward. In the second half of the nineteenth century, the development went even further; for, now, certain "auxiliary" verbs could be expanded to cover a whole category of similar phenomena. For example, the verb оказать was defined in a dictionary of 1847 as meaning "demonstrate," "show"; in Dal''s dictionary two more meanings were added, "reveal," "express"; gradually, the verb lost all its active, concrete, semantic coloring and came to be used in a whole series of phrases: оказать помощь, содействие; оказать давление, действие; etc. The proliferation of this kind of construction was abetted by a parallelism between active and passive constructions: подвергнуть испытанию–подвергнуться испытанию; давать применение–находить применение. One thus arrives at whole sets of semantic parallels: влиять, повлиять–испытывать влияние, подвергнуться влиянию.

Such periphrastic constructions compensated for the occasional absence of a direct designation (ввести в заблуждение), and also made semantic differentiation possible, as between предложить and сделать предложение (make a proposal of marriage), ходить and иметь хождение (concerning money).

In this fashion, abstract formulas were created which could develop specialized meanings. Synthetic forms of expression were replaced by analytical ones—on the model of West European languages.

8. THE INTENSIFICATION AND SPREAD OF ARTIFICIAL AND BOOKISH FORMS OF EXPRESSION IN THE RUSSIAN LITERARY LANGUAGE OF THE SECOND HALF OF THE NINETEENTH CENTURY

The official, scientific, and publicistic styles developed an artificial, periphrastic, syntactically complex manner of expression. Words were divorced from their objective base. Between the word and the object there developed an intermediate sphere of conventionalized, descriptive, expressive devices. In *Dnevnik pisatelja*, Dostoevskij ironically characterized this stylistic phenomenon as follows: "Someone assured us that, if some critic nowadays wants a drink, he won't say принеси воды; he will, most likely, say something like the following: принеси то существенное начало овлажнения, которое послужит к размягчению более твердых элементов, отложившихся в моем желудке. This joke in part reflects the truth." Contemporaries cited even more fearful (and genuine) examples, particularly from the language of jurisprudence. In this connection, Čexov's advice to the author L. Avilova is interesting: "It is necessary to construct the phrase, therein lies the art. The phrase should be purged of по мере того, and при помощи. One must think about its musicalness, and not allow стал and перестал to appear almost next to each other in the same phrase."

In this artificial, bookish language, semantic accuracy tended to be lost and pleonasms were the result. One example from the scholarly language of the beginning of the twentieth century should suffice: превыше всяких *человекоуподобительных персонификаций*. Stock rhetorical phraseology caused words to lose their concrete semantic content. Again, Čexov's advice to Avilova is interesting: "Throw out the words идеал and порыв. To hell with them!"

This studied bookishness of expression penetrated into jargons and into the language of the half-educated and of the bourgeoisie (where it often took on grotesquely artificial forms). An example may be taken from Dostoevskij's *Podrostok*, where a girl leaves a suicide note in the following style: Маменька милая, простите меня за то, что я *прекратила мой жизненный дебют*. One of the characters in the novel, Versilov, comments on the language of the note:

Выражение, конечно, неподходящее, совсем не того тона, и действительно могло зародиться в гимназическом или ... каком-нибудь условно-товарищеском ... языке, али из *фельетонов каких-нибудь*, но покойница употребила его в этой ужасной записке совершенно простодушно и серьезно.

9. THE BASIC TENDENCIES IN THE USE AND TRANSFORMATION OF CHURCH SLAVONICISMS

The structure of publicistic and even, occasionally, of artistic styles evolved in the direction of artificial bookishness and a heavy, mannered "scientificalness" of exposition. At the same time, however, it absorbed forms from the spoken, even from the familiar, language and endowed bookish words with new semantic nuances. The publicistic language of the raznočinec intelligentsia developed characteristic devices for transforming and "debasing" Church Slavonicisms. Methods were developed for ironically unmasking the official style. And new methods were found for the hybridization of colloquial and bookish elements.

The position of Church Slavonicisms within the literary language as a whole and within the publicistic language in particular, in the second half of the century, is interesting. There were two basic tendencies. First of all, a number of Church Slavonicisms, representing a disorderly mass of lexical and phraseological fragments, enjoyed various stylistic uses in both the literary and, to some extent, the spoken language. They were phrases and idioms such as the following: алчущие и жаждущие; альфа и омега; бить себя в грудь; бросить камень в кого-нибудь; вкусить от древа познания; глас вопиющего в пустыни; грехи юности; злоба дня; знамение времени; ни на йоту; каинова печать; камень преткновения; камни возопиют; не оставить камня на камне; кимвал бряцающий и медь звенящая; книга за семью печатями; манна небесная; во мгновение ока; метать бисер перед свиньями; не от мира сего; нищие духом; Ноев ковчег; земля обетанная; отрясти прах от ног своих; запретный плод; в поте лица своего; святая святых; суета сует; умыть руки; Фома неверный; поцелуй Иуды; etc., etc. Undoubtedly, many such expressions were the result of a democratic, raznočinec broadening of the concept of "literariness": избиение младенцев; злачное место; притча во языцех; темна вода во облацех; etc.

The other tendency in the use of Church Slavonicisms was characteristic of the language of the liberal, and especially the revolutionary, intelligentsia. It consisted in the frequent use (often ironic or satirical) of archaic and cultish Church Slavonicisms, and the mixture of these with colloquial "vulgarisms," as in the following: from the language of Saltykov-Ščedrin—Писемский как не обтачивает своих болванчиков, а *духа жива* вдохнуть в них не может; *обнимем друг друга и возопием;* from the language of N. G. Pomjalovskij—много в том месте, *злачнем и прохладнем,* паразитов; из нижних этажей на улицу купечество выставило свое *тучное чрево;* or, from G. Uspenskij— *елико* хватило сил; и *несть числа и меры* всему благородству.

The process of "vulgarizing" Church Slavonicisms was supported by a process of mixing them morphologically and semantically with colloquial elements. It can be illustrated by the following quotation from Nekrasov's "Komu na Rusi žit' xorošo":

> Удар искросыпительный,
> Удар зубодробительный,
> Удар скуловорот.

Such devices led to restorations and neologisms like the following: злопыхательство, благоглупость, очковтирательство, зверинствовать. Compare also the spread of familiar, caressingly pejorative formations in **-енция, -тура, -истика, -логия**, such as старушенция, поведенция, верхотура, ерундистика, глупистика, болтология.

10. THE PROCESS OF STYLISTICALLY DISORGANIZED MIXING OF BOOKISH ELEMENTS WITH COLLOQUIAL SPEECH

The literary language of the second half of the nineteenth century, based on publicistic, official, and popular-science styles, enjoyed a rapid development at its peripheries—even at the expense of the semantic structure of its core. The stylistic boundaries of the previous period disintegrated; the conception of what was "literary" was rapidly expanded. It is characteristic that the second half of the century witnessed no codification of rhetorical norms to replace the Slavonic and aristocratic norms which had been already rejected in the forties. Two factors were primarily responsible: writers now came from very different social backgrounds, and the choice of subjects had broadened. The hypertrophy of artificial bookishness coexisted with a democratic broadening of the literary language.

A very instructive, though bizarre, indication of the state of affairs is the profusion of words associated with drinking. In the noble tradition, the lexicon of drunkenness either was connected with the folk (нализаться, как зюзя; хлебнуть лишнее) or with military and card-playing argots (зарядиться, быть на втором взводе, под мухой, нарезаться), or had a punning studiedness (под шефе, заложить за галстук). In the language of the bourgeoisie, the concept was connected either with the vulgar city colloquial language on the one hand—often with a nuance of jargon (ковырнуть, нажраться, дернуть, долбануть, налакаться, раздавить мерзавчика, хлебнуть малую толику, садануть, тюкнуть, царапнуть)—or with bookish, often Church Slavonic or official, periphrases on the other (вонзить в себя, двинуть от всех скорбей, нарезаться в досто-должном порядке, разрешить вино и елей). Compare this passage from Turgenev's novel *Nov'*:

И *Русский Вестник*, пожалуй, тоже с некоторых пор, — говоря современным языком, — *крошечку подгулял*. Калломейцев засмеялся во весь рот; ему показа-лось, что это очень забавно сказать: "подгулял," да еще "крошечку."

This stylistic "openness" of the literary language of the second half of the nineteenth century and the beginning of the twentieth also found expression in the explanatory dictionaries of the period. Some of them admitted colloquialisms, while others restored archaisms and obsolete Church Slavonicisms.

11. SOCIAL DIFFERENCES IN THE CONVERSATIONAL LANGUAGE OF RUSSIAN SOCIETY. THE CITY COLLOQUIAL LANGUAGE AND PEASANT DIALECTS

Different combinations of bookish and colloquial elements, as well as differences in their sociological nature, produced sharp differen-tiations between literary styles. The literary language retained its national unity, but it became stratified into many different styles which depended on sociological contrasts in everyday speech. The spoken and written language of the upper classes of the nobility continued to be oriented toward the semantics of West European languages, sometimes with an admixture of the peasant language. We have already seen evidence of this West European orientation in the language of L. Tolstoj.

The conversational language of the intelligentsia was not, how-ever, free of sharp social differences, based on professional differen-tiation within society, on the character of the literary influence on the everyday language, and on the attitude of different social groups toward the peasant language and toward the colloquial language of the city. The colloquial language of the city undoubt-edly occupied one of the central positions in the everyday spoken styles, and one can cite a number of literary examples which illustrate its composition. L. Tolstoj, for instance, has Anna Karenina carry on the following conversation with a country doctor of the sixties and seventies:

Вы были там? — я был там, но *улетучился* — с мрачной шутливостью отвечал доктор ... — Ну, а здоровье старухи? Надеюсь, что не тиф? Тиф не тиф, а *не в авантаже обретается* ...

The lexical complexity of the language of the raznočinec intelligentsia is very clearly illustrated in the language of Bazarov, in Turgenev's *Otcy i deti:* разовьют в себе *нервную систему до раздражения;* этакое *богатое тело,* хоть сейчас в *анатомический театр.* Everyday colloquial forms (with a tinge of vulgarity) are used: *обломаю* дел много; *для ради* важности; пора *бросить эту ерунду.* And there are statements opposing "high" romantic rhetoric: Романтик сказал бы: *я чувствую, что наши дороги начинают расходиться,* а я просто говорю, что *друг другу мы приелись.*

Colloquial word formation is ironically illustrated in the conversation of Nihilists in N. Leskov's novel *Na požax:*

Он нагрубил мне и *надерзил.* — Что это за слово, *надерзил?* — А как же надо сказать? — *Наговорил дерзостей.* — Зачем же два слова, вместо одного? Впрочем, ведь вы поняли, так, стало быть, слово хорошо ...

The expressive and stylistic singularities of the colloquial language of the city are clearly illustrated in the letters of the actor F. Burdin to A. N. Ostrovskij, which contain these constructions: Эта комедия совершенно *замазала рот* распускателям нелепых слухов; Леонид *осушает опрокидонты* и опоручивает хозяйку; *отлупили* комитет; *сочинили загул* жестокий; чем-то *шибко подсолили;* Борбунов *сшит по рукам и ногам,* а это—полное *олицетворение личности;* публично *оплюй* их; *стукни их в морду.*

In the language of the democratic intelligentsia, colloquial forms were interlarded with forms from the language of the chancery, with Church Slavonic, and with bookish expressions. All of these elements appear, for example, in the language of G. Uspenskij.

The city colloquial language had connections, of course, with the peasant language. To be sure, the language of the peasantry was accepted into the language of the city only to the extent that it was close to city social dialects or that it satisfied bourgeois tastes. But the peasant language had a great influence on the literary language even without passing through the filter of the city. In this connection, one must always remember folk poetry, which played such a great role, for example, in Nekrasov's creative work. Moreover, certain circles of educated society had deep and direct connections with the language of the peasantry. L. Tolstoj, in trying to create an easily understandable, simple, literary style in opposition to the publicistic style, freely used peasant expressions even in his own narrative prose: e.g., Мы все в жизни как *неуки-лошади, обратанные и введенные в хомут и оглобли*. Of course, the peasant language did not always function the same way in the language of all the writers who were connected, by birth or profession, with country life or the provincial town.

Turgenev's use of folk speech is of uncommon interest for the history of the Russian literary language. His narrative style contains many elements from the living conversational language as well as provincialisms. In using the latter, he never forgot the one essential criterion—clarity. Uncommon words are always explained in the text or in notes. If the words are not explained, their meaning can be deduced from the whole context. Guided by his artistic sense and by the desire to be understood, he only took what was close to the literary language. He adopted terms which were known to the whole of the peasantry and not to just one or another grouping within the peasantry. He did not decorate his language with provincialisms in the manner of V. Dal', and he advised young writers to reduce the number of localized words in their language. In general, he only utilized the language of the more cultured and progressive peasantry.

Even the more conservative nobility had its own well-defined esthetic attitude toward peasant word forms. In his novel *Nov'*, Turgenev introduced the following clever touch into the picture of Kallomejcev:

Калломейцев уверял, между прочим, что пришел в совершенный восторг от названия, которое мужики — oui, oui! les simples mougiks! дают адвокатам. "Брехунцы! брехунцы! — повторял он с восхищением: — ce peuple russe est délicieux!

Of course, writers from the Populist or raznočinec democratic camps had a totally different attitude toward the language of the peasants. People like G. Uspenskij viewed it as a basic source for the renewal of the literary language and as a wellspring of national originality.

The question of reproducing peasant speech in artistic literature is not to be confused with the question of the relationship of the literary language to that of the peasantry. N. G. Černyševskij complained that, in the artistic literature of the fifties and sixties, the peasant was made to speak in such a fashion that not a single phrase was normal, and not a single word was pronounced without being distorted. In 1873, Dostoevskij grumbled that writers were going about with notebooks, registering items from the speech of merchants, peasants, and the like, for later use in character depictions in their novels, and the end result was that the characters in novels spoke a language that no actual merchant or peasant ever spoke.

The interaction between the literary language and the language of the peasantry, in the second half of the nineteenth century, was of great importance, but it did not have a decisive influence. The role of the spoken language, and particularly the language of the democratic strata of society, was of much greater importance.

12. THE STYLISTIC NORMS OF A NATIONAL DEMOCRATIZATION OF THE LITERARY LANGUAGE. V. I. DAL''S "TOLKOVYJ SLOVAR'"

In the second half of the nineteenth century, the literary lexicon continued to adopt elements from the colloquial language of the city and from the folk language (occasionally in its regional varieties). Words and expressions which, in the thirties and forties, crept into literature by way of the "oral" tale and the dialogues of heroes, now openly entered the general system of literary expression.

The democratization of the literary language found its clearest expression in Dal''s *Tolkovyj slovar' velikorusskogo jazyka* (1863), which, despite its somewhat provincial, dialectological tendency, had a great influence on literary word usage in the second half of the nineteenth century and the beginning of the twentieth. Dal''s dictionary, in keeping with his literary practice, was intended to "transform the national language into a cultured one." It was to prove that "the living national language, which has preserved, in vital freshness, a spirit which gives language firmness, power, clarity, integrity, and beauty, must serve as the source and storehouse for the development of a cultured, intelligent Russian speech in place of our present language—a eunuch." At the same time,

Dal' included in his dictionary terms from professional dialects and the sciences, an abundance of phraseological illustrations (consisting of more than thirty thousand proverbs, sayings, folk expressions, and riddles), and a great deal of ethnographic material describing folk beliefs, customs, and various aspects of the cultural and economic life of the Russian peasant and artisan. It was thus a sort of encyclopedia of national life of the middle of the century.

Nevertheless, the dictionary had certain polemical and normative goals. It was intended as an attack against the "written jargon" of "high" society, which had betrayed the spirit of the Russian language by introducing Europeanisms; and, on the positive side, it was meant to be a study of the "spirit" of the language, and to serve as a model for word formation. It therefore included words "which have not been written until now, and perhaps not even spoken." In addition to newly created words, the dictionary endowed words with new meanings. In this fashion, Dal' tried to improve the literary language and show the way toward a synthesis of the literary and the folk languages. With this end in view, he put forward six basic principles:

(1) *The principle of replacing the barbarisms of the "aristocratic" language with national Russian equivalents of differing stylistic value.* In actuality, Dal' opposed the principle that a West European expression should be rendered into Russian with an exact equivalent in semantic range and stylistic nuance. In his opinion, the problem of translation consisted in finding a national (and usually folk) expression and bestowing on it the meaning of the foreign term, without worrying about expressive or stylistic divergences between the native and the foreign expression. The method may be illustrated with items from his dictionary: *акушер*—родовспомогатель, родовспомогательный врач, родопомощник, повивальщик, бабич, приемник; *консерватор*—боронитель, сохранитель, охранитель, охранник; *реальный*—дельный, деловой, прикладной, опытный, насущный, житейский; etc. It is clear from such examples that Dal' intentionally obliterated the boundary between literary words and his own neologisms, as well as between bookish forms and colloquial ones.

(2) *The principle of a national, democratic justification of words and morphological elements in the literary language.* Dal' limited the Church Slavonic types of word formation. He lamented, for example, the

number of abstract terms in **-ость, -вость,** suffixes which the folk language rarely used. He therefore suggested the following kinds of substitutions: *мертвенность*—мертвизна; *предохранительный*—охранный; *собственность*—собь; *кругозор*—овидь, озор; etc. Here we also see a mixture of the bookish and the "folk." Dal' did not, after all, accept the "native" elements in their entirety; he made a selection of them, even though, when he was carried away, he would announce that "native words can be directly transferred into the written language."

(3) *The principle of morphological and semantic assimilation and mutual contamination of literary and colloquial forms.* Dal' reasoned that, although the language of the folk had few abstract expressions, the terms which it did have could be utilized in an abstract sense. He recommended that cumbersome compounds be banished from literature and replaced with short words utilizing native suffixes and, occasionally, prefixes: "From молоко, for example, the folk have composed молочник, молочница, молочная (комната), молокан, молочай молоки; and, without any strained effect, one can form молочняк, молочанка, молочан, молочец, etc." Using the word-forming resources of the folk language, Dal' produced all sorts of forms from one root.

(4) *The principle of a democratic unification of the literary language through destruction of the traditional stylistic categories.* Dal' wanted the folk element to erase the boundaries between the former styles and genres of the literary language. In his opinion, the idea of a faultless "literariness" was purely negative. To be sure, the language of the folk lacked many terms simply because the concepts did not exist. It therefore was necessary to create neologisms. One means of doing so was to create derivational "nests." Another was to freely translate European expressions. The absence of abstract and scientific terms was not "the fault of the national language, but the fault of its makers."

(5) *The principle of purging and selecting folk elements.* (Concerning this principle, see above, pp. 193–95.)

(6) *The principle of making the phonetic, morphological, and semantic structure of the folk lexicon more literary.* Dal' recommended that regional forms be adapted to the orthographic and orthoepic principles of the literary language. The very orthography of the word was supposed to reveal "the root, its origin, and its connection with the general Russian language."

For a characterization of the general process of democratization of the literary language (a process which took place in by no means all styles, and which never turned sharply in the direction of regional elements), it is worthwhile to quote a few examples from the "normal" language of various authors: from Dostoevskij—этот приговор дан *зазнамо;* вся каторга, как один человек *осаживала выскочку;* from G. Uspenskij—не может он не видеть, что кроме почерка у него нет никакой *заручки;* from V. Korolenko—получил на свой пай хорошую цензурную *затрещину* и прикусил язык.

13. THE PROCESS OF FILLING THE LITERARY LANGUAGE WITH PROFESSIONALISMS AND ARGOTISMS

As the colloquial language of the city increased its literary functions, it brought with it many words and idioms from jargons and professional dialects. City social strata now found a clearer reflection in literary genres. The relationship between literary genres and various kinds of everyday speech became more tense. The professionalization of the literary language did not, however, lead to its disintegration, because a huge stock of literary clichés, phrases, idioms, and compositional schemata were not only defended but were considered the hallmark of literariness.

The process of professionalization, which had begun between the thirties and the fifties, continued in the second half of the century. Factory and industrial jargons played a role, but the leading role was taken by those professional languages which were closer to the everyday interests of the nobility, the bourgeoisie, and the intelligentsia. The tempo of assimilation and semantic change of expressions was rapid. For example, the term втереть очки, which originally came from the argot of cardsharps and designated the changing of the face value of a card with a special powder, now came into general literary use with the transferred meaning of "to deceive for purposes of personal gain."

Since the co-opting of professionalisms into general literary usage depended on social interests, there were great differences in the manner in which it was done and in the methods used. In the sixties, the expression закусить удила entered the literary language as a result of the increase of horse-breeding among the landowners.

The colloquial term и никаких гвоздей had its origin in the cavalry command Смирно, и никаких движений. The original context was lost, the word гвоздей was added, and the term came to mean "there's nothing more to be said; that's enough."

Alongside such terms, there was a great flood of professionalisms of a more democratic origin. From the argot of thieves, there came валять дурака, тянуть волынку, жулик, etc.; from theatrical argot, этот номер не пройдет, etc.; from the argot of singers, подголосок, спеться, etc.; from school argot, ни в зуб толкануть, провалиться (cf. German *durchfallen*); and so on. One should also note, on the one hand, such bourgeois phraseology as разменяться на мелкую монету, ставить (вопрос) ребром, ударить по рукам, нагреть руки, вылететь в трубу, and, on the other hand, such metaphorical reflections of scholarly terminology as привести к одному знаменателю, отрицательная величина, центр тяжести, вступить в новый фазис, достигнуть апогея, etc.

As a consequence of such processes, the phraseological system of the Russian literary language of the second half of the nineteenth century was unstable, complex, contradictory, and stylistically undifferentiated.

14. CHANGES IN THE GRAMMATICAL SYSTEM

The grammatical system of the literary language also underwent great changes in the second half of the century. These were of two kinds. Grammatical doctrine, which had condemned the "folkish" features of the older grammar (such as nominative plurals for neuter nouns in **-ы, -и**), nonetheless still allowed those conversational grammatical forms which did not sharply contradict the orthoepic system of the written language. The drive to establish national standards for grammatical categories thus became stronger. On the other hand, however, the tendency toward bookishness in scholarly and journalistic writings, and the instability of the boundaries between the written and conversational languages, led to a development of new grammatical forms based on the old categories of the literary language. A process of granting equal literary rights to opposing grammatical categories thus came into being. The basic morphological changes of the period were as follows:

(1) In the declension of masculine nouns, the use of the nominative plural in **-a** expanded even further, encompassing even such nouns as had formerly retained the endings **-ы, -и**. The stress could be on any syllable, and very often the nouns denoted animate beings, as in учителя, офицера, профессора, инспектора. From the language of commerce came the form счета, "accounts," to differentiate it from the form счеты, "abacus." Grammatical codification thus encountered two opposing tendencies—the collapse, in colloquial speech, of masculine nominative plural noun endings into **-a**, and the need, in certain cases, for a morphological expression of differences in meaning.

(2) In compound numerals, there was a tendency to consider all digits except the last as indeclinable, and even the last digit, which bore the grammatical functions of governance and agreement, often was not declined and thus lost its syntactic connections with surrounding words. Purists deplored newspaper expressions of the type решено послать шестьсот сорок две сестры instead of ... шестьсот сорок двух сестер, and свыше шестьдесят домов instead of свыше шестидесяти домов. The literary language was thus influenced by the language of mathematics, which utilized only syntactic sequence, not morphology.

(3) Possessive adjectives in **-ов, -ин** began to acquire a descriptive nuance and, in certain cases (such as the masculine and neuter genitive and dative singular), began to take the endings of long-form adjectives: возле матушкиного кресла (Turgenev), пособить сестриному горю (S. Aksakov). In the seventies, a teacher of Russian grammar objected to such constructions as не имеющих своего состояния ни жениного.

(4) In the participles, there was a continued development of descriptive, adjectival meaning. This was true of the active participle as well as the passive. Compare such adjectival usages as the following: с вызывающим видом, вопрошающий взгляд, угрожающее положение.

(5) In conjunction with the tendency to adjectivalize participles, there developed a tendency to form adverbs from them. Such adverbs evoked sharp protests in the seventies. Note the following examples: невыносимо нагло и вызывающе подействовал (Tolstoj); концы усов угрожающе торчали (Korolenko); кричали торжествующе; взглянул испытующе (L. Andreev).

(6) Adjectival forms in **-ящий, -ущий,** which had arisen by analogy with participles, and which had remained in the official language, in the familiar colloquial language, and in literary stylizations of the "folk" language, now entered the general literary language. There were forms such as работящий, завабящий, гулящий, злющий. Compare, in the language of Turgenev, черна, как сапог, и злюща, как собака. Note also forms of the superlative degree in **-ущий, -енный**: большущий чайник (Dostoevskij), здоровенный работник немец (Tolstoj).

(7) Present passive participles now stabilized their forms with the thematic vowels **-и-, -е-** before the participial ending **-мый**. The dying out of present passive participles in **-омый**—a process which had begun in the thirties and forties—continued. A. X. Vostokov's grammar of 1831 still contained many participles, such as рвомый, сосомый, пекомый, which were not used at all in the second half of the century. There was a growing tendency to form such participles from derived verbs: for example, not зовомый but называемый.

(8) In newspaper and chancery language, there was an increased tendency to form passive participles from intransitive verbs. The phenomenon was a result of French and German influence and of the general lack of distinction between the grammatical functions of the participle. Note the following examples: из сумм, *заведываемых* земством; совет, *председаемый* генералом.

(9) There were aspectual changes in the verb, including a growing polarization of the verb into two basic aspects, perfective and imperfective, and a consequent decrease in the use of iterative verbs. These apparently continued to exist longer in those narrative styles which imitated either folk poetry or the language of the peasant. Note verb forms such as the following, in Turgenev's language: дирывались, зачуевал, вострепещивалось.

(10) There was a broad development of the stem vowel **-a-** (instead of **-o-**) in denominative imperfective verbs which had heretofore kept the original vowel. This process, too, was opposed by purists. Note the following: устраивать, успокаивать, зарабатывать (L. Tolstoj); задабривать (A. K. Tolstoj); замораживать (S. Aksakov); затрагивать (Korolenko).

(11) Imperfective verbs with the suffix **-ну-,** and with a stable stem accent, tended to lose the suffix in the past tense and past

active participle (in contrast to semelfactive perfectives with the same suffix). Note forms like поверг, высох, etc.

(12) Within the past tense forms of the verb, there arose a sharp differentiation between an aoristic and a perfect meaning (particularly in perfective verbs). Compare the aoristic value of such forms as пришел, увидел, победил with usages such as скалы, нависли (i.e., hang) над морем. In the present and future forms, complex semantic displacements became established: for example, the present or future could be used in the past, the present could be used with future meaning, etc.

(13) There were changes in the function of prepositions and prefixes, largely because of German influence. The use of two prepositions with one noun became established, with only one preposition (usually the second) governing the noun: *до и вслед за чем; за и против чего-нибудь*. Since they were used in such fashion, the prepositions acquired greater freedom from the noun, became somewhat adverbialized, and could be used as adjectival prefixes, as in до- и послеобеденного времени.

(14) At the same time, the expansion of prepositional, analytic constructions (which had begun at the end of the eighteenth century) continued apace. Prepositions such as в, на, с, для acquired a host of abstract meanings. Many verbs came to govern by means of a preposition (instead of directly, as before). In many constructions, prepositions lost their concrete meaning and assumed the role of a sort of "prepositional inflection."

Thus, as a result of these morphological changes, Russian acquired the analyticism of West European languages (mainly French and English) and limited the forms of its own synthetic structure.

15. THE CONTEST BETWEEN PETERSBURG AND MOSCOW FOR THE ROLE OF MODEL OF THE GENERAL LITERARY PRONUNCIATION

Petersburg pronunciation differed from Muscovite pronunciation in that it was more bookish, more orthographic, and had fewer connections with its ethnographic surroundings. It did not as consistently palatalize consonants in certain clusters (e.g. [láfk'i], not [láf'k'i]); it restored many spelling pronunciations (such as the group [čn], where Moscow had [šn], and the nominative singular masculine of the adjective, where Moscow had [-kəj], [-xəj], and the like); and it differed from Moscow in some of its rules for *akan'e* and in its general intonational patterns.

In fact, the question of the normal literary pronunciation remained unresolved, although the Muscovite tradition held the advantage because its pronunciation was cultivated and supported by theatrical tradition.

16. THE NORMS OF THE LITERARY LANGUAGE AND THE COLLOQUIAL LANGUAGE OF THE CITY MASSES

If one omits professional dialects (which only served narrow social spheres), there were two broad language systems opposed to the "normal" system of the literary language in the second half of the nineteenth century: the language of the peasantry, with its local varieties, and the language of the city masses (which interacted with the peasant language). Various "orthoepic" dictionaries noted the "irregularities" present in the colloquial language of the city and attributed them to "Russianized foreigners." The attribution was called forth by nationalistic considerations and social antagonisms and was, in fact, wrong, since some of these "irregularities" were common to all varieties of the city language. The peculiarities of the language of the city (seen from the point of view of the literary norms of the second half of the century) were as follows:

(1) *Phonetic peculiarities* (apart from dialect pronunciations and intonational differences) consisted mainly in accentual deviations from the literary norm. In this area, six kinds of phenomena may be differentiated: (a) Foreign borrowings often underwent a change of place of stress due to complicated efforts to make their accentuation conform to established patterns. It is an interesting fact that all the orthoepic dictionaries of the period reproduced almost the same list of words: e.g., докýмент, инструмéнт, магáзин, пóртфель, рóман, etc. (b) Bookish words occasionally had either an accent shift or a preservation of an archaic accentuation, as, for example, деятельный. Note, in the language of Lermontov, С деятельной и

пылкою душой. Note also such accentuations as до́говор, при́говор. (c) In past passive participles, the accent was systematically moved from the suffix to the stem: вве́дено, занесе́но, определе́нный, переве́денный, привезе́нный, etc. (d) In the same fashion, there was a shift of accent in non-past forms (with the exception of the first person) of verbs with infinitives in -и́ть and with a fixed stress on the ending, in order to make them conform to verbs of the type заплати́ть–запло́тишь: зво́нишь, зво́нит, зво́нят, instead of звони́шь, etc. (e) Many past tense forms shifted their stress from the ending to the stem: гна́ла, отда́ла, instead of гнала́, отдала́. Note also дра́лся instead of дрался́. (f) A few words had a dialectal, rather than a literary, stress: случа́й, сиро́та, по́нять, мо́лодежь, etc.

(2) *Morphological peculiarities* consisted of the following deviations common to all varieties of city language (deviations caused by peasant influences are excluded): (a) There were differences in the gender of nouns: бланка, эполета, ставня, rather than бланк, эполет, ставень, etc. (b) There were differences in noun number. Some nouns which had lost their singular in the literary language—дрязги, for example—still retained it in the everyday language of the city. (c) There was a limitless expansion of the masculine nominative plural ending -а, going far beyond the norm imposed on the literary language. (d) There was greater fusion of declensional types. For example, feminine and neuter nouns took the genitive plural ending -ов: блюдечков, делов. (e) There were differences in formation of adjectives: for example, бабский, губатый, instead of бабий, губастый. (f) Reflexive forms of the verb, particularly the participle, were often replaced by non-reflexive forms, and vice versa: загоревший сарай, млекопитающийся, instead of загоревшийся сарай, млекопитающий. The phenomenon was already present in the bourgeois prose of the eighteenth century. (g) There were analogical levelings of the present stem of verbs which had consonant alternations: гордюсь, ляжу, instead of горжусь, лягу; and зажгешь, зажгет, instead of зажжешь, зажжет. (h) There was a freer mixing of verbal sub-classes: пахаю, пахаешь, instead of пашу, пашешь. (i) There were imperative forms such as едь, едьте, instead of поезжай, поезжайте. (j) There were forms of the past passive participle in -тый instead of the normal literary forms in -нный: вырватый, порватый, etc.

(3) *Syntactic peculiarities* consisted of such phenomena as the

following: (a) There were certain differences in verbal government, with or without a preposition: for example, беспокоиться про кого, про что or за кого, за что, in contrast to the normal literary construction with the preposition о; and радоваться о чем instead of радоваться чему. (b) There were different nuances in the meaning of prepositions, or broader use of prepositions in certain meanings: for example, the preposition чрез was used in the meaning "because," "on account of." (c) After the preposition по, in its distributive meaning, the dative case of numerals was replaced by the accusative case: по шестьдесят instead of по шестидесяти.

(4) *Lexical and phraseological peculiarities* were even more significant. It is interesting that some words which were originally considered to belong to the language of the city gradually entered the literary language during the course of the century: for example, столоваться instead of иметь стол. Note also the following items, which were considered typical of "low" city colloquial language (corresponding literary forms are put in parentheses): крепко (очень), смирный (скромный), уворовать (украсть), ни к чему (попусту), кушать (есть), утекать (уходить), позавчера (третьего дня), всего на всего (всего на все), гладкий (толстый), дружить с кем (быть в дружбе), справить (приобрести).

Throughout the second half of the nineteenth century and the first decade of the twentieth, various social classes strongly opposed the granting of literary rights to the language of the city. The very history of the city language is unclear in many respects, and it is difficult to assess what various social groups contributed to it. The above sketch gives only the more glaring deviations from the standard literary norm. A deeper study would show that the language of the city had a general, over-all system with social and professional sub-categories. It entered the arena of literature after the revolution and played a great role in the organization of the post-revolutionary literary language.

Index

adjective morphology, xiv, xxi, xxv, 27, 39–40, 48, 63–6, 105–8, 130, 142–3, 167, 263–4, 267
Adrianova-Peretc, V. P., xvii, xxiv
adverbs, 8, 134
akan'e, 23, 29, 108, 266
Aksakov, I. S., 117
Aksakov, K. S., 18
Aksakov, S. T., 204, 230, 263, 264
Aleksej, Tsarevich, 35
Aleksej Mixajlovič, Tsar, 4, 23, 26, 29
alphabet, xxii–iii, 46, 47–8
Andreev, L., 263
Anna Karenina, 247
Aonidy, 108
aphorisms. *See* sayings
"Arabeski" 219, 223
"Arap Petra Velikogo," 152
argot, 261–2
Aristotle, 17
Atala, 167
"Ataman," 163
Avilova, L., 252
Avvakum, 22–5

Bacon, F., 88
Baratynskij, E. A., 103, 158, 161, 162, 177
barbarisms. *See* loan words
Barsov, A. A., 64
"Baryšnja krest'janka," 135, 137
Batjuškov, K. N., 92, 103, 130, 161, 205
Baudouin de Courtenay, J., 241

Beckij, I. I., 77
Bednaja Liza, 104, 107
Bednye ljudi, 196
"Bèla," 176
Belinskij, V. G., 83, 111, 122, 177, 180, 188, 190, 195, 199–202, 212, 239
Belyj, A., 245
Benediktov, V. G., 158, 180, 202, 222
Berynda, P., 14
Bestužev-Marlinskij, A. A., 121, 122, 150, 161, 162, 173, 174, 180, 188, 190, 191, 192, 217, 222
Biblioteka dlja čtenija, 179, 189
"Bitva u Zenicy-Velikoj," 155
Bogdanovič, I. F., 76, 81
Boris Godunov, 129, 133
"Boris Godunov," 219
"Borodino," 166, 170
"Borodinskaja godovščina," 134
borrowings. *See* loan words
braiding and weaving of words, xxiii, 8, 22, 42
Brigadir, 87, 95
Brjusov, V. Ja., 245
Bulgarin, T., 121, 122, 195, 201
Burdin, F., 256
Buslaev, F. I., 180
Butkov, Ja. P., 189
Byloe i dumy, 200
Byron, G., 245

calques, xii, xxiii, 7, 19, 20, 21, 60, 72, 75, 88–9, 95, 137, 138, 200, 250–1

269

Catherine the Great, 92, 149
"Čerkesy," 161, 162
Černyševskij, N. G., 241, 258
Čexov, A. P., 173, 239, 252
chancery language, xxv–vii, 4, 18, 28,
    30, 38, 49–50, 51, 75, 80–1, 101, 103,
    176, 197–8, 210, 214, 216–7, 226,
    227–8, 233–4, 249–51
Chateaubriand, F. R., 167
Čistoserdečnoe priznanie, 74
compounds, xxiii, 8
conjugation. See verb morphology
conjunctions, 41, 71, 82, 99, 103–4,
    115, 134, 144, 147, 176
"Čto beleetsja na gore Zelenoj," 156
Čto naše, tovo nam i ne nada, 116
Čulkov, M. D., 93
Cygany, 129, 222

Dal', V. I., 173, 183–4, 185, 189, 193,
    194, 201, 221, 229, 234, 236, 241–2,
    257, 258–61
Darwinism, 244
"Dary Tereka," 166, 169
"David," 115
Davydov, D. V., 148, 158
Decembrists, 115, 132
declension. See adjective morphology;
    noun morphology
Dejanija Petra Velikogo, 143
Del'vig, A. A., 161
"Dem'janova uxa," 172
"Demon," 164, 165–6
Derevnja, 194
"Derevnja," 198
Deržavin, G. R., 65, 81–3, 85, 100, 105
Dimitrij, Metropolitan of Rostov, 38
Dmitriev, I. I., 73, 161, 162, 179
Dmitriev, M. A., 116
Dnevnik (of Kjuxel'beker), 161
Dnevnik pisatelja, 251
Dobroljubov, N. A., 240
Dobrynin, G. I., 86, 112
Dobrynin, N., 21
Domik v Kolomne, 151, 152
Domostroj, xxv–vi

Dostoevskij, F. M., 152, 176, 177, 196,
    197, 204, 235, 236, 237, 239, 251,
    252, 258, 261, 264
Dubrovskij, 140
Duchesne, 167
Dušen'ka, 76, 81
"Dva goluba," 124
"Dva sravnenija," 222
"Dvojnik," 196, 197
Dvorjanskoe gnezdo, 188
Dym, 202, 240

École furieuse, 217
Èjxenbaum, B. M., 159, 162, 164, 165,
    174, 244
"Èlegija 2," 115
Elizabeth, Empress, 71, 92
Entretiens sur la pluralité des mondes, 33
Epifanij Premudryj, xxiii
"Èpigramma," 140
Evgenij Onegin, 129, 130, 136, 138, 139,
    146, 151, 159, 172
Ezda v ostrov ljubvi, 50

"Fatalist," 175, 176
"Feodor i Elena," 155
Fontenelle, B. de, 33
Fonvizin, D. I., 74–6, 84, 87, 95, 105
"Fortuna i niščij," 123
"Fortuna v gostjax," 123

Ganc Kjuxel'garten, 210
Gavriiliada, 130, 131, 132, 142
"General'nyj plan vospitatel'nogo
    doma," 77
Gercen, A. I., 188, 200, 223, 245
Geroj našego vremeni, 174, 176
gerunds. See verb morphology
Gistorija carja Petra Alekseeviča, 36
Gogol', N. V., 82, 99, 142, 152, 157,
    173, 177, 180, 190, 191, 194, 198,
    201, 203, 205, 209–36
Golikov, I. I., 143
Golyšenko, V. S., xviii
Gončarov, I. A., 189, 204, 239
Gore ot uma, 117

Gor'kij, M., 239
"Gorodok," 130, 131, 147
"Gospodin Proxarčin," 197
Greč, N. I., 106, 107, 108–9, 119, 203, 204
Griboedov, A. S., 115, 117
Grigorovič, D. V., 194, 196, 197–8, 204
Grot, Ja. K., 242, 243
Gudzij, N. K., xvii, xviii, xxiv, xxvi
Gukovskij, G. A., 84
"Gusar," 153

Hegel, G., 200, 202, 240
Hegelianism, 200
Hugo, V., 167

Igroki, 230
Ispancy, 162
"Ispoved'," 174
Istomin, K., 8
Istorija Gosudarstva Rossijskogo, 104
I to i sio, 93
"Iz A. Šen'e," 134
Izbornik 1076 goda, xviii
Izbrannye raboty po russkomu jazyku, xvi
"Iz Goracija," 145
Izmail-Bej, 159
"Iz Pindemonti," 147

Jabeda, 76
jakan'e, 23
Jakubinskij, L. P., xix
"Janko Marnavič," 154
"Janyš Korolevič," 155
Javorskij, S., 39
Jazykov, N. M., 154, 158
Judif', 19
Junost', 179, 247
Jurij Miloslavskij, 121

Kamenev, G. P., 91, 93
Kamennyj gost', 139
Kamenskij, P., 180
Kantemir, A., 33, 42, 59
Kapitanskaja dočka, 143, 152
Kapnist, V. V., 76, 161

Karamzin, N. M., 61, 67, 74, 85, 91–104, 107, 108, 110–1, 131, 137, 139, 143, 178, 179, 183, 198, 222
Karamzin school, 116, 120, 126, 128, 129, 139, 141, 145, 147–8, 180, 184, 203
Katenin, P. A., 114, 115, 132
"Kavkazskij plennik," 159, 161, 167
"Kazač'ja kolybel'naja pesnja," 169
"Kazak," 147
Kazaki, 191
"Kaznačejša," 172
"K Čaadaevu," 140
"K Del'vigu," 139
Kireevskij, I. V., 211, 238
Kjuxel'beker, V. K., 110, 114–5, 132, 161
Kleist, H., 198
"K nej," 140
Kniga ratnogo stroenija, 18
Kniga tolkovanij i nravoučenij, 23
Knjaginja Ligovskaja, 167
"Knjaginja Natal'ja Borisovna Dolgorukaja," 161
"Knjažna Mèri," 176
"Kol'na," 138
Komovskij, V. D., 154
"Komu na Rusi žit' xorošo," 254
Kop'ev, A., 116
Korolenko, V. G., 261, 263, 264
"Kotel i goršok," 124
Kotošixin, G., xxvi, 18
Kozlov, I. I., 158, 161, 165
Kratkij očerk istorii russkogo literaturnogo jazyka, xxvi
"Krest'jane i reka," 123
"Krest'janin i ovca," 123
"Krest'janin i razbojnik," 123
"Krovavyj bandurist," 217
Krylov, I. A., 122–5, 128, 172, 203
"K tipografskim naborščikam," 71
Kukol'nik, N. V., 158, 180, 185, 235
Kulikov, N., 201
Kurakin, V. I., 36

"Lan' i derviš," 124

Lažečnikov, I. I., 173, 204
Lermontov, M. Ju., 158–77, 201, 203, 205, 266
Leskov, N. S., 238, 242, 256
Levin, V. D., xxvi
lexicon, xii, xv–vi, xx, 7, 12, 27, 42–3, 44, 46, 58–60, 82, 91, 94–5, 101, 106, 118, 120, 124, 130, 135, 184, 186–7, 196, 197, 223, 241–2, 258–61, 268
"Literaturnye mečtanija," 111
"Litvinka," 173
loan translations. *See* calques
loan words, vii, xxiii, 7, 14, 15, 16–7, 19–21, 28, 31, 32–4, 35, 36–9, 46, 50, 56, 60, 72, 75, 80, 85, 86–9, 93, 167, 199–201, 206, 240–1, 243–5, 259, 266
Lomonosov, M. V., 17, 54, 56–74, 78, 79, 81, 84, 92, 101, 103, 111, 113, 114, 128, 161, 179, 183
Lomonosov school, 97, 105
"Loterejnyj bal," 198
Louis XIV, 100
Lovers of Wisdom, 199–200, 217
Ludolph, H. W., 4, 26–7
Lukin, V I., 76
Lunatik, 194

Majkov, V. I., 64, 65, 76
Makarov, P., 92
Maksim Grek, 3
"Mansurovu," 147
"Marko Jakubovič," 155
Mazepa, I., 17
"Mcyri," 165
Mednyj vsadnik, 136, 144
Medvedev, S., 10, 15, 16, 17
Menschen und Leidenschaften, 162
Mérimée, P., 141
Mertvye duši, 142, 190, 210, 218, 219–31
Metamorphoses, 17
"Metel'," 135, 142
Mirabeau, V. R., 84
Mirgorod, 213, 214
"Moemu Aristarxu," 147
"Moe zaveščanie," 138

Mogila, P., 15
"Moja rodoslovnaja," 146, 152
Molenie Daniila Zatočnika, xviii
Monastyrskij, Father Superior, 17
Monomax, V., xvii, xix, xxi
Moskovskij telegraf, 150, 179, 193
Musin-Puškin, V. A., 43
Musset, A. de, 167
"Muxa i dorožnye," 123

"Nabeg," 191
Nadeždin, N. I., 122, 182, 211
Na nožax, 242, 256
"Napoleon," 130
"Na smert' Bibikova," 82
Natural School, 152, 235
Nedorosl', 74, 149
Nekrasov, N. A., 163, 176, 196, 235, 236, 239, 244, 250, 254, 257
"Nevskij prospekt," 215, 216, 223
Nihilists, 244
"Noč' pered Roždestvom," 212, 214
"Nos," 216
noun morphology, xiv, xxi, xxv, 8, 27, 32, 39–40, 48, 49, 62–6, 79, 82, 104–7, 130, 168, 186, 203–4, 254, 262–3, 267
Nov', 244, 245, 255, 257
Novikov, N. N., 221
"Novyj russkij jazyk," 121
numerals, 63, 65, 82, 263

Obyknovennaja istorija, 189
Očerki russkoj literatury, 188
"Oda na vosšestvie na prestol Petra III," 70
"Oda na vzjatie Xotina," 70
Odoevskij, A. I., 158, 161, 163
Odoevskij, V. F., 173, 189, 200, 210
Odyssey, 235
O ispravlenii v preždepečatnyx knigax minejax, 9, 12
okan'e, 23, 61
Old Believers, 21, 22–5
"Olegov ščit," 134
"O muza plamennoj satiry," 152

O pol'ze knig cer'kovnyx v Rossijskom jazyke, 57, 58
"Orakul," 124
O Rossii v carstvovanie Alekseja Mixajloviča, xxvi, 18
ort-, etc., groups, xiii
orthography. *See* alphabet
"Osel," 124
"Osen'," 146
"Osen' vo vremja osady Očakova," 83
Ostrovskij, A. N., 157, 236, 239, 256
"Osvoboždenie Moskvy," 162
Otcy i deti, 239, 244, 256
"Otcy pustynniki i ženy neporočny," 134
"Otkupščik i sapožnik," 123
"Otvet Kateninu," 151
Ovid, 17

Panaev, I. I., 195, 235
parataxis, xiv–v, xxv, 144
participles. *See* verb morphology
particles, 106
Paul I, 112
Pavlov, N. F., 173
Pavskij, G. P., 205
Peretc, V. N., 50
"Pesni zapadnyx slavjan," 134, 154–6
"Pesnja," 163
Pesnja pro ... kupca Kalašnikova, 169
"Peterburgskie ugly," 196
Peter the Great, 26, 29, 30, 31, 35, 36, 40, 41, 43, 44, 80, 93, 212
phonetics, xix, 11–2, 23, 27, 28–9, 39, 60–2, 76, 108–9, 116–7, 130, 206–7, 265–7
phraseology. *See* syntax
Physics (of Aristotle), 17
Pikovaja dama, 140, 141, 142, 152, 168
"Pirujuščie studenty," 131
Pisemskij, A. F., 236, 240
Pis'ma russkogo putešestvennika, 93, 96, 104
Pis'mo o pravilax rossijskogo stixotvorstva, 56
"Pod''jezžaja pod Ižory," 138
Podolinskij, A. I., 158, 161

"podražanija drevnim," 134
"Podražanija Koranu," 134
Podrostok, 252
"Poedem, ja gotov ... ," 145
Pogodin, M. P., 189, 211, 241
Pogorel'skij, A., 173
"Pole Borodina," 170
Polevoj, N. A., 126, 150, 173, 184, 187–8, 193, 196, 211
Poležaev, A. I., 158, 161, 163
Polikarpov, F., 8, 9, 31, 42–3, 48
Poljarnaja zvezda, 150
Polockij, S., 10, 15, 22
Poltava, 130, 133, 139, 152
Pomjalovskij, N. G., 239, 253
Popov, M. I., 93
"Pora, moj drug, pora," 147
Porošin, S. A., 88
"Portret," 215, 217, 219, 223
Pososškov, I. T., 40
"Poučenie," xvii, xix
Povesti Belkina, 211
Povest' vremennyx let, xvii
Praktičeskaja russkaja grammatika (of N. Greč), 106
prepositions, xv, xxv, 41, 97, 140, 265, 268
Prokopovič, F., 39, 45
pronunciation. *See* phonetics
"Prorok," 131
"Proščenie ljubvi," 49
proverbs. *See* sayings
Prutkov, Kuz'ma, 239
"pseudo-majestic school," 180, 185
Puškin, A. S., 54, 83, 84, 85, 97, 99, 103, 121, 125, 127–57, 158–60, 163, 164, 166, 167, 168, 169, 173, 175, 177, 185, 188, 190, 191, 199, 203, 205, 211, 215, 216, 217, 221, 222
Putešestvie iz Peterburga v Moskvu, 84

Radiščev, A. N., 83–5, 105
Raevskij, V., 115
Rassuždenie o starom i novom sloge rossijskogo jazyka, 86, 97
Raynal, G., 84

Razgovor ob ortografii, 48
Razgovor o pol'ze nauk i učilišč, 42
raznočinec, 178–80, 188, 244, 253, 256
"Refutacija Beranžera," 153
Revizor, 214, 230
Rifmologion, 10, 15
Ritorika, 17, 67, 68–71
"Rodoslovnaja moego geroja," 135
Rossijskaja grammatika, 60, 63
Rostovskij, D., 16
Rousseau, J. J., 84
Rozanov, V. V., 244
"Rumjanyj kritik moj," 151–2
Ruslan i Ljudmila, 132, 139, 148
Russkaja pravda, xvi
Russkij jazyk; Istoričeskij očerk, vii
Ryleev, K. F., 115, 158

Saltykov-Ščedrin, M. E., 226, 236, 237, 239, 241, 249, 253
Sand, George, 194
"Sapožnik," 145, 156
"Saška," 165, 166
sayings, 125, 172, 228, 239, 253, 259
"Scena iz Fausta," 136
Ščepetil'nik, 76
Schelling, F., 199, 240
Schismatics. *See* Old Believers
Schopenhauer, A., 244
Scott, Walter, 210, 213
second South Slavic influence, xxii–iii
semantics. *See* lexicon
Semejnoe ščast'e, 191
Senkovskij, O. I., 173, 182, 193, 195, 217, 220
Sentimental Naturalism, 235
Sevastopol'skie rasskazy, 171
Ševyrev, S. P., 158
"Siluèt," 160
Simeon, Tsar, xi
"Šinel'," 219
Šiškov, A. S., 61, 86, 94, 96, 97, 101, 102, 112, 113–4, 119, 128, 137, 142, 179
"Skazka dlja detej," 166
"Skazka o mertvoj carevne," 131, 153

"Skazka o zolotom petuške," 154
Škola natural'naja, 201
Slavineckij, E., 7–8
"Slavjanka," 161
Slovar' Akademii Rossijskoj (1789–1794), 120
Slovar' Akademii Rossijskoj (1805–1822), 118
"Slovo v novuju nedělju po pascě," xvii
"Smert' poèta," 164, 165
"Smirdin school," 217, 220
Smotrickij, M., 5, 8–10, 20, 48
"Sobač'ja družba," 123
Sobolevskij, A. I., 20
Sobolevskij, S. A., 141
"Sofokl," 115
Sokraščenie filosofii kanclera Bakona, 88
Sollogub, V. A., 235
Somov, O., 178, 211
"Soročinskaja jarmarka," 218
"Sosedka," 171
"Sovet myšej," 128
Sovremennik, 241
spelling. *See* alphabet
Spravočnoe mesto russkogo jazyka, 186, 206
"Stancionnyj smotritel'," 135
Stanevič, E., 94
"Stansy," 163
"Starosvetskie pomeščiki," 215, 218
"Strannik," 134
Sumarokov, A. P., 45, 47, 54, 59, 62, 66, 71, 72, 73, 76, 77–81, 90–1, 105
Svetov, V. P., 65
synonyms. *See* lexicon
syntax, xiv–v, xxv, 8, 9–10, 12, 13, 16, 20, 21, 23, 27, 35, 38, 41–2, 66–8, 75, 80, 84–5, 89–91, 95–9, 103–4, 123–4, 135, 139, 140–7, 154–5, 159–60, 167, 173–6, 182, 187, 205, 247–9, 250, 265, 267–8

Tallement, P., 50
"Taman'," 176
Taras Bul'ba, 213, 214
Tatiščev, V. N., 42
"Telega žizni," 153

"Ten' i čelovek," 123
Thomson, J., 198
Timofeev, A. V., 158, 180, 235
Timofeev, I., xxiv
Tjutčev, F. I., 158, 239
Tolkovyj slovar' živogo velikorusskogo jazyka, 184, 258–61
Tolstoj, A. K., 239, 264
Tolstoj, L. N., 171, 176, 177, 179, 190–2, 199, 204, 230, 237, 238, 239, 244, 246–9, 255, 257, 263, 264
Tomaševskij, B. V., 142
tort, etc., groups, xii, xix, xxiii
Trediakovskij, V. K., 40, 44, 46–7, 48, 49, 50–4, 59, 61, 62, 66, 74, 78, 79, 88, 89, 90–1
Trejazyčnyj leksikon, 42
Turgenev, A. I., 205
Turgenev, I. S., 157, 176, 177, 180, 185, 188, 194, 200, 202, 204, 230, 235, 236, 237, 238, 239, 240, 244, 245, 246, 255, 256, 257, 263, 264
Turovskij, K., xvii, xx

"Učitel'," 214
Uedinenie, 244
Uloženie, 4
"Umirajuščij gladiator," 164
Ušakov, V., 211
Uspenskij, G. I., 249, 250, 253, 256, 257, 261
"Utoplennik," 145, 153

Vadim, 167, 168–9, 173, 174
"Valerik," 160, 171
Večera na xutore bliz Dikanki, 212, 213, 216
Vel'tman, A. F., 173, 194
Venevitinov, D. V., 211
verb morphology, xiv, xxi, xxv, 3, 8–9, 23, 32, 39–40, 46, 48, 49, 62–6, 81–2, 108, 168, 203–5, 263–5, 267
"Vešnee teplo," 52
"Videnie," 115
"Videnie korolja," 154, 155
Vigny, A. de, 167
"Vij," 214, 231
Vinokur, G. O., xvi, xxv

virši, 5, 17, 28
vjakan'e, 23
Vjazemskij, P. A., 103, 120, 128, 133, 150, 158, 162, 173, 177, 203, 230
"Voevoda," 146
Vogüé, E. de, 167
Vojna i mir, 171, 192, 238, 244, 246–7
"Volja," 163
Voskresenie, 192
Vostokov, A. X., 155, 205, 264
Voyage de l'île d'Amour, 50
Vremennik Ivana Timofeeva, xxiv
Vybrannye mesta iz perepiski s druz'jami, 233, 235
"Vystrel," 141
Vzdornye ody, 72, 78
Vzgljad na moju žizn', 73, 179

winged words. See sayings
word order. See syntax

Xomjakov, A. S., 158
"Xozjain i myši," 123
Xrestomatija po drevnej russkoj literature, xvii, xviii, xxiv, xxvi
"Xristos voskres, pitomec Feba," 131

Zagoskin, M. N., 121, 173, 180
"Žalobnaja pesn' blagorodnoj Asan-Aginicy," 155
"Zametki o Borise Godunove," 149
Zapiski (of G. Dobrynin), 112
Zapiski (of S. Porošin), 88
"Zapiski sumasšedšego," 216
Zapisnye knižki (of Gogol'), 198, 229, 230–1
"Želanie zimy," 82
"Ženix," 152
Ženixi, 214
"Ženščina," 218
Žitie Stefana Permskogo, xxiv
"Živ, živ Kurilka," 151
Zotov, I., 44
Žukovskij, V. A., 99, 103, 108, 145, 154, 158, 161, 163, 165, 185, 203, 205, 217, 235
"Žurnal Pečorina," 176